Agrotourism and the Rural Environment

Agrotourism and the Rural Environment

Ramesh Kant Rajput

RANDOM

RANDOM PUBLICATIONS

NEW DELHI (INDIA)

Agrotourism and the Rural Environment

ISBN 978-93-5111-541-0

Published in 2015 in India by

RANDOM PUBLICATIONS

4376-A/4B, Gali Murari Lal, Ansari Road
New Delhi-110 002
Phone : +9111-43580356, 011-23289044, 011-43142548
e-mail: sales@randompublications.com,
info@randompublications.com, randomexports@gmail.com

Type Setting by : Friends Media, Delhi-110089
Digitally Printed at : Replika Press Pvt. Ltd.

Preface

Since its creation in 1961, the OECD Tourism Committee has endeavoured to grasp the overriding trends, including structural change, in the tourism, travel and recreation industry, to give governments a clearer understanding of their role and of how they must tailor their action. Accordingly, in 1987 the Committee began to probe how tourism strategies could contribute to rural development. Since 1990, this examination has been carried out within the broader context of the OECD Group of the Council on Rural Development, following the wish of the Council at its 1990 meeting at Ministerial level.

For many years a number of rural areas have been beset by population loss and declining services. These problems are now exacerbated by changes that have brought job losses and falling income to the farm sector. In contrast to this downturn, tourism has blossomed into a prosperous, fast-growing activity, and has indeed turned out to be a significant factor for economic growth in the countries in which it has developed.

It was therefore important to determine whether tourism's growth potential could be harnessed as a strategy for rural development, in particular by drawing upon resurgent interest in the countryside, its traditional way of life, and landscapes and the architectural heritage, referred to as amenities. The Tourism Committee devoted several of its sessions to these issues, undertaking in particular to ascertain, in the light of national experience, whether rural tourism had any distinguishing characteristics, whether it could develop in all rural areas, whether it was truly capable of generating employment and attracting capital to such areas, whether it presented drawbacks for the countryside and whether it required action on the part of national or local governments.

I would like to thank my team for standing beside me throughout my career and writing this book. My special thanks go to "Random Publications" who have published the book.

– Ramesh Kant Rajput

Contents

1

Agritourism: Ideas and Resources

Since 1997, the National Agricultural Statistics Service has reported a contin-uous decrease in the number of farms and the number of acres being farmed. Thousands of agricultural acres have been redesigned into housing develop-ments or manufacturing sites. How-ever, Virginia agriculture is still ranked as the No. 1 state industry and is using every measure to maintain its economic impact on the state. One resource that local farms are finding to be highly suc-cessful is development of agricultural attractions that invite local residents and tourists onto their land to experi-ence the peaceful but energized farm environment.

Agritourism is recreation at its finest! Visitors might tour a vineyard, explore winemaking, or discuss the pro-cess of transforming grapes into high-quality Virginia wines. Younger guests (as well as many adults) may discover that goats are not dogs with horns, donkeys are different from horses, and milk does not originate in a plastic container in the grocery store. Tours of farm fields have enabled many people to realize that peanuts grow underground, and cotton grows on a plant – not in a bale. Visitors can pick pumpkins, apples, cherries, and other produce; or they can navigate corn mazes. Virginians are adding hayrides, barnyard animal visits, and ice-cream treats from a local dairy to the top of their "fun-things-to-do" lists.

THE DEFINITION

Virginia law defines agritourism as *"any activity car-ried out on a farm or ranch that allows members of the general public, for recreational, entertainment, or educational purposes, to view or enjoy rural activities, including farm-ing, wineries, ranching, historical, cultural, harvest-your-own activities, or natural activities and attractions. An activity is an agritourism activity whether or not the participant paid to participate in the activity."*

For most people, agricultural tourism refers to a visit to a working farm or any agricultural, horticultural, or agri-business operation in order to enjoy, be educated by, or become actively involved in the activities of the farm or operation – in other words, getting a *true farm experience*.

CREATE A NEW ADVENTURE

"Living on an Acre" (U.S. Department of Agriculture, 2003) suggested that farmers develop a "rent-a-tree" operation. This idea would work very nicely for an orchard: The customer selects a tree and pays a rental price, and the farmer cares for the tree throughout the season.

The customer could pick the fruit or contract with the farmer to harvest it. Creative ideas for agritour-ism activities are unlimited. However, before you start implementing a new farm adventure, you will need to analyze the liability issues and the financial feasibil-ity in relationship to the farm's character, values, goals, and financial resources.

Some of the best ideas for agritourism are published by the National Sustainable Agricultural Information Ser-vice. However, numerous conversations and farm visits around the state have resulted in a variety of ideas for your consideration as part of a farm agritourism plan.

POTENTIAL AGRITOURISM ACTIVITIES

- Agricultural museum and displays
- Archery
- Barn dances
- Bed and breakfast accommodations
- Biking trails
- Bird watching
- Birthday parties
- Breweries
- Cabin living
- Campfires (don't forget the marshmallows)
- Camping
- Canning produce
- Canoeing
- Corn mazes
- Corporate and group events
- Cut flowers (picking, arranging, and planting)
- Cut-your-own Christmas tree and evergreens
- Farm cooking contests
- Farm scavenger hunts
- Farm stores and markets
- Farm vacations (a day or a week on the farm: living, working, enjoying)
- Fee-fishing pond (fishing, cleaning, and cooking)
- Flower arranging workshops
- Haunted barns
- Hay wagon rides

- Heirloom plant and animal exhibits
- Herb walks
- Heritage trails
- Hiking paths (walking, identifying vegetation, deter-mining a tree's age, picnicking)
- Historic reenactments
- "How-to" clinics
- Hunting
- Ice cream parlor or bakery
- Jam- and jelly-making demonstrations
- Meeting barnyard animals (participating in educational programmes focusing on each animal: shear the sheep, milk the "demonstration" cow, or participate in "cattle college")
- Music events, concerts, and festivals.
- Orchards and pick-your-own (picking, sitting, picnics under the trees)
- Pancake breakfasts
- Plant a garden
- Pony and horseback riding
- Pumpkin patch (picking, painting, carving, and buying)
- Quilting/weaving exhibitions
- Restaurants/dining (farm food, slow dining, Sunday brunches, or local foods)
- Snow sledding
- Sorghum milling
- Stargazing and moonlight activities
- Storytelling/story swaps
- Straw bale maze
- Tours for children and families
- Vegetable contests
- Virginia Standards of Learning and the farm
- Weddings
- Winemaking and tasting
- Wineries

AGRITOURISM PARTNERS

Agritourism is a growing industry within the common-wealth that is supported by the partnership of Virginia Tourism Corporation, Virginia Department of Agricul-ture and Consumer Services (VDACS), and Virginia Cooperative Extension. Farm owners considering agri-tourism as a tool to sustain or expand farm profitability must examine the business model, entertainment options, operation logistics, and liability issues and coverage.

Agritourism operations are challenged by the cost of and access to insurance and liability coverage, unpre-dictable weather, the seasonal nature of the operation, health and code inspections, and the struggle to provide customer service to the sometimes not-so-agreeable public. These factors cannot be addressed in detail in just one document; they require the involvement of mul-tiple experts and numerous face-to-face discussions.

GET STARTED

Think about your options and the impact your choices will have on reaching your goals.

There are some key steps to developing and implementing a successful plan:

- Create a plan. What farm experience can you offer the public that will make your operation unique, in compliance with all local ordinances and codes, and profitable? Your local Extension agent and farm management agent can help you iden-tify alternatives. In addition, *Agritourism*, Virginia Cooperative Extension publication 310-003, *pubs.ext.vt.edu/310/310-003/310-003.html,* provides an excellent guide for developing a plan.
- Plan to grow your business. After developing the initial plan to establish an agritourism business, you need to consider how to continually create new adventures to attract new guests and entice those who have already visited the farm to return. When consid-ering growth, assess space limitations, availability of parking, maximum number of people who can be safely transported, time required to travel around the activity area, and seating capacity for activities.
- Understand your liability. When visitors arrive on your property, liability increases. Identify risk-man-agement issues, implement safety plans to prevent identified risks, and obtain the necessary insurance coverage for your specific operation. Wise agritour-ism entrepreneurs consult their attorneys and insur-ance agents prior to opening their doors to guests.
- Develop partnerships. Talk to neighbours about your plans and ask for their support. Inform your economic development office and Chamber of Commerce about your plans to open a new business enterprise. Review road signage and confirm that directions to the farm are clearly marked.
- Inventory existing attractions. Ask the local tour-ism office to provide assistance in reviewing your publicity plan and linking to other local activities. Determine if other farms in the region are engaged in agritourism activities and explore the idea of all the farms developing a publicity partnership.
- Add your operation to tourism web sites. Contact the Virginia Tourism

Corporation at *www.virginia.org*, and scroll to the bottom of the page to select "Add/Update a Listing." Also be sure to list your opera-tion with VDACS.

- Know your customers. Long-time agritourism entrepreneurs know that their customers want to slow down, relax, and truly enjoy a farm experience.
- Set guiding rules for all farm visitors and com-municate them clearly. You will want to make the visit a wonderful experience for each guest. How-ever, guests must follow the rules for handling ani-mals, traveling through open fields, and avoiding areas that are not visitor-safe.

CONDUCT RESEARCH

Compiled a list of agricultural tourism publications and web sites packed with suggestions, experiences, and facts. Hopefully the following resources will provide you with a strong base of information on agritourism and the data needed to guide your decision-making process.

This resource list is just the beginning. It can spark unique ideas that – combined with energy and enthusiasm – can be implemented to make your agrito-urism adventure a one-of-a-kind destination.

AGRITOURISM IN THE UNITED STATES

Agritourism is widespread in the United States. Agritourists can choose from a wide range of activities that include picking fruits and vegetables, riding horses, tasting honey, learning about wine and cheesemaking, or shopping in farm gift shops and farm stands for local and regional produce or hand-crafted gifts.

According the USDA Cooperative State, Education and Extension Service, "Tourism is becoming increasingly important to the U.S. economy. A conservative estimate from the Federal Reserve Board in Kansas, based on 2000 data, shows that basic travel and tourism industries accounted for 3.6 per cent of all U.S. employment. Even more telling, data from the Travel Industry Association of America indicate that 1 out of every 18 people in the U.S. has a job directly resulting from travel expenditures".

Through the Small Farm Center at the University of California, "Agricultural tourism or agritourism, is one alternative for improving the incomes and potential economic viability of small farms and rural communities. Some forms of agritourism enterprises are well developed in California, including fairs and festivals. Other possibilities still offer potential for development". The UC Small Farm Center has developed a California Agritourism Database that "provides visitors and potential entrepreneurs with information about existing agritourism locations throughout the state".

The publication *Promoting Tourism in Rural America* explains the need for planning and marketing a rural community and weighing the pros and cons of tourism. According to the publication, local citizen participation is helpful and should be included in starting any kind of a tourism programme. Citizen participation in planning tourism can contribute to building a successful programme that enhances the community. Additional web sites that promote and publicize agritourism in the United States include Rural Bounty, founded by agritourism consultant Jane Eckert, Farm Stay U.S., a nationwide directory of farm stays, and The Farm Stay Project, a blog that profiles farm stays and tracks agritourism news.

PUBLIC AWARENESS

People have become more interested in how their food is produced. They want to meet farmers and processors and talk with them about what goes into food production. For many people who visit farms, especially children, the visit marks the first time they see the source of their food, be it a dairy cow, an ear of corn growing in a field, or an apple they can pick right off a tree.

Farmers and ranchers use this interest to develop traffic at their farm or ranch, and interest in the quality of their products, as well as awareness of their products

DUDE RANCHES

Dude (or guest) ranches offer tourists the chance to work on cattle ranches, and sometimes participate in cattle drives. The fact sheet, *Promoting the Farm and Ranch Recreation Business*, gives farmers and ranchers information on marketing and developing strategies to win tourism dollars. Dude ranches are common in the United States and Australian Outback.

NATURE-BASED TOURISM AND AGRITOURISM TRENDS: UNLIMITED OPPORTUNITIES

Rural tourism has been increasing rapidly over the lasttwo decades. Many factors have contributed to this trend.Briefly, people are taking more and shorter trips, doingmore traveling by car, combining business travel withvacations, looking for new experiences, adding diversityto their experiences, traveling as a family, and looking to"get back to their roots."

In most cases, one family memberhas a grandparent who grew up on a farm/ ranch or in arural community. These are the "roots" tourists want to visit.I have five take-home points I would like you to learnfrom my presentation: (1) What are alternative enterprisesand agritourism? (2) tourism trends and projections, (3)income-producing ideas, (4) available resource material,and (5) tourism ideas for Oklahoma. My goal is to get youto think outside the box about your farm/ranch and ruralcommunity. How can you use your natural and humanresources differently for income-producing opportunities?Or, as George DeVault of the Rodale Institute says, "Getsmall and get in."

What are Alternative Enterprises and Agritourism?

- An "alternative enterprise" is marketing what you produce differently, adding value to the product you produce or adding a new enterprise. It is also using your natural or other resources differently or using the same resource in multiple ways.
- Agritourism is an alternative enterprise where you invite the public onto your farm or ranch. It can also be defined as "a set of activities that occur when people link travel with the products, services, and experiences of agriculture." The product itself can be an "experience."
- Agritainment is the fun side of agritourism and includes mazes, petting farms, pumpkin picking, haunted houses, horseback riding, and the like.
- Agrieducation is teaching your visitors about agricultural production, how food and fibre are produced, rural values, and quality of life. It is building support for agriculture through educational experiences. I have no data to prove this point! But I firmly believe that farmers and ranchers like you teach more people about agriculture than any other form of education in the United States. When they visit your farm, you have children.s undivided attention for twenty minutes to an hour to teach them about their food and how farmers and ranchers produce it. At the same time you teach, you also provide an experience about cultural and heritage tourism, two of the fastest-growing tourism niches.
- Nature-based tourism ranges from hunting and fishing (consumptive tourism) to bird watching, flower/ tree/rock identification, hiking, rock climbing, or just being with nature (non-consumptive tourism), and
- Avitourism or bird watching is the fastest growing nature-based tourism activity in the nation.

Industry Structure

Today's agricultural production, marketing, and distributionsystem can be described as an hourglass. We havemore than two million farmers/ranchers producing thenation's food who sell to a few firms that add valuethrough processing, packaging, and transporting, like theneck of the hourglass, and then sell it to the 290 milliondomestic and foreign consumers.

These firms incur thecosts, risks, and management, add value, and store andtransport these products before they are sold.With alternative enterprises, the farmers "add value"to their own products and realize a larger income byperforming marketing activities and incurring the risksby processing, packaging, storing, transporting, and sellingdirectly to the consumer. The farmer becomes a competitorwith agribusiness firms for a larger share of the consumer'sdollar.In 1913, farmers received 46 per cent of the consumer'sdollar compared to less than 20 per cent today.

Thisoccurred because many small farmers carried out themarketing at the local level such as delivering milk,manning the butcher and bake shop, and selling "in-seasonproduce," or consumers visited farms to buy directly fromthe farmer/rancher.

In 1950, farmers received 50 to 80percent of the consumer's dollar spent on fruits andvegetables. Today, the figure is less than 30 per cent.A farmer or rancher entrepreneur who diversifies intovalue-added agriculture or agritourism has several marketopportunities. These can be categorized as: food (processing,packaging, branding, specialty markets, farmers. markets),roots (heritage and culture), agrieducation (schools,retreats, conferences), experiences (farm stays, ranchstays, B&Bs pick-your-own), agritainment (petting farm,mazes, hayrides), and nature-based adventure (horsebackriding, rock climbing, hunting, fishing).

Most entrepreneursdevelop several of these activities as alternative enterprisesor as their agritourism activity grows. It is a natural fit.You have a very important and responsible job: You aredeveloping friends for agriculture forever! It is not just forthe profit! This fits nicely into the values of rural America.

INCOME-PRODUCING OPPORTUNITIES FOR YOUR FARM OR RANCH AND COMMUNITY

Agritourism or any other alternative enterprise is adifferent business than farming. Two major changes willoccur. First, you are no longer a price-taker but a pricesetter.You are not going to the elevator or livestock auctionand asking, "What will you give me?" Now, you aretelling the consumer how much you want for your productor service.

Secondly, you are now in the people business.You are working directly with the consumer in a relationshipjust as important if not more important than the productyou are selling. Someone in your family must enjoy workingwith people to succeed at agritourism or other alternativeenterprises. You are marketing directly to the consumer.You are producing memories, adventure, experiences, andfriendships.Thinking about the "customer" is probably moreimportant than thinking about "production" in this scenario.When you think about your customer, you must thinkabout how you operate your business. When are yougoing to be open?

How many people will you hire? Whattype of facility will you need? How small can you be tostart? These are just a few of the questions you will needto answer when developing an agritourism or other alternativeenterprise.

These farm or ranch income-producing opportunitiesmay be put into fourteen groups:

- Farm Markets and Specialty Products. These markets provide an excellent opportunity to sell all types of value-added products from food to crafts, depending upon the rules of the farmers. market. Specialty product markets exist everywhere. The Internet has made this a more easily accessible market. Also, many farmers are now marketing to restaurants, schools, and nursing homes. Many state government and local communities support this type of activity. If they don't help them get started!
- Product Processing. These products include maple syrup, wood products, dairy products, and wine production, to name a few. They can become an education activity as well as resulting in product sales. The ideas are almost limitless as to what you can do with product processing and packaging. Customers like to shop, so you need to provide them with the opportunity to take something home for themselves or for friends.
- Fairs, Festivals, and Special Events. Farms hold festivals as well as communities. People just need something to rally around. These festivals range from food and crafts to nature, flowers, art, heritage, and cultural themes. Farmers have found festivals to be a very profitable way to attract customers. Many economic development or chamber of commerce groups will sponsor these events. Plan your activities around these festivals or hold your own.
- Horses and Other Farm Animals. This can range from petting farms to the training of horses or raising buffalo. These enterprises can be educational, produce food, fibre, and fun, or develop skilled horsemen. Exotic animals often attract many visitors. Many entrepreneurs raise llamas, sheep, and other fibre producing animals. They market the fibre in both the finished and unfinished form and sell the meat and in some cases milk to local customers. Some dairy goat producers deliver milk more than three hundred miles. Others have raised ostrich and emus. The changing diversity of the American population has led to the development of many niche markets for goats, sheep, and other livestock products.
- Unique Dining Experiences. Opportunities exist for farms and ranches to serve food to the public. You may have a special location and setting with a view, provide plays, or other entertainment, develop a catering service, or have a dining/fun experience on the farm with great country cooking. People are looking for a new experience, and dining on the farm is a "new experience." Dining is the number-one tourist activity!

- Wildlife and Fish. This includes fish production, bird watching, hunting, and fishing. You can raise several different species and release the game birds for hunting or mange your land for improved game habitat. You can offer guided or unguided hunts.
- Nature-based Recreation. Opportunities exist on farms and ranches to market natural resources as nature-based recreation for a fee. These include hiking, biking, walking, snowmobiling, all-terrain vehicles, swimming, canoeing, float trips, boating, picnicking, water-skiing, paint balling, and other outdoor team sports. Water-based activities are a very popular form of outdoor recreation.
- Floriculture. The raising and marketing of flowers at farmers. markets, community supported agriculture groups, and other markets have increased rapidly in the past decade. Fresh flowers on the table have a high priority in most of our homes today. In addition, one can raise bedding plants for the wholesale and retail markets as well as wildflowers and herbs. There are many niche markets for floriculture products. It is surprising how much people will pay for fresh cut flowers.
- Education. Education can become a part of almost every agritourism and alternative enterprise. Education may even be the focus of the enterprise. Either approach provides for many income-producing opportunities on the farm and ranch. Public and private education systems are looking for ways to broaden students. educational experiences. Most schools are open to an invitation to visit your farm once you explain your education programme. Be sure to have different programmes for the various age groups, from preschool to senior citizens.
- Heritage and Culture. This is one of the fastestgrowing tourism activities. American and foreign visitors are very interested in the history of the United States. Since most people come from an agricultural ancestry, they want to learn more about what their great grandparents or grandparents did for a living. This is a great opportunity to sell the rural "quality of life." Agriculture has a tremendous heritage and culture that can also be marketed to tourists by people staying and/or working on the farm or ranch. The more original the better, including the antiques, claim cabins, homesteads, and the like.
- Arts and Crafts. Tourists. second-favorite activity is shopping. Local arts and crafts have always been in demand by domestic and foreign tourists. This includes food items and other value-added food products produced on the farm. Quality products are needed to attract and keep tourists coming back. There are several regions in the United

States where journeyed crafters live and market their products. They have succeeded in establishing high-quality products and experiences for the customer.

- Farm/Ranch Stays. There are three types of stays: vacation (visitors are looking for rest and relaxation), working vacation (visitors participate in the farm/ranch daily chores and work), and dude ranches/ farms (visitors are specially treated by staff members, who do all the necessary preparation for the activities during their stay).
- Tours and Touring. These enterprises are generally tied to activities involving a group of farms/ranches or community festivals or events. Tourists travel to see foliage or blossoms or farm harvest activities such as maple syrup, cheese, or ice cream processing or events such as threshing bees or fall harvest activities. Either a group of farmers or a community/county sponsors such events. It is a time to open your enterprise to the public.
- Pick, Cut, Gather or Grow Your Own. Farmers have been selling the pick-your-own fruits and vegetables events for decades, and some have been renting land to people who want to grow their own. Arelatively new enterprise is rent-a-tree, cow, or bush. Here the farmer still maintains complete control in the production management aspects and the customer pays the farmer for these services. For example, you can rent/lease an apple tree to a customer. You still prune, spray, and perform the functions involved in production. The customer is invited to watch the pruning, see the apple blossoms, and watch other production practices. When the apples are ready to pick, the customer can bring friends and pick whatever quantity they want from the tree they rented. The farmer then harvests the remainder for himself.

This type of programme allows the farmer to get thecustomer to visit his farm several times a season, providingopportunities for sales of other value-addeditems and development of a loyal relationship.We have just identified several agritourism and alternativeenterprises possible on your farm or ranch. I suggesttalking these ideas over with neighbours, your local extensionagent, or other entrepreneurs. This is a difficult timefor most farmers/ranchers; they are concerned theirneighbour will do the same thing if they talk to them abouttheir ideas. This should not be a concern because researchhas proven that the more tourist attractions there are inan area, the more people will come. Customers recognizethey have an opportunity to pick and choose. Don.t beafraid of getting your neighbour involved in an alternativeenterprise a little bit different than yours.

This is whereteamwork really pays off.As you start to develop your business, you will need toconsider the type of customer you want to attract orserve. For example, do you want to lease your place tohunters who guide themselves and hunt whatever gameis in season for about $1,500 per week, raise and releasegame, or manage your game so there are more trophyanimals available and provide guided hunts for $12,000per week? These decisions need to be made when you aredeveloping your business and marketing plan.Some people get very nervous as they think aboutthese new and different enterprises.

You need to look atit the same as you do new farm and ranch productionpractices: Read about them, attend seminars, talk to peers,read research reports, and discuss with technical staff.Finally, try to test your new business by selling yourservices or products to family, friends, church groups,and other civic groups. Don.t make a big investmentimmediately. Build and learn.The NRCS has a put together a publication (seeresource list) describing seventeen success stories. Thestories tell you how people started and built their business,the mistakes they made, and how they took advantageof things that went right.

TIPS FOR STAYING ON TRACK AND GETTING STARTED (RECOMMENDED FOR A ONE TO TWO-YEAR PERIOD)

1. Assess your resources.
   - Look at the notes you have made in considering alternative enterprises and use them to make a more in-depth assessment of the resources available to you and your family.
2. Get informed.
   - Attend seminars, workshops, trade shows, and schools.
   - Purchase books, videos, newsletters, magazines, and other publications.
   - Go to the library and do some research. Use the Internet to get the most up-to-date information. If you don.t have an Internet connection at home, one should be available to you at the library.
   - Look through the resources listed in the NRCS "Alternative Enterprises and Agritourism: Farming for Profit and Sustainability" tool kit available at your area Resource Conservation and Development Office.
3. Find out what other entrepreneurs are doing.
   - Talk to neighbours, friends, and strangers about their businesses.
   - Visit businesses in your surrounding area and in neighbouring counties and see what they are doing.
4. Consult potential customers.
   - Ask your relatives, friends, and neighbours about the product(s) you are thinking of providing through your new enterprise. Are they interested?
5. Research the market for your products.

6. Network.
   - Join organizations or groups for people involved in enterprises similar to the one you are interested in.
   - Join the chamber of commerce, rotary, and other business and planning organizations or committees in your community.
   - See if other local entrepreneurs would like to join you in your business venture or start their own agritourism or alternative enterprise.
7. Get help.
   - Visit resource people in your county, region, or state. County agents, RC&D coordinators, state Extension staff, Department of Agriculture staff, state tourism directors and staff, small business development center staff, and other specialists should all be willing to answer questions and help you get started.
8. Develop a business and marketing plan.
   - Various books, worksheets, and programmes designed to help you develop a successful business and marketing plan are available through
   - The Internet
   - Your local library
   - Your local outreach programme
   - Your local college
   - SCORE
   - SBDC
   - Your local RC&D office
9. Create a financial plan.
   - Decide how you will finance your business.
   - Find out about financial assistance (grants and loans) available to you.
10. Start small, learn from your experience, and expand the business.

2

Rural Tourism Development: Constraints and Possibilities with a Special Reference to Agri Tourism

Global economic restructuring has created a climate in which many local economies have to adjust, in order to maintain or enhance their socio-economic viability. As Butler et al. note economic and social forces operating at the global level are determining both the nature and form of the rural landscape and how we value and use it. These changes, coupled with new ideas and approaches to leisure and recreation time are encouraging tourism development in rural areas at an ever increasing pace.

Rural tourism development in areas not traditionally considered tourism destinations per se occurs incrementally; either as a result of entrepreneurs developing businesses that attract visitors or as a result of visitors discovering the area and thereby generating a demand for tourism related activities to which local entrepreneurs respond.

The development of tourism in a rural area is not simply a matter of matching tourist demands with local product supply but a matter of evaluating local suitability and acceptability. *The Indian Agriculture and Tourism Industry Scenario* India is known as "Land of villages". More than 77 crore farmers live in 5.5 lakhs of village. Agriculture contributed about 18.5 per cent of the national income as compared to a high 50 per cent in 1950.85 per cent of population of India still depends on Agriculture hence Agriculture is not mere business, but is still the "True Culture of India".

INDIAN AGRICULTURE SCENARIO

Today the Indian Agriculture has to face tremendous competition because of the driven global trends. To add to this the agriculture crop growth is also weakened due to the uncertain climatic conditions. There is no minimum support price guarantee also. These changes have altered the form and practices of farming operation. Farmers are looking beyond traditional farming to generate income via various forms of direction farm marketing and farm based non-agriculture business.

INDIAN TOURISM INDUSTRY

The Indian Tourism sector contributes 5.3 per cent of India's GDP 2006-07. The tourism industry shows that India had 367 million domestic tourists and 3.92 million international tourists. The Forex earnings from the tourism industry were 25,000 crores.

The tourism industry created 38.8 million direct and indirect jobs. The tourism trend shows as per the 10th five year plan Indian government is willing to spend overRs.2900 crores in the next five years to boost the growth in this sector. It is also seen that domestic tourism has displayed greater buoyancy and resilience. The centre has committed to contribute 765 crores for the state tourism development.

DOMESTIC TOURISM GROWTH

India has achieved great prosperity in tourism as a product. India being the home to many leading religions of the world has many important pilgrim sites of different religions scattered throughout the country. Besides the average Indian is also an avid sightseer. As per the study report of FICCI A.F. Ferguson and Co. 2004, every additional ₹.10 lakhs invested can create 47.5 direct jobs and each direct job can create11 indirect jobs. It also stated that every 30 million additional tourist translate into ₹.4300 crores in revenue. It also stated that farm tourism if developed along unique indigenous lines could have a multiplier effect and high revenue capital ratio. Within last 15 years, domestic tourism has grown by more than 304 million from 63 million in 1990 to 367million in 2005 registering a growth of 20 per cent p.a. The World Travel and Tourism Council has rated India as one of the five fastest growing tourism economies in the world.

TOURISM POTENTIAL IN MAHARASHTRA

Maharashtra is the third largest state of India, both in area and population. It is located on the West Coast of India with a 720 km long coastline along the lush green Konkan region of Maharashtra, with its dense forests is home to several wild life sanctuaries and nature parks. Maharashtra abounds in numerous tourist attractions ranging from ancient cave, temples, unspoiled beaches, ancient forts and monuments, forest and wild life unique hill stations, pilgrimage centers, a rich tradition of festivals, art and culture. The tourism market in Maharashtra is estimated to be around 250 million domestic tourists in 2005.

RESEARCH METHODOLOGY

The research methodology involved both the desk research and the field research which was widely used to understand the concept of Agri tourism and the various aspects that are involved in the successful development of Agri tourism. For the field research, a questionnaire was used comprising of both open-ended questions as well as close ended questions. The sample size used for the study was 100. The sample was selected in a random manner and the respondents were personally interviewed by the authors. Additionally discussions were also held with the officials of the district and other taluka levels to understand the government policies etc. The subject being vast, we have limited the study to the project at Malegaon, Baramati, and Maharashtra.

DEFINING RURAL TOURISM

The definition of rural tourism has been the subject of many debates in the literature without arriving at any firm consensus. First of all, rural areas where rural tourism occurs are difficult to define since criteria used by different nations vary enormously; secondly, not all tourism which takes place in rural areas is strictly "rural" – it can be urban in form, and merely be located in a rural area; thirdly, different forms of rural tourism have developed in different regions and hence it is hard to find characteristics that are common to all of the countries; fourthly rural areas are in a complex process of change due to the impact of global markets, communications and telecommunications that have changed market conditions and orientations for traditional products.

Besides, though some rural areas have experienced depopulation there are many of them that are experiencing an inflow of people to retire or to develop new non-traditional businesses:

- Rural tourism and agri-tourism (each of these categories is a derivative of the subsequent one, like concentric circles).
- Tourism is termed rural when the rural culture is a key component of the product on offer. Depending on the primary activity component of this product, the terms used are agri-tourism, green tourism, gastronomic, equestrian, nautical, hunting, adventure, historical/ cultural tourism and so on.

Tourism activities revolving around large holiday home developments, big hotels, golf courses are difficult to integrate into the concept of rural tourism. The distinguishing feature of tourism products in rural tourism is the wish to give visitors personalized contact, a taste of the physical and human environment of the villages and, as far as possible, allows them to participate in the activities, traditions and lifestyles of local people. There is also a strong cultural and educational element in this form of leisure tourism. Hence a rural tourist destination could be defined as a wider area dominated by the natural and/or farmed/forested environments where specific natural, economic and socio-cultural features, such as tradition, local cooperation, trust and reciprocity are harmoniously embedded and as such create a unique tourist product that is predominantly small scaled, nature friendly, "ethno-cultured", in other words 'sustainable". Since tourism is predominantly a consumer activity, most of the studies are demand driven, concentrated on the visitors and their needs and motivation.

Hence the motives attracting people to the villages are seen as are flections of a growing interest in the outdoors, and a number of other general trends of tourist motivation. The attractiveness of rural areas for tourism and recreation can first be associated with the image of rurality. Here rurality is closely related to the traditional and romantic idea of the "good old days" pure and simple lifestyle, intact nature and perfect integration of man in his natural environment.

Thus nostalgia of the origins, the need for recuperation of the lost link with nature and the basics of life in an increasingly complex, highly organized, anonymous, congested, stressful urban and inhumane surrounding constitutes the principal attention of rural area. The importance of rural tourism as a part of the overall tourism market depends on each country's recreation/ tourism resources, infrastructure image, market access and the presence of other types of tourism products. Even if rural tourism may be minor in relation to the overall tourism market of many countries its importance to the development of specific rural areas may be critical.

Thus, the multiplier effect is often more impacting in rural areas where the entire rural lifestyle is looked for a main attraction.

Rural tourism includes:

- *Agri–Tourism:* Tourism on the farms enables farmers to diversify their activities while enhancing the value of their products and property. Farm tourism also helps to reconcile farming interests and environmental protection through integrated land management in which farmers continue to play a key role. Tourists who choose farm accommodation rather than other kinds of accommodation facilities look for genuine rural atmosphere where they can share intimacy of the household they live in, learn traditional crafts and skills with their hosts, make friends which is a quality, modern times have almost forgotten and above all enjoy home made food and drinks. Some specific food labels can help consumers establish a local produce and can be used as a selling point to tourist who want to taste home grown quality food and drink.
- Heritage and cultural Tourism in rural areas comes in a wide range of forms most of which are unique to an individual local and a valuable component of the rural tourism product. Heritage and cultural tourism includes temples, rural buildings but may be extended to local features of interest including war remnants, monuments to famous literary, artistic or scientific people, historic remains, archeological sites, traditional parkland etc.

- Eco Tourism: Many tourists visit rural areas for the purpose of bird and animal watching and learning about local flora and fauna. Rural tourist destination as a product is definitely very fragile in ecological, social and cultural sense. Its development requires very specific approach that could help it remain sustainable in the long term.

RURAL TOURIST DESTINATION – A PRODUCT

There are some critical factors responsible in the evaluation and development of rural tourism as a product.

Some of these are:

- Changes in the preferences and needs of visitors.
- Destination of the natural and manmade environment.
- Change or disappearance of those attractions, which brought tourists to the area.
- Identification of potential consumer.
- Understanding the rural tourists buying behaviour.

To be competitive rural tourism destination must possess basic tourist requirements:

- Such as hygienic accommodation and catering.
- It should be connected with the farm accommodation.

DEFINING AGRI TOURISM

Agri Tourism is defined as travel, which combines agricultural or rural settings with products of agricultural operations all within a tourism experience. The product can be "experience itself". Agritourism can be defined as "A range of activities, services and amenities provided by farmers and rural people to attract tourist to their area in order to generate extra income for their businesses".

STATUS OF AGRI-TOURISM INTERNATIONALLY WITH SPECIFIC FOCUS ON EUROPE

Most of the European countries pay lots of attention to rural tourism. The growth of rural tourism is difficult to quantify because few countries collect statistics in a way, which separates purely rural fro mother forms of tourism. The concept of Agri-Tourism developed in 80's in Europe, the participating farms have doubled in countries like Italy, the United Kingdom, and France. The number of agri-tourismaccommodation units exceeds 600.00.

In the middle of the 90s, 12 European countries: Belgium, Denmark, Greece, Netherlands, Portugal, Spain, Ireland, Great Britain, Italy, Austria, France and Germany had more than 100.00 farm enterprises involve with different tourism activities. It is obvious that most of the European countries have positive attitude towards rural tourism development because of the advantages this strategy has on rural areas and their overall development.. Agritourism in India: Innovative Income generating activity for Enterprising Farmers Agriculture is backbone of Indian economy.

This sector's contribution towards GDP is decreasing and farmers are finding it difficult to carry the agricultural activities without an additional income. Whereas tourism is termed as an instrument for employment generation, poverty alleviation and development, Agri-Tourism brings in together the declining and booming sector.

Advantages of Agri-Tourism:

1. It brings major primary sector Agriculture closer to major service sector tourism expected to create win-win situation for both the sectors.
2. Tourism sector has the potential to enlarge.
3. Agriculture sector has the capacity to absorb expansion in Tourism sector.

Scope of Agri-Tourism:

1. *An inexpensive gateway:* The cost of food, accommodation, recreation and travel and tourism is low, widening the scope of tourism.
2. *Curiosity for the urban about farming industry and life style:* Agri-tourism, which involves villages and agriculture, has the capacity to satisfy the curiosity of the urban segment by providing scope for re-discovering the rural life, which is rich in diversity.
3. *Strong family oriented recreational activities:* Through rural games, festivals, food, dress.
4. *Finding solace with nature friendly life style:* Peace and tranquility are in-built in Agri-tourism.
5. *Nostalgia for their roots on the farm:* For tourists it is like returning back to their roots.
6. Educational value of Agri-Tourism spreading knowledge about Agriculture science where urban students are moving with the pace of technology.

Basic Principles of Agri-Tourism:

1. *Have something for visitors to see:* Animals, birds, farms, culture of the village, dress and festivals.
2. *Have something for visitors to do:* Participating in agricultural operations, riding camel, buffalo, cooking and participating in the rural games *i.e.* gillidanda, gotti (marble etc.).
3. *Have something for visitors to buy:* Rural crafts, dress materials, farm gate fresh processed food are few items.

Three important factors, which contribute to the success of Agri-Tourism as service:

1. *Farmer:* Majority cases farmer is less educated, less exposed and

innocent for him outsider as guest is (like god) and is treated wholeheartedly without any commercial motive. He entertains the guest while entertaining himself in the process he fills all the service gaps. This makes him a natural businessman.

2. *Village:* Village being located far from the city lacks urban facilities but is rich in natural resources. The investment is the natural resources itself.
3. *Agriculture field:* Each field is unique which adds to the attraction of the urban population. This is the incentive wealth of the rural people.

FORMATION OF AGRI-TOURISM DEVELOPMENT CORPORATION

ATDC's mission is "To promote agriculture tourism to achieve income, employment and economic stability in rural communities in India. To help boosting a range of activities, services and amenities provided by farmers and rural people to attract urban tourists to their area. Thus providing opportunity to urban people to get back to the rural roots".

ATDC'S ROLE IN AGRI-TOURISM

- Prepare Agri Tourism project report and business plan for each applicant agriculture farm.
- Help to facilitate the financial support from Nationalize banks, institutes and government agencies to built agri and rural tourism facilities and infrastructure like accommodation, sanitation, approach road etc.
- Conduct Agri Tourism Business Training Programme.
- Conduct Seminars and conferences on agri-tourism business.
- Provide sales and marketing support.
- Co-ordinate tours from urban areas to the farms.

The trust decided to experiment Agri-Tourism concept on a pilot scale on its own 110 acres model farm, Malegaon, Baramati. Prior to setting up the successful Pilot Agri and Rural Tourism Project in Maharashtra, Malegaon, Baramati Taluka, Dist. Pune in October, 2005 a market survey was conducted by ATDC with sample size of 2,440.

The analysis of the survey was:

- 35 per cent do not have relatives in village.
- 43 per cent never stayed or visited village.
- 57 per cent never visited dairy farm.

This survey promoted to experiment Agri-Tourism in the 110 acre model farm of the agriculture development trust:

- The Agri Tourism Destination Malegaon village, Taluka Baramati, Dist. Pune, Maharashtra, India (Pilot Project)

- This Agri Tourism destination belongs to "Agricultural Development Trust Malegaon". The detailed study has helped in bringing to light the following facts about the model project at Malegaon, Baramati.

CONNECTIVITY

The Agri Tourism Unit in Malegaon is well connected by Airways; Railways and Roadways.

- Nearest International Airport: Pune Airport 102 kms.
- Nearest Railhead: Baramati 10 kms.
- Roadways: Mumbai – Pune – Hadapsar – Saswad – Jejuri – Morgaon – Karhawagaj Chowk – Malegaon
- Kurd – Agri Tourism Destination; (Malegaon Sheti Farm) (ADTM) total distance: 95 kms. Driving time is approx: 2 hrs.

The nearest bus stop is just 1 km from the farm and main bus station is just 5 kms at Baramati Town wherein there is regular non-stop bus service to Pune every after 30 min that reaches to pune in just 2 hrs. In case very emergency event the Agri Tourism Development Corporation will organize private transport facility (at extra cost)

ATTRACTIONS

Agri Tourism activities include farm tours; tractor and bullock cart rides; grapes, mangoes, and other horticulture farms and by-product farms; birds and animal farms; There are lot of things the visitors or guests can enjoy in this agri tourism unit/farm. Total area under cultivation here is of 110 acres, primarily use for agricultural purposes, out of which 65acres is used for Horticultural plantations and cultivation, consisting of various seasonal fruits farms. The added attractions here are the poultry farm; dairy farm; goat farm; and most visited point silk processing unit. The visitors here can also visit the gram panchayati village office and school; village fairs and markets, near by Jaggery making unit; Emu bird Farm; Sugar factory; Taluka Milk Collection Centers and some of the oldest religious temples and also Museum.

ACCOMMODATION

The over night stay arrangement is at the farm itself, there are 12 rooms and 1 big hall. The occupancy is quadruple sharing every room having 4 single beds. One Room is allotted to each Family. The accommodation facilities are basic but very hygienic neat and clean. Two toilets (one western style) (and one bathroom attached to block of every three rooms, this arrangement is purposely kept to experience the joint family atmosphere. The Solar Water heaters at the rooftop are fitted to provide the running hot water for bathing in the morning. There is also the facility of dormitory hall, wherein more than 250 people can easily accommodate.

OUTDOOR RECREATIONAL ACTIVITIES

The outdoor recreational activities for children and adults during daytime are farm tours and agricultural education programmes, how to grow sugarcane, grapes, pomegranate, guava, watermelon, other fruits and what are the food values of each fruits, how to take care of the cattle, nature education programmes, domestic animals and emu bird farms visits and education of the different trees, demonstrations such as goat and cow milking, honey making, silk making, jaggery making, rural games that they can play as gotya; bovhra; surparanbhya; vittidandu; Buffalo ride; bullock cart ride; tractor rides; watching domestic animals; clay molding; painting the nature scenery; tree climbing or simply run with the cycle tree.

ENTERTAINMENT PROGRAMMES

The Evenings are generally fun filled, star gazing activity and the rural Maharashtra folk dances and folksong programmes is organized. Bonfire/ campfire during winter seasons, family games, children games, and lots of fun filled programmes.

MEALS FOR TOURISTS

The food served is pure vegetarian Maharashtrian style, for breakfast Poha, Upma, or Shira, for the lunchusually jawar or bajra bhakri, chapattis, rice, varan, pickle, papad, kurdaya, bhaji, thecha, wangeche bharit, jhunka/pitla, any fresh green vegetable sabji, matki/ chawli usual shabji, etc.

SAFETY AND SECURITY ASPECTS

The Agri Tourism unit at Malegaon is very safe and secure for all the guests and visitors, there is only one main entrance gate, during daytime almost 400 people work in the farm, plus the entire area of 110 acres is barbed wire fenced and over and above there is adequate 24 hours security persons at the main entrance gate and for the entire area.

MEDICAL FACILITIES

This Agri Tourism unit is just 1 km from the Malegaon village. Apart from the onsite medical doctor there are specialist doctors available 24 hours on call.

RISK AND LIABILITY IN CASE OF ACCIDENTS

ATDC has examined the risks associated with some of the activities of agri-tourism. For example: one may decide to ride the bullock cart ride or tractor tailor ride which is not risk free, since there is always a possibility that a guest will fall off the bullock cart or the tractor tailor, however ATDC has established rules and regulations that protects the guests from potential risks. Sometimes accidents cannot be avoided during agri tourism visits at the farms, However, ATDC makes sure that the operations and the farm activity and the sight seeing tours at the farm and outside the farms to sugar factory, jaggery making unit is safe as possible and they have taken appropriate safety precautions.

DISCUSSIONS

Based upon a detailed analysis of the case, the following positive outcomes at the Malegaon Village Khurd, Baramati Taluka can be highlighted:

1. Lives of the farmers changed considerably with the agri-tourism destination venture.
2. The farmers today have developed themselves into entrepreneurs.
3. They have learned soft skills to handle customer service and to market their product.
4. The entire agri-tourism venture has raised the self-esteem of the farmers.
5. The agri-tourism venture has a positive effect among the community from a drought prone area where the suicide cases were increasing.
6. Today the Agri-Tourism destination has more than 4,300 tourists from urban cities every year from 2005. Besides the year end of 2006 also saw Korean companies coming to enjoy the destination.
7. Efficient utilization of the existing natural resources.

A careful analysis and observation of the Case Study of Baramati brings to light certain issues and challenges which need to be addressed by any agri-tourism development body.

These are:

1. Danger of over exploitation of natural resources.
2. Uncertainty of demand for agri Tourism especially in the light of the fact that other type's tourism is becoming popular.
3. Providing and maintaining hygienic conditions in the agri-tourism destination.
4. Danger to Plant life in the form of infectious diseases.
5. Lack of sufficient government support.
6. Training the farmers.
7. Large scale power-cuts.
8. Security aspects.
9. Accessibility and approachability of the area with respect to basic facilities like (medical facilities, transport facilities, availability of water etc.)
10. Marketing Agri-Tourism as a product effectively and consistently.

The study indicated that the critical factors involved in the successful development of the rural tourism industry are:

1. Establishment of a rural environment especially an Indian rural

environment. Many of the tourists wanted to establish their roots in India.

2. The setting of the destination should indicate a rural bias including cultures and artifacts.
3. Hygienic accommodation and catering is a must.
4. It should be connected with the farm accommodation.
5. Attitude of the Central and the State Governments especially with respect to the seed money required, subsidies required or even tax exemptions. This aspect is very important as can be seen through the tax exemptions etc given in European countries.

The success or failure of any tourism in the ultimate analysis depends on the involvement of the local community and also the deep routed networking requirements not only at the local levels but also the state levels. This networking is one of the key issues in making rural tourism sustainable in the long run. The study with special reference to the Agri tourism destinations at Malegoan, Baramati district of Maharashtra indicated that for the Agri tourism to succeed, the following are a MUST: Creation of a Model Demonstration Farm Unit

- Coordinated tours from urban areas to the farms.
- Connectivity by land, air (as well as sea if possible)
- Attractions
- Outdoor Recreational activities
- Accommodation
- Good Meals (preferably a typical Maharashtrian or a Local meal, of course tempered for suitability of the foreign tourists—less spicy etc)
- Hygienic Conditions
- Medical Facilities
- Security, etc.
- *Looking ahead:* The Agri-Tourism Development Corporation has identified 25 new destinations in Maharashtra for initiating Agri-Tourism and has also framed a full fledged training programme module for the farmers.

SUGGESTIONS AND RECOMMENDATIONS

For any agri-tourism venture to be successful some important pre-conditions need to be fulfilled.

These are:

- A complete tourism package can be provided through initiation by the local government bodies of activities such as beautification campaigns, sponsorship of special events that tie in with local tourist attractions and participation of all businesses in the area.
- Good community leadership; Successful tourism promotion and

development requires good leadership by open minded and enthusiastic persons from local government, community groups, the business community and non-profit organizations such as chamber of commerce and convention and visitor bureaus.

- Support and participation of local government; The role of local government is especially important in the following areas; funding for tourism development and promotion, creating and maintenance of infrastructure necessary for tourism, zoning and maintenance of the community so that it looks clean and appealing to tourists and educational support for farmers.
- Sufficient funds for tourism development; Most of the rural communities depend on public funds that are very often insufficient to cover all the needs of the rural community; private funds are something that most often can't be reached since local people do not have sufficient incomes by themselves to invest; therefore it is very important to explore for other sources of funding and assistance.
- Strategic planning; Planning is fundamental for the efficient and effective use of resources and funds, especially in rural areas that have few funds and resources. Good planning for tourism development and promotion can help develop and support local businesses connected to tourism. Planning for tourism development should be integrated into a community's overall economic strategy because of the interdependence of the community and key aspects of tourism development and promotion. Hence, planning for tourism requires the involvement of various stakeholders in the community.
- Coordination and cooperation between businesspersons and local leadership; for tourism development and planning to work, coordination and cooperation between local government and entrepreneurs is crucial. While strength of rural communities is their strong personnel networks, coordination and cooperation between local government and the business community do not always occur easily, if at all.
- Coordination and cooperation between rural tourism entrepreneurs; Tourism requires different types of businesses to work together because, by its nature; tourism has intertwined relations between different types of business such as shops, accommodation facilities, restaurants and tourist attractions. They may create different types of networks, both formal and informal. Tourism network allows for a standardized, yet high quality, business management, which small enterprises lack. Strategic planning and tactical decisions such as pricing, product differentiation and yield management can be handled much well by a qualified management. A tourism network can

substantially improve small tourism business performance by transforming their sporadically scattered products into a one-stop-shop selling a wide variety of functionally interrelated tourism products.

- Information and technical assistance for tourism development and promotion; Different types of information for tourism development and promotion are especially important to agri-tourism development because small communities usually cannot afford to hire experts To this end the role of the above explained networks is also of the utmost importance.
- Widespread community support for tourism; Community support for tourism development and the attitudes and hospitality of local tourism workers are important for successful tourism. It is obvious that management and marketing of tourism often require a community effort because of the nature of tourism; the community as a whole and its image must be marketed, not just one attraction.

CONCLUSION

Development of agri-tourism in Maharashtra rural areas is still in its nascent stage. Maharashtra has perfect opportunities to enhance its agri-tourism offer and it also represents one of the few states, which unifies different climates, natural characteristics and socio-cultural entities. Though there has not been much initiative by the state government for agri-tourism development, it has been successfully initiated through the farmers' efforts.

For the Agri tourism to succeed, it is imperative that the tourists must have:

1. *Something to see:* Animals, birds, farms, culture of the village, dress and festivals.
2. *Something to do:* Participating in agricultural operations, riding camel, buffalo, cooking and participating in the rural games *i.e.* gillidanda, gotti (marble etc.).
3. *Something to buy:* Rural crafts, dress materials, farm gate fresh processed food are few items.

3

Tourism's Relationship with the Rural Environment

CHANGING PERSPECTIVES ON TOURISM'S RELATIONSHIP WITH THE ENVIRONMENT

The reliance of tourism upon the natural and cultural resources of the environment means that its development induces change which can either be positive or negative. Today there is a growing interest in the environmental effects of tourism from governments, non-governmental organisations (NGOs), the private sector, academics and the public. This interest is reflective of a marked change in attitudes to our interaction with the environment that has occurred during the second half of the twentieth century.

Society's concerns after the Second World War rested primarily with rebuilding the economies of Europe and environmental priorities were subsequently low.

By the late 1960s, as the effects of the pursuit of economic growth upon the environment became more evident, environmental issues began to gain more prominence. The first break-up of a major oil-tanker, the Torrey Canyon, leading to the release of oil onto the south-west coast of England caused a high level of public concern and highlighted the fact that increased consumer consumption was not free of environmental risk.

The increasing industrialisation of farming in the USA was also heavily criticised in Rachel Carson's (1962) book, *Silent Spring*, for the ecological damage caused by the use of agro-chemicals on farmland. This book subsequently had a major influence on public consciousness and eventually on regulatory policy, with the banning or restriction of use being placed on twelve of the pesticides and herbicides Carson identified as being most dangerous, including the notorious DDT. Academic interest in the environment was also heightened during the 1960s, and the disciplines of chemistry, physics, mathematics, ecology and biology began to be applied to the environment in an integrated manner within the field of environmental sciences.

However, tourism remained largely immune from environmental criticism, the image of tourism being predominantly one of an 'environmentally friendly' activity, the 'smokeless industry'. This perception was enhanced by the imagery of tourism, embracing virtues of beauty and virginity, as portrayed in landscapes of exotic beaches and mountain areas framed in sunshine.

Nevertheless, there were one or two dissenting observations about the 'smokelessness' of tourism. Milne (1988) comments that in 1961 there was concern being expressed over the possible ecological imbalance that could result from tourism development in Tahiti in the Pacific. The observation of the effects of increasing numbers of people descending upon beautiful areas in the 1960s led Mishan (1969:141) to write:

Once serene and lovely towns such as Andorra and Biarritz are smothered with new hotels and the dust and roar of motorised traffic. The isles of Greece have become a sprinkling of lidos in the Aegean Sea. Delphi is ringed with shiny new hotels. In Italy the real estate man is responsible for the atrocities exemplified by the skyscraper approach to Rome seen across the Campagna, while the annual invasion of tourists has transformed once-famous resorts, Rapallo, Capri, Alassio and scores of others, before the last war no less enchanting, into so many vulgar Coney Islands.

By the 1970s people were becoming more aware and concerned over environmental issues. In 1972, the results of research by a group of scientists and business leaders into population growth, resource use and other environmental trends were published in the 'Limits to Growth: A Report for the Club of Rome Project'. Predictions in the report of pollution, resource depletion and heightened death rates resulting from a lack of food and health services, raised public consciousness over environmental issues. In 1979, the near meltdown of the nuclear reactor at Three Mile Island in Pennsylvania, and the subsequent threat of a major environmental catastrophe, alerted the public to the dangers of the civil nuclear power programme.

Opposition to nuclear power became a central focus of the environmental movement in the 1970s, based upon both the environmental consequences of the programme and its strong link to the development of nuclear weapons. During the 1970s, questions about the environmental impacts of tourism began to be raised more widely, as tourism expanded internationally and the negative effects of its development became more obvious.

Recognition of the problems that could be caused by tourism led the Organisation of Economic Cooperation and Development (OECD) to establish in 1977 a group of experts to examine the interaction between tourism and the environment. Negative effects on the environment from tourism such as the loss of natural landscape, pollution, and the destruction of flora and fauna were already being noted. These concerns were also expressed in academic circles, with the publication of *The Golden Hordes* by Turner and Ash (1975), in which the whole process of tourism development was questioned. By the 1980s, global environmental problems resulting from the human actions had begun to become popular media items. Global warming, associated with the burning of the earth's carbon stocks for energy and the associated release of CO2 had become a major concern, as had the depletion of the ozone layer.

The predicted climatic changes associated with global warming, and the increased risk of skin cancer resulting from the depletion of the ozone layer, became matters of both interest and concern to many members of the public. There was a growing realisation that the pursuit of economic growth and increased material consumption was having a profound effect upon our environment and threatening the long-term well-being of humankind. Concern was also being increasingly and vociferously voiced over the depletion of the tropical rain forests of the world for agriculture and logging.

Nuclear power remained a concern as the world had its worst nuclear disaster at Chernobyl in the Ukraine in 1986 and the effect of the nuclear fall out was felt all over Europe. It is not a coincidence that in 1989 the Green Party in the United Kingdom recorded 15 per cent of the vote in the European elections.

During the 1980s, the spread of mass tourism beyond the Mediterranean basin into new areas, including south-east Asia, Africa and the Caribbean, meant that there was increasing focus on tourism as a form of economic development in less developed countries. Besides economic aspects of development, this focus also included concern over the environmental and cultural consequences of tourism development. The awareness that tourism could have negative effects was increasingly being recognised by NGOs.

Pressure groups such as Tourism Concern, the UK-based campaigning group for humane tourism development, and the Ecotourism Society in the USA were established in the 1980s to promote ethically based tourism for both indigenous peoples and nature. Local pressure groups, concerned by the effects of tourism development on their physical and cultural environment were also formed, such as the Goa Foundation in India.

The Goa Foundation have opposed tourism because of the loss of access to resources for local people and other associated human rights violations associated with its development, as is described later in this chapter. There was also evidence of increasing dissatisfaction by tourists with areas that were perceived as being overdeveloped or having lost their original attractiveness.

For instance, Barke and France (1996:302), commenting on the problems facing tourism in the Costa del Sol region of Spain in the late 1980s, state: 'Environmental decay and poor image have combined with overcrowding and low safety and hygiene standards, together with the popularity of cheaper forms of accommodation and catering, to reduce the perceived attractiveness of the region.'

During the 1990s, new environmental concerns became prominent, reflecting both local and global concerns. An ethical dimension was increasingly introduced into environmental campaigning over the rights of non-human life, with high profile and sometimes violent actions being taken for the liberation of animals from experimentation. Protests against road building became a central focus for environmental campaigners in Britain and other European countries as concerns over the loss of countryside and nature grew.

The enthusiasm and popular support for this campaign led the British government to a major rethink of its strategy over transport, particularly the role of the private motor car and road building, leading to the cancellation of numerous road-building projects. Green politics in Europe gained increasing recognition through formal political routes in the 1990s, notably the formation of a governing red-green coalition in Germany, and by the end of the decade green politicians were in charge of the environment ministries of Germany, France, Italy and Finland.

Concerns over the practices employed by farmers were also heightened with the outbreak of bovine spongiform encephalopathy (BSE) in Britain, which not only threatened animal life, but could also be transmitted to humans in the form of Creutzfeldt - Jakob disease (CJD). Worries over genetically modified crops were also raised in Europe and there was a subsequent increased demand for organically produced vegetables, fruits and meats.

Major protests were also made over the global inequality in world trade and the role of the World Trade Organization in encouraging the removal of trade barriers and import tariffs. By the end of the 1990s, tourism development had for the first time been attacked directly by eco-warriors. Ski facilities were burnt down in Vail in Colorado at the beginning of 1999 because of their possible impacts upon wildlife. In the 1990s, the tourism industry began to take action over the environment, with many tour operators, hotels and airlines attempting to improve their environmental credibility.

Growing concern over the use of the environment for tourism also found its way into the popular press; for example, the English newspaper the *Guardian* raises environmental issues associated with tourism almost on a regular basis in its weekend travel section.

Tourism and the need for a more sustainable approach to its development also led non-governmental organisations not directly associated with tourism, such as the World Wide Fund for Nature, Voluntary Service Overseas and Oxfam, to become increasingly interested in tourism development.

A growing number of tourists also became more interested to varying degrees in the environmental aspects of tourism. 'Green tourism', 'eco-tourism' and 'sustainable tourism', became favourite phrases in the industry. A summary of the changing attitudes of society towards the environment and tourism over the last five decades is shown.

THE ENVIRONMENTAL IMPACTS OF TOURISM

This section of the chapter discusses the environmental impacts of tourism. As will be illustrated tourism will have either negative or positive impacts upon the environment; rarely, if ever, will it have a neutral relationship with the environment.

Although the discussion will attempt to be as holistic as possible, our knowledge of the impacts of much of human action upon the environment, and subsequently the amount we know about the effects of tourism, is limited.

The limitations of the discussion that need to be taken into account can be summarised as follows:

- Research into impact studies is relatively immature and a true multidisciplinary approach to invest-igation has yet to be developed.
- Research into the environmental consequences of tourism tends to be reactive and therefore it is not always easy to establish a baseline against which to monitor changes.
- It is not always easy to separate out the environm-ental impacts attributable to tourism from the effects of other economic activities or anthropogenic factors, such as human habitation, and non-anthropogenic causes, such as natural environmental change.
- It is not always possible to separate the source of impacts upon the environment between local residents and tourists.
- The consequences of tourism are difficult to assess because tourism development is often incremental and the effects are cumulative.
- Spatial discontinuities are inherent to tourism. For example, the effects of air pollution caused by air and car emissions associated with tourism may contribute to acid rain which destroys forests hundreds of kilometres away.

The impacts of tourism upon the environment can be separated into two broad categories of negative and positive changes. To provide a structure to the discussion, the first part of the following section deals with the negative consequences of tourism and the second part with the positive effects for the environment.

This ordering is reflective of much of the observation and commentary that has been expounded on the impacts of tourism, which has raised awareness of the negative environmental aspects that can result from tourism development, whilst the positive environmental aspects are less well defined.

This imbalance in the literature is also a reflection of the fact that any change to the natural environment by human action is likely to be viewed as harmful, involving at the very minimum damage to individual flora and fauna, and sometimes threatening the existence of species and whole ecosystems.

However, it should be realised that within the context of the discussion on impacts, the extent to which we determine impacts to be either positive or negative ultimately relies on value judgements. From an anthropocentric viewpoint, these judgements need to be balanced with the consideration that through the usage of natural resources for development, the standard of living for humans can be improved.

This is a particularly relevant consideration for societies that live in material poverty and struggle to meet their basic needs for food, clean water and shelter. Nevertheless, this is not to condone the negative effects of tourism upon the environment, as in many situations these result from a mixture of human ignorance and greed, rather than from a philanthropic desire to improve the living conditions of human beings.

THE NEGATIVE IMPACTS

There are a broad range of negative physical and cultural environmental impacts resulting from tourism development, which can be categorised into three major types of concern: resource usage; behavioural considerations; and pollution.

RESOURCE ISSUES AND TOURISM

The development of tourism requires physical resources to facilitate its expansion. One of the most noticeable developmental aspects of tourism in generating and destination areas is airport construction. Airports are an essential part of the international tourism system and can generate major employment opportunities for local people. The expansion and development of airports is also beneficial to the tourist by offering easier access to a wider choice of destinations.

However, the resultant effects for the environment, including the people who live near to airports, are not always as beneficial. For instance, airport development and expansion often involves the transformation of agricultural and recreational land which is covered by runways and terminal buildings. According to Friends of the Earth (1997), major international airports, like Heathrow in London, have paved areas equivalent to 320 kilometres of three-lane highways or motorways. In destination areas the extensive amount of land used for both airport and seaport development can also be problematic.

For example, in 'small island developing states' (SIDS), the loss of agricultural land for airport and seaport development can lead to an increased reliance upon food imports to meet local needs.

The development of an airport also requires additional infrastructure, such as new roads and railways, which again necessitates land-use changes and adds to the pollution of surrounding areas. As the demand for international tourism increases, the demand for the expansion of airports is likely to grow.

According to Whitelegg (1999), air transport demonstrates the biggest growth rate of any form of transport and the International Air Transport

Authority (IATA) estimate that the rate of growth in air passengers will continue at 5 per cent per annum until the year 2010.

Within destinations, the development of the tourism superstructure, such as hotels and attractions, and its associated infrastructure, also requires land. Tourism is often a competitor for land use with other economic activities, such as agriculture, and in some cases extractive industries like logging and mining.

Subsequently, the use of land for tourism development is at the denial of other forms of economic activity, thereby incurring what economists refer to as 'opportunity costs', that is the potential economic benefits resulting from another type of development other than tourism are denied. The danger of unplanned and unregulated tourism development, in response to market conditions in which there is a high demand for tourism, can mean there is an overuse of resources for tourism and a lack of development of other forms of economic activity.

This can lead to an economic overdependence upon tourism and a lack of diversification of the economic base. The danger of this situation is that if tourism demand to a destination decreases, there is a lack of development of other economic sectors to support the local economy. This is likely to lead to high levels of unemployment and associated social problems.

Another key natural resource that is essential for tourism is water. The addition of hundreds or thousands of bed spaces in a destination, combined with the lifestyle demands of western tourists, such as a daily requirement for showering, clean sheets and bath towels, means that tourism is responsible in some destinations for the consumption of copious amounts of water compared to the needs of the local population.

Salem (1995) remarks that 15,000 cubic metres of water will supply 100 luxury hotel guests for 55 days, whilst the same amount will supply 100 nomads or 100 rural farmers for three years, and 100 urban families for two years. The effects of the development of tourism in areas where water resources are limited can mean that local people are denied the access to the water resources they previously used, for example to irrigate crops.

They may find that streams previously used for irrigation have been diverted further upstream to service tourism development, or that the water-table level has been lowered by overextraction to service tourism establishments, rendering their wells useless. Where it is impossible to continue to extract enough fresh water locally, hotels can pay to have the water imported, whilst local people suffer water shortages. Unsurprisingly, access to water resources has sometimes led to conflict over tourism development between the developers and the local community.

CONFRONTATION OVER WATER RESOURCES

In Tepotzlan in Mexico, the place from which Zapata led the peasant army in the Mexican Revolution of the early twentieth century, the residents who are mostly Nahua Indians protested against plans to build a golf course, five-star hotel and 800 tourist villas. Apart from the fact that such a development will be exclusive of local people in terms of employment opportunities, it is calculated that the development will use up to 525,000 gallons of water a day, threatening shortages in the town. Using slogans of 'Zapata lives' and 'Land and Liberty', the locals took over the town hall periodically, and barricaded the streets with barbed wire and boulders in protest against the scheme.

In Goa, in India, tourism development has also caused discord over resource issues between developers and local people. This has resulted in local people organising protest groups against tourism development and open antagonism towards tourists.

CLASHES OVER RESOURCES IN GOA, INDIA

The development of tourism in Goa raises many issues over the interaction between local people and tourism. Goa is a state in western India facing the Indian Ocean. It possesses the typical 'exotic' image of paradise for westerners with over 65 kilometres of sandy beaches and coconut palms. The area began to develop its international tourism (it was already very popular for domestic tourism) potential in the 1980s with the first German charter arriving in 1987.

The development of tourism has been characterised by investment from outside the region and the building of large four- or five-star hotels. Unfortunately, this style of development has meant that tourism has excluded some local people from the resources that they need for their livelihoods. Nicholson-Lord (1993) gives examples of the 'Cidade de Goa Hotel' which built a 2.4-metre wall around a beach to deny local people access, and the Taj holiday village and Fort Aguada beach resort hotels, where guests are guaranteed water twenty-four hours a day whilst nearby villagers are denied access to the pipeline for even one to two hours a day.

Many villagers face electricity and water shortages, with one five-star hotel consuming as much water as five villages, and one fivestar tourist consuming twenty-eight times more electricity than a Goan. Many of the hotels were also built directly on the beach, damaging the dunes, and human sewage was put directly into the water without being treated. The extent of the feeling of exclusion of local people from the benefits of tourism has led to the growth of protest groups against tourism development, notably the Jagrut Goenkaranchi Fauz (Vigilant Goan's Army) and the 'Goa Foundation', an environmental group.

Occasionally there has been open aggression towards tourists, such as the pelting of German tourist buses with rotten fish in the late 1980s, and ten tourists were beaten up by a group of villagers in Nuven village after knocking down two pedestrians.

Besides possibly having restricted access to water resources, local people may also find that they are excluded from other areas that they used to use for natural resources and recreation, such as beach areas. A typical sign on beaches that have been privatised to accompany up-market hotel development, especially in less developed countries, taken on the island of Langkawi in Malaysia.

Tourism development can also lead to the displacement of people from their homes, particularly of poorer people in less developed countries, many of whom possess no rights of land ownership and have limited or no access to legal representation. One of the most notable examples of the displacement of indigenous people associated with tourism was the exclusion of the Maasai people from their traditional lands, when the Maasai Mara reserve in Kenya was established. However, the exclusion and displacement of local people from lands for tourism development is not something that is specific to Kenya.

The development of the Chitwan National Game Reserve in the Terai area of Nepal was also achieved by the exclusion of local people, and on the island of Langkawi in Malaysia, the compulsory reclamation of land by the state government led to the splitting up of a long established community and a loss of livelihood for many villagers. Displacement of people from the land for the development of 'golf villages' in South-East Asia has also occurred.

The development of these golf villages usually involves the transformation of agricultural land, the development of condominiums, conference centres and other leisure facilities. Their size can be up to 80 times the size of a typical European golf course. It is difficult to have a global perspective on the numbers of people that may be displaced from the land for tourism development. However, it is evident that tourism development can be an exclusive process, and as landowners and entrepreneurs become aware of the financial opportunities to be gained from tourism, then the pressure on local tenants to leave their land is likely to increase.

CORAL REEFS AND GAME PARKS, ISSUES OF TOURISM DEVELOPMENT IN KENYA

The country of Kenya in east Africa is endowed with natural resources that should make it an attractive tourism destination for decades into the future. It has both fantastic game reserves, a beautiful coastline with coral reefs, and cultural diversity. However, many of these resources are being put under threat from tourism development. The most popular area for holiday tourism in Kenya is along the coast, north and south of Mombassa.

The coast has a diverse range of ecosystems including coral and mangrove swamps. However, the development of tourism has placed the coral under threat from sewage pollution from hotels, tourists walking on the coral and killing it, local people breaking it off to sell as souvenirs to tourists, and boats dragging their anchors through it. Mangrove swamps which form the basis of another vital ecological chain are also being cleared in an unsustainable fashion. They are being cut for construction poles, timber and fuel wood, as well as being removed for aquaculture farms. As a result of the demand by tourists for lobsters, crabs, prawns and fish, there has been overfishing and a decline in fish stocks, and subsequently lobsters and prawns now have to be imported from Tanzania.

Nor is tourism faring much better in some of the safari parks in Kenya, tourists being attracted by the 'Big Five' game animals: elephant, rhino, buffalo, lion and leopard. Indigenous people were displaced to create the parks in the 1940s, notably the Maasi people from the Maasi Mara park. This has radically altered their way of life and resulted in some of the Maasi having to migrate to the coast to sell their handicrafts to tourists. The consequences for the wildlife of increasing numbers of tourists in some of the parks have been the disruption of their breeding and eating patterns.

Tourists are taken too close to the animals, elephants have been poisoned from eating zinc batteries thrown out in the rubbish from the tourist lodges that have been established, and there is also erosion of the vegetation from the excessive numbers of minibuses crossing the parks threatening the grazing of herbivores. Other problems in the parks include the pollution of water through lack of adequate sewage and other waste disposal facilities.

This has led to wild animals and vultures feeding on the waste food and drinking from open sewers. Besides adversely affecting the access of local people to resources, the physical environment can also be threatened by tourism development. A natural feature of many holiday destinations is the beach, but even it may be used as material for hotel construction ultimately leading to its disappearance.

For example, in Antigua in the Caribbean, miles of pristine sand have been removed by sand-mining companies for use in constructing tourism projects, and sand has also been shipped to the Virgin Isles to build other beaches.

Similarly, coral reefs, the second most biologically diverse ecosystem on the earth after tropical rainforests and subsequently a great attraction for tourists, have come under threat from tourism development. Coral reefs are home to approximately 25 per cent of all marine species despite covering only 0.17 per cent of the ocean floor.

Their growth requires specific environmental conditions, including a water temperature of between 25 and 29 degrees centigrade, a relatively shallow platform of less than a 100 metres below sea-level to grow upon, highly oxygenated water, and areas free from sediment or pollution. There are three main types of coral reefs: 'fringing reefs', which connect directly with the shore; 'barrier reefs', which are separated from the shore by a lagoon; and 'atolls', which consist of a ring of coral reefs around a lagoon. The reefs are composed of a thin veneer of living corals that exist on the top of the skeletons of previous biological growths. Coral is placed under threat from different aspects of tourism, including the construction of tourist facilities, inadequate sewage disposal measures to deal with human waste, and the behaviour of local people and tourists.

Coral reefs have been mined for building materials in Sri Lanka, India, Maldives, east Africa, Tonga and Samoa. Besides being used for building materials, reefs may also be placed under threat from the dust created by construction which gets blown onto the reef, for example as in the Red Sea off the coast of Egypt.

The addition of untreated sewage into the water results in nutrient enrichment or eutrophication, which stimulates the growth of algae, which can cover coral reefs, in effect suffocating them. For instance, the discharge of partially treated sewage into the sea off the Hawaiian island of Oahu stimulated the growth of the alga *Dictyosphaeria cavernosa*, which overgrew and killed large sections of the reef.

Similarly parts of the Great Barrier Reef off the coast of Australia are being destroyed by the proliferation of 'crown-of-thorns' starfish, *Acanthaster planci*, which feed on the reef and have become abundant as a consequence of pollution and overfishing of their predators.

According to Jenner and Smith (1992) millions of starfish have been observed, each one able to eat its own area of coral in a day, and as much as one-third of the Great Barrier Reef has been adversely affected to some degree. The Queensland tourism industry has been devastated, and the world's first floating hotel called the 'Barrier Reef Floating Hotel' operated for only a few months in 1988, before being towed back to Ho Chi Minh City from where it had come owing to a lack of tourist demand. The behaviour of local people and tourists towards the reefs can also damage the coral. One country in which tourism has resulted in negative effects upon its coral reefs, and other types of natural resources is Kenya.

According to Pattullo (1996) over 90 per cent of the world's coral reefs are said to have been damaged by various forms of human activity. The extent of tourism's involvement in this damage is generally thought not to be large compared to other industrial sectors, although as Goudie and Viles (1997) point out, 73 per cent of the coral reefs off the coast of Egypt are thought to have been adversely affected by tourism.

Nevertheless, the blame for the demise of the world's coral reefs cannot solely be laid at the door of tourism. Tourism is a contributory factor to the destruction of coral reefs along with other natural and human causes. These include storms and hurricanes, El Niño, overfishing, increased sedimentation produced by the deforestation of land and industrial pollution.

Hurricanes can kill living coral by flinging it up to the top of the reef, whilst El Niño which is an ocean current occurring off the coast of Peru every two to ten years, causes changes in ocean currents and sea temperatures. Changing sea temperatures have also been attributed to the effects of global warming.

The raising of sea temperatures can threaten the food supply of coral, which is dependent upon microscopic algae called *Zooxanthellae* turning the sun's energy into sugars, to provide energy for the coral polyps. The algae are very temperature sensitive, and as the temperatures of the ocean rise the algae will leave the polyps denying them food, which may subsequently lead to the mass death of the corals. It is thought that with continued global warming and increasing ocean temperatures, this process of coral bleaching may occur more regularly.

Additional threats for coral are also posed by more aggressive kinds of human actions. The reefs of French Polynesia in the tropical Pacific face the constant threat of nuclear bomb testing by the French, whilst the residual radiation remaining on some of the atolls from the American and British nuclear tests in the 1960s means they cannot be used for habitation or tourism. Industrial activity can also threaten the well-being of coral, for instance increased silting as a consequence of dredging for tin poses a threat to coral reefs in Thailand. The destruction of coral reef not only means a loss of biodiversity but also threatens other environmental resources upon which tourism depends.

In the same way that tourism was likened to a spider's web, major natural features such as coral, form part of interlinked and complex ecosystems. Coral not only provides an abundance of food for fish but also acts as a natural breakwater to help protect coastline and beach areas from erosion. Without this natural breakwater, beach erosion will occur at a much quicker rate than normal, especially where palm trees, the roots of which help to stabilise the beach, are removed to make space for hotel construction.

The potential damage that unaware and unplanned tourism development can do to coral and beach environments, developed from the work of Edington and Edington (1986). An actual example of the type of construction, which is a photograph of tourism development on the coastline of the Indian Ocean. The construction of tourist facilities would seem to be happening at a rapid pace, leading to the removal of palm trees, and destabilising the beach area.

Another important ecosystem in terms of making the earth a habitable place to live for humans, are coastal and inland wetlands, which cover approximately 6 per cent of the world's surface. Wetlands not only house a wide range of biodiversity and act as vast carbon-storing areas for the world, but also operate as a form of local flood control measure by absorbing vast amounts of water at times of high rainfall, and discharging it to adjacent areas in a slow and measured way.

However, the restricted availability of land for tourism development in coastal areas, combined with the engineering ability to reclaim wetlands, means that wetlands are increasingly being used for tourism development. For instance, in the Languedoc-Rousillon region of France, five new coastal areas were developed on reclaimed wetland sites, in response to the lack of available land for building on the French Riviera. One of the coastal areas, 'La Grande Motte', has subsequently become the third largest French resort in the Mediterranean after Cannes and Nice. The engineering project was enormous, involving the draining, dredging and filling of coastal marshes and saltwater lagoons, leading to the complete disappearance of the wetland fauna.

A similar scheme to reclaim wetlands including mangrove swamps has taken place in the Caribbean, to accommodate the Sir Donald Sangster International Airport in Jamaica. After coastal areas, the second most popular location for tourism is in mountain areas. Just as tourism has resulted in detrimental environmental effects in coastal areas, it has also caused negative impacts in many mountain areas. Mountain areas are physical environments which are sensitive to change, characterised by short growing seasons as a result of the cold temperatures, and soils which tend to be thin and nutrient deficient. The combination of these factors makes subsequent regeneration of damaged vegetation difficult.

Mountain areas have become popular destinations for activity-based tourism, and mountain systems worldwide are being used increasingly for activities such as downhill skiing and snowboarding, mountain biking, paragliding, white water rafting and trekking. One particular form of mountain tourism that is very popular, estimated to account for 3 to 4 per cent, or approximately 24 million of the recorded total of international tourist arrivals in 1997, is wintersports.

The economic benefit associated with sports such as downhill skiing and snowboarding has meant that their development has actively been encouraged through government policy in some countries, as a means of developing upland rural areas. Although the development of downhill skiing has aided the creation of economic prosperity in many mountain areas, it has also resulted in many negative consequences for the physical environment.

The development of mountain tourism requires the construction of hotels, apartments and associated infrastructure, placing increased pressure on land resources and animal habitats. The removal of trees to create ski runs, besides resulting in a loss of habitat for wildlife, also means that rainfall falling on the mountain slopes is not absorbed in the same quantity as before. The removal of trees causes a loss of cohesion and stabilisation of the soil by the tree roots, and subsequently the mountain slope is more prone to slippage.

The combined effects of increased amounts of water running across the surface of the slope, its weakened stability and the force of gravity, has led to mountain areas becoming vulnerable to landslides. The effects of these landslides can be quite dramatic, sometimes involving the loss of human life. For example, Simons (1988) describes the avalanches of mud that swept down mountainsides during the summer of 1987 in northern Italy and southern Switzerland, in which 60 people died, 7,000 were made homeless and 50 towns and villages and holiday centres were wrecked.

The cause of these landslides was attributed to the removal of mountainside forest for ski development. Another mountain area to suffer deforestation and subsequent landslides as a consequence of tourism is Nepal. These landslides can be on a large scale, sometimes leading to whole mountainsides tumbling into valleys. The landslide in this photograph occurred at Tatopani in the Annapurna area of Nepal, and was on such a scale it dammed the powerful Kali Gandaki River behind it, necessitating the dynamiting of the blockage to let the river flow.

A major cause of deforestation in the Annapurna area is the influx of mountain trekkers into the area during the last thirty years. The traditional resource used in the mountain valleys of the area for cooking and to heat water is wood. The continued growth in the number of trekkers to the area has put increased pressure upon forest resources as trekkers demand hot food and often a shower every day.

HUMAN BEHAVIOUR TOWARDS THE ENVIRONMENT

An integral part of the tourism system is tourists and local people. The behaviour of both groups will be highly influential in determining the extent to which the consequences of tourism upon the non-human world are either negative or positive. The behaviour of tourists to the culture of the destination they are visiting will also be influential in determining whether tourism is viewed as a positive or negative force for change by local people.

A major natural attraction for tourists is wildlife but wildlife can be adversely affected by certain aspects of human behaviour. The viewing of wildlife species in their natural habitats has become an attractive activity for an increasing number of tourists, resulting in the intrusion of humans into environments which had previously been the exclusive preserve of wildlife.

Ironically, the desire of the tourist to enhance their perceptions of nature by observing wildlife at close quarters can bring disruption to the natural behaviour of the wildlife they want to see. According to Duffus and Dearden (1990) cited in Roe *et al*. (1997), the extent of the impact of tourism on wildlife can be related to the type of tourist activity and the level of tourism development. Mathieson and Wall (1982) also add that the resilience of wildlife to the presence of humans will influence the degree to which tourism proves harmful to a particular species.

THE ENVIRONMENTAL IMPACTS OF TREKKING IN NEPAL

Nepal is a small land-locked country situated between India and the People's Republic of China and is one of the world's poorest nations with a large foreign debt. It possesses outstanding natural resources for tourism, notably the Himalayan mountain range, and is becoming an increasingly attractive tourism destination for international travellers. The number of international arrivals has risen from 6,179 in 1962 to 393,613 in 1996.

One type of tourism that Nepal has become renowned for is trekking, with 23 per cent of the tourists who go to Nepal participating in this activity. The most popular trekking area is Annapurna, with 59 per cent of all trekkers going there, compared to 19 per cent who go to the Everest Region and 9 per cent who go to Langtang. The Annapurna area is rich in biodiversity containing both rare fauna and flora.

However the arrival of over 40,000 trekkers per annum has put extra pressure upon the natural resources of the area. Unplanned development has led to the construction of 700 tea houses and lodges in which trekkers can stay. Large areas of the outstandingly beautiful rhododendron forests that grow in the area have been removed to provide timber for construction, and fuel to heat food for tourists, and provide them with hot water for showers. Deforestation of the mountains has resulted in tremendous landslides becoming a regular feature of the area.

Waste disposal problems are also an issue. Inadequate sanitation facilities results in pollution of water supplies, and non-biodegradable litter is thrown into streams and piled in rubbish heaps on the edge of settlements, again leading to pollution and hygiene problems. Cultural problems have also been created in the area, with children begging from trekkers, and the development of an inferiority complex amongst some local people in comparison to the 'richer' tourist.

For example, the type of safari tourism practised in the Serengeti Park on the Kenyan/Tanzanian border is representative of a highly developed level of tourism, involving local operators taking tourists into the park in minibuses, and animals being surrounded by thirty or forty vehicles full of tourists taking photographs.

The invasion of the territorial space of the animals, and the associated increase in noise levels, raises the stress levels of animals which is disruptive to their breeding and eating patterns. For example, cheetahs and lions are reported to decrease their hunting activity when surrounded by more than six vehicles. The drivers of the minibuses are encouraged to ignore laws governing the proximity of their vehicles to the animals by the extra tips they receive from tourists for getting close to them.

Sometimes the threat to wildlife from tourism can be more direct, especially in communities where the level of environmental education is low, and an insensitive view of the environment is held by locals. For example, commenting on the backpacker operations that take tourists into the rainforest in Ecuador, Drumm (1995:2) writes:

Only 20 per cent of local guides have completed secondary education, and very few are proficient in a language other than Spanish. Together with a social context which embues them with a settler frame of mind, antagonistic to the natural environment, the negative impacts of this operation are significant. Hunting wild species for food and bravado is commonplace during tours as well as the occasional dynamiting of rivers for fish. The capture and trade in wildlife species including especially monkeys and macaws is also very common.

Besides wildlife, other natural resources may be placed under threat from the action of local people. For instance, coral is damaged by local people who break it off to sell as souvenirs, as in the Bahamas and Granada, where rare black coral is made into earrings for sale to tourists. Local operators taking tourists out in boats to visit reefs sometimes drag their anchors through the coral causing localised damage, whilst tourists harm the coral by touching and standing on it. Additionally, shells are sometimes collected by local people to sell to tourists, as in areas of the Red Sea, the Caribbean and off the coast of Kenya. Key factors influencing the attitudes of local people to the surrounding environment, are poverty levels, economic opportunity and the extent of the provision by government and the private sector of environmental education.

Careless behaviour by tourists can also adversely affect wildlife and ecosystems. A common problem associated with tourists is littering, which can potentially result in the death of animals eating the litter, and also lead to the attraction of predators of endemic species into areas where they would not normally go. For example, elephants have been killed by eating zinc batteries thrown onto rubbish heaps surrounding the outskirts of lodges in the Maasai Mara in Kenya.

In the Cairngorm mountains in Scotland, foxes who are predators of the indigenous ptarmigan and grouse have been enticed into the area, leading to a decline in bird numbers. However, as Shackley (1996) points out, although tourism can be detrimental to wildlife, the habitat of much wildlife is under a more widespread threat from other phenomena, such as agricultural development, urban expansion, and extractive industries like logging and mining.

The behaviour of tourists can also cause cultural changes in the societies they visit. One of the possible consequences for cultures that are exposed to tourism, especially in less developed countries where there is likely to be a marked difference between the lifestyle of the tourist and the local population, is what anthropologists term the 'demonstration' effect. According to Burns (1999:101) the 'demonstration effect' applied within the context of tourism can be explained as:

This effect refers to the process by which traditional societies, especially those who are particularly susceptible to outside influences such as youths, will 'voluntarily' seek to adopt certain behaviours (and accumulate material goods) on the basis that possession of them will lead to the achievement of the leisured, hedonistic lifestyle demonstrated by the tourists.

Seemingly there exists a desire for some groups living in non-western cultures, to imitate western lifestyles by acquiring the same symbols, a phenomenon also referred to as 'blue-jean' culture. The imitating of western lifestyles may however, go beyond the purely superficial, to appropriating the more materialistic and individualistic values of western society. The adoption of such values will undoubtedly cause change in societies whose previous cultural value systems are likely to have emphasised religion, co-operation, the family and the community.

The copying of tourists' fashions can also lead to cultural conflicts between different groups in communities. For example, post-pubescent Muslim girls living on the Mombassa coast in Kenya who see western women dressed in bikinis, may wish to dress the same way, even though their religion dictates they should be completely covered. In societies with strong traditional values, such a situation is likely to result in conflict with the elders and men of the community.

Another criticism that is often made of tourism's effect upon local cultures is that it can lead to their commercialisation and commoditisation.

This can result in established rituals and ceremonies becoming a parody of the authentic culture, to satisfy the demands of tourists, in effect turning into 'pseudo-events'. Tourists are unlikely to understand the significance and meaning of the event they are watching or participating in, and with the passage of time it is also possible that the performers may lose sight of the original cultural importance of the practice.

Similarly, the same criticism can be made of local handicrafts, which instead of being handcrafted for their cultural significance, can end up being mass produced for sale to tourists. Yet as Burns (1999) points out, it is often difficult to separate out cultural changes resulting from tourism from those attributable to the wider process of modernisation, such as the geographical spread of global television networks.

However, the material wealth and lifestyle of the tourist can have the effect of making one's own culture feel comparatively worthless and limiting. What local people fail to understand, as no one usually informs them, is that the behaviour of the tourist is atypical of how they behave during the rest of the year.

The fact that western society suffers from increasing levels of family breakdowns leading to social isolation, high crime rates, drug addiction and suicides and that there is a developing underclass of impoverished and isolated people, are not points often made to people in less developed countries.

This was illustrated by Marcel-Thekaekarka who had spent ten years working with the Adivasi, the indigenous people of the Nilgiri mountains of

Tamil Nadu in India, on rural development schemes before she visited Germany with six of the Adivasis.

Although in material poverty themselves, the Adivasi were shocked by the lifestyle of people in Germany, even though they were materially much wealthier. The Adivasis expressed sympathy for their lifestyles which seemed urbane and isolated as Marcel-Thekaekarka (1999:3) writes: '"It's very nice to be here", Chathi, one of the six told me. "But I couldn't live here. It's not my place. A man needs his family, his community, his own people around him. Just money can't give you a life. You'd shrivel up and die."'

Sometimes the problems that arise from tourism are what the majority of societies would perceive as being socially unacceptable, involving crime, prostitution and drugs. For example, the development of sex tourism in Thailand and other parts of south-east Asia has resulted in increased levels of Aids amongst the population. It has also led, as is the norm in prostitution, to the exploitation of women by men.

POLLUTION

Pollution of the physical environment resulting from tourism can occur on different spatial levels, including tourism generating and destination areas, and other localities not directly connected with tourism but to which pollution is displaced.

However, it is important to point out that tourism is a contributing factor to local and global pollution, along with a whole range of other services and industries. The pollution associated with tourism may be categorised into four main types: water, air, noise, and aesthetic pollution.

WATER POLLUTION

Water pollution is a major problem in many tourist regions of the world. For instance, in the most visited tourist area of the world, the Mediterranean, only 30 per cent of over 700 towns and cities on the coastline treat sewage before discharging it into the sea. In the Caribbean Basin, where 100 million tourists annually join the 170 million inhabitants, only 10 per cent of the sewage is treated before being discharged into the sea.

The most worrying aspect is that, compared to other areas of the world, these figures are actually good. Other regular international tourist destinations such as east Asia and Africa and the islands of the South Pacific, with a few exceptions, have either no sewage treatment or treatment plants that are totally inadequate for the size of the population.

The problem of water contamination from human sewage is not caused exclusively by tourism but is reflective of an inadequate infrastructure to meet the needs of both local people and tourists. Besides the consequences it can have for human health, causing diseases ranging from mild stomach upsets to typhoid through the intake of water contaminated by faeces, human sewage also causes eutrophication (nutrient enrichment) of the water. This can pose a particular threat to coral and associated ecosystems as explained earlier in the chapter. Eutrophication of water may also lead to a downturn in tourism demand as experienced on the Romagna coast of Italy in 1989.

According to Becheri (1991), the total number of tourist bookings on the Romagna coast fell by 25 per cent in 1989 compared to 1988, owing to the eutrophication of the Adriatic and the spread of algae on the surface of the water. The source of the pollution was from agricultural, urban and industrial wastes, which were deposited in the River Po and subsequently outflowed into the Adriatic.

Similarly, the fear of a typhoid outbreak in Salou in Spain in 1988 resulting from contaminated water, led to a 70 per cent decline in tourist bookings the next year.

By the late 1980s, many Spanish beaches were considered dirty, with only three beaches on the Costa del Sol being considered clean enough for Blue Flag status in 1989. The decline in water and beach quality contributed significantly to a slump in tourism receipts in Spain in the late 1980s.

Besides the pollution resulting from the inefficient disposal of human waste, water pollution is also caused by fertilizers and herbicides, which are widely used on golf courses and hotel gardens. The water containing the chemicals seeps through to the groundwater lying 5 to 50 metres below the earth's surface and through aquifers it eventually reaches rivers, lakes and seas.

Other sources of water pollution are caused by motorised leisure activities such as power boating, and even suntan oil being washed off tourists when swimming can result in localised pollution. However, although tourism may seem to be a culprit of much of the planet's water pollution it is important to realise it is a contributory factor. The major sources of water pollution come from oil spills, industrial waste pumped into sea, and from chemicals used in agriculture.

AIR POLLUTION

A major source of air pollution within the context of tourism is associated with transport for tourism. Both air and car transport contributes to local and global atmospheric pollution through the burning of fossil fuels. The release of carbon dioxide (CO_2) is widely thought to be a major cause of global warming, and the emission of sulphur dioxide (SO_2) contributes to problems of acid rain which destroys forests and historic monuments such as the Parthenon in Athens.

Per passenger, aviation produces more pollution than any other form of transport, accounting for 3 per cent of the total amount of the world's carbon dioxide emissions or equivalent to the entire CO2 output of British industry.

The growth in air travel since the 1950s has been rapid, with the annual rate of passenger growth averaging 5 to 6 per cent per annum, over almost a 50-year period. Besides contributing to global warming, air transport emits 2 to 3 per cent of the total global emissions of nitrogen oxides, which are believed to reduce ozone concentrations in the stratosphere (Friends of the Earth, 1997). Emissions of nitrogen oxides and hydrocarbons at lower levels also contribute to regional smog problems by forming low-level ozone on calm summer days, which is harmful to health.

Air pollution is also associated with the development of airports for tourism. Health issues associated with airports include respiratory problems caused by emissions from aircraft and car traffic, and stress associated with noise pollution from air traffic.

According to Whitelegg (1999) aircraft produce significant amounts of nitrogen oxides during take off and landing. He adds that Kennedy and La Guardia airports in New York are amongst the largest sources of pollution in the city, and that Midway Airport in Chicago generates more toxic pollutants than any other form of industry in the city.

The effects of this pollution on health are dramatic, with aircraft engines being held responsible for 10½ per cent of the cancer cases in south-west Chicago caused by toxic air pollution.

A common mistake is to equate transport in tourism solely with airlines, as it is often assumed that most tourism is undertaken by using air travel. However, this is not the case; for example, within Europe, the car accounts for 83 per cent of the total passenger kilometres. A very common pattern of summer holiday travel in Europe is for tourists from the countries of northern Europe such as Germany, Scandinavia, and the Benelux countries to drive down to the Mediterranean coast for their vacation.

When domestic tourism is also taken into account, then the effect of the motor car becomes even more prominent, as the majority of domestic trips are undertaken by its use. For those people living in transport transit areas, the effects of tourism are predominantly ones of inconvenience, associated with pollution and safety concerns.

Although the social and health effects of transit traffic upon local communities is an underresearched area, Zimmermann (1995:36), commenting on transit traffic through the European Alps, remarks: 'The transit traffic is one of the most evident problems within the Alpine area. In several regions local populations' endurance levels have already been reached or exceeded.'

Within destination areas the air quality may deteriorate as a result of both extra traffic and construction. Dust generated during the construction of tourist facilities contributes to air pollution, for example Briguglio and Briguglio (1996) remark that the demolishing of existing buildings and the construction of new ones for tourism has generated vast amounts of dust in Malta.

Yet, as with water pollution, tourism can also be adversely affected by displaced air pollution originating from sources elsewhere. Forests used for tourism in developed countries that are situated close to large industrial centres are particularly under threat from acid rain, caused by emissions of sulphur dioxide from coal-burning power stations. For instance, Mieczkowski (1995) refers to the Black Forest in Bavaria becoming the 'Yellow Forest', and Jenner and Smith (1989) comment that as a result of the damage to the forest caused by acid precipitation, there has been a loss of tourism income.

It should also be noted that as tourism was a contributory factor with a range of other human activities to water pollution, the same is true for air pollution. The use of the motor car in everyday life for commuting and shopping, and the burning of fossil fuels to produce electricity, is larger air polluting activities than tourism.

NOISE POLLUTION

In psychological studies of humans, noise pollution has been found to affect behaviour in a detrimental fashion. According to Mieczkowski (1995) most complaints associated with tourism relating to noise are from air traffic. Noise pollution is particularly a problem for those residents who live around busy international and domestic airports, and the proposed development of airports may sometimes lead to violent opposition by local people and protest groups, as was the case with the construction of Narita Airport in Tokyo.

Noise pollution from tourism will be particularly noticeable in destinations where tourists are searching for quietness and peace. Airflights in remote areas where quiet is expected, such as the Grand Canyon in the USA and the Himalayas, can cause disruption to tourists and recreationists.

Noise pollution from the construction of tourism facilities can also be a problem for residents and tourists. Briguglio and Briguglio (1996) observe that intense noise is generated by the building of hotels and other construction activity in destinations. Night clubs open until the early morning, and increased car traffic from tourism movements, all add to the noise pollution experienced by both residents and tourists in tourism destinations.

AESTHETIC POLLUTION

The development of tourism facilities can also lead to a decline in the aesthetic quality of the environment. Commenting on the development of tourism in the Guadeloupe and Martinique islands situated in the Lesser Antilles, Burac (1996:71) comments: 'The most worrying problem now prevalent in the islands relates to the anarchic urbanisation of the coasts. ... Also, the built-up areas by the seaside are often not aesthetically attractive due to the diversity of architectural styles, the disappearance of traditional creole homes and the disorderly way in which public posters are displayed.'

Often tourism development is based upon maximising profits whilst ignoring aesthetic concerns. This has led to a uniform style of development along many coastlines of the world, that ignores local architectural styles, building traditions and materials. In mountain areas tourism has also created unsightly development. Besides hotel and apartment construction, the development of ski lifts and pistes has also been heavily criticised as a form of aesthetic pollution.

For instance, the Scottish Office (1996:7) make the following remarks about the development of downhill ski facilities in Scotland: 'In addition [to adverse ecological effect], the infrastructure and uplift facilities associated with skiing can have a visual impact on what would otherwise be an unspoilt and undeveloped landscape.'

Harm to fauna and flora resulting from tourism development is an emotive topic. Yet tourism can bring economic benefits to people who are in poverty, such as the money to buy medical supplies and food. To what extent is a reduction in biodiversity important (especially if aesthetic appreciation is not harmed) if economic benefits are being brought to an area from tourism?

THE POSITIVE EFFECTS

It is unlikely that any kind of human action has a beneficial effect for the natural environment it interacts with, other than to protect it from more damaging forms of human behaviour. Therefore, when we talk about the beneficial effects of tourism for the environment, we are in essence talking about tourism being used as a way of protecting the environment from possibly more damaging forms of development activity, like logging and mining. The exception to this situation is tourism's interaction with the built environment, where in post-industrial landscapes, tourism has been used as a catalyst to aid urban regeneration and improve the quality of the environment.

The development of tourism will, however, normally place an increased emphasis on the maintenance of a 'good-quality' environment in a destination, if tourism is intended to play a long-term role in the local economy. Yet the meaning of what is a 'good-quality' environment is highly value-ridden and debatable. Nevertheless, it is certain that the long-term economic success of tourism is often dependent upon maintaining a level of quality in the natural environment, which will satisfy the demands of tourists.

As Mieczkowski (1995:114) comments: 'The very existence of tourism is unthinkable without a healthy and pleasant environment, with well preserved landscapes and harmony between people and nature.' The consequences for tourism destinations that do not maintain a high-quality environment were illustrated by the examples of Salou in Spain, and on the Romagna coast in Italy, earlier in the chapter. This relationship between the economic success of tourism, the environment.

This diagram emphasises that the environment, including both its cultural and physical resources, is the key to satisfying the needs of the tourists and building long-term economic prosperity for tourism. It is therefore in the interest of the destination community to ensure that the landscape remains well preserved and that they provide stewardship of the environment.

Importantly, tourism can play a role in the conservation of the environment by giving it an 'economic value' through the revenues from tourist visitation. Given that development decisions are predominantly based upon an economic rationale, the revenues from tourism can help to protect habitats and wildlife from other more environmentally harmful forms of development, such as mining and logging, or from other forms of destructive human activity, such as poaching.

Within the context of this section of the chapter, one of the most positive examples of where tourism has been used to conserve a particular species is the mountain gorilla project in Rwanda, which was proving very successful until the outbreak of civil war that took place there between 1990 and 1994.

One type of environment, in which some of the best examples are to be found of tourism making a positive contribution to environmental improvement, is in post-industrial urban environments. Although tourism can bring problems of traffic management, overcrowding and associated problems, such as littering to urban areas, it can also play in active part in the restoration of redundant industrial areas and of historic sights.

Many of the post-industrial towns of the western world suffered the loss of traditional manufacturing industries, such as iron and steel, shipping and coal mining in the 1980s. Subsequently, tourism was turned to by many local governments as a catalyst for urban regeneration and as a means of providing new employment opportunities.

The pioneer of using tourism to regenerate urban areas was Baltimore in the USA, where the decision was made in the 1980s to rejuvenate the waterfront through the development of shopping and recreation, to arrest inner city decline.

Despite the numerous commendations that have been made of the redevelopment of Baltimore through tourism, Law (1993) criticises the success as being only skin deep, suggesting that poverty and housing problems still remain in the city.

However, there is little doubt that environmental improvements have resulted from the development of tourism in depressed urban areas. This is particular the case for the waterfront areas of major cities, such as Sydney in Australia, and Liverpool in England.

One advantage of improving the environmental quality of the urban environment, especially where it is combined with improved infrastructure development, is that it enhances the image of the city and makes it more probable that other businesses and services will be attracted to relocate and invest there. Besides the advantage of attracting secondary investment, tourists who come to the area also spend money, which induces a multiplier effect generating further demand for goods and services in the local economy.

GORILLAS IN RWANDA

One of the most cited examples of how tourism can be used to aid conservation is in Rwanda in central Africa. The Parc National des Volcans in Rwanda is home to more than 300 of the world's estimated 650 mountain gorillas. They were particularly under threat from poachers, an export trade of gorillas' hands for ash-trays to the Middle East was one lucrative outlet, and also from the encroachment of agriculture leading to the removal of their habitat.

The gorillas were popularised by the film *Gorillas in the Mist*, about the life of Dian Fossey who was an active researcher and conserver of the gorillas, ultimately resulting in her murder. There is little doubt that the film aided the development of tourism in the park.

Tourist visitation of the gorillas is controlled by the Office Rwandaise du Tourisme et de Parcs Nationaux, and part of the revenues generated from tourism go to conservation agencies, notably the Mountain Gorilla Project and Dian Fossey Gorilla Fund. Visitors are taken out in small groups (maximum of eight) by well-informed local guides to see the gorillas in their natural habitat of dense bamboo forest.

The total annual visitation to the park is between 5,000 to 8,000 tourists. Importantly, the project has been proven to be a financial success, critically benefiting local people, who in turn have taken a more active interest in conservation.

However, the civil war in Rwanda between 1990 to 1994 unfortunately brought visitation to a standstill. In 1994 when 750,000 refugees were escaping from Rwanda to Zaire (now named the Democratic Republic of Congo), tens of thousands of people per day passed through the park, bringing with them their cattle and belongings.

Many took refuge in the park. The occupation posed particular problems for the gorillas, including land-mines being placed in the forest, and gorillas being trapped in response to a lucrative black market for meat that had developed in response to famine. Between 1994 to 1998 rebel militias still held out in the park. The future of gorilla tourism in Rwanda therefore remains uncertain because of political unrest.

The redevelopment of urban areas through tourism can also be aided by the development of tourist attractions which are rooted in the local heritage and history of the area. For instance, at Wigan in England, the town that was the source of inspiration for George Orwell's novel *The Road to Wigan Pier*, the local municipality developed a heritage centre called 'Wigan Pier'.

Reflecting the day-to-day life of an industrialised Wigan at the beginning of the twentieth century the centre attracts over 500,000 visitors per annum.

Importantly the involvement of local people in establishing the centre helped regenerate local pride and interest in their heritage. The development of heritage attractions to attract tourists to urban areas has now become a global phenomenon; for example Holden (1991) remarks that in Singapore a large historical and cultural theme park based upon the ancient Tang Dynasty of China has been developed, including 1,000 replicas of the Terracotta Warriors.

However, the development of such attractions has led to criticisms of inauthenticity, especially where the theme seems to have little to do with the area it is situated in, or the attraction attempts to recreate life as it was in a historical period.

As with all forms of tourism, the benefits of urban tourism will only continue to be enjoyed if it is carefully planned and managed to ensure that areas do not become totally overcongested, as in the case of Venice, which is literally sinking under the weight of tourists.

The influx of large numbers of tourists has been a contributory factor to a deterioration in the quality of life for residents in Venice, which has led to some of them leaving the city.

As for all forms of tourism, urban tourism has threshold limits beyond which the environment will be perceived as having declined in quality, with consequences for both local residents and tourists.

THE FUTURE OF TOURISM'S RELATIONSHIP WITH THE ENVIRONMENT

The raised awareness of the impacts society was having upon the global environment, including issues such as resource usage, pollution, animal and human rights, meant that by the end of the twentieth century some individuals were beginning to change their attitudes to consumerism and demand products that were more 'environmentally friendly' and 'ethically correct'.

This change in buyer behaviour was given the name 'green consumerism'. This chapter considers the extent of the influence of green consumerism upon tourism, examines 'new' forms of tourism, and proceeds to consider the future of tourism into the twenty-first century.

THE GROWTH OF 'GREEN' CONSUMERISM

The late 1980s in the developed countries of the world marked the beginnings of a change in consumer behaviour, with concerns over the environmental effects of products being expressed in the buying patterns of a significant market segment of consumers. Cairncross (1991) takes the view that the extensive media coverage of environmental concerns, such as climatic change, the burning of rainforests and the vanishing ozone layer, was highly influential in getting people to think about the environmental effects of what they were buying.

Martin (1997) takes the view that the rapid economic growth experienced in Britain during the early 1980s was influential in moving people's concerns on from basic economic needs to wider ethical considerations of consumerism. Generally, levels of public concern over the environment tend to reflect economic cycles, that is, when the economy is buoyant environmental concern is at its highest (Martin, 1997).

Evidence of this shift in concern of consumerism towards environmental issues was demonstrated by the *Green Consumer Guide* becoming top of the list of best-selling books in Britain in September 1988. This publication was a seminal consumer guide, in that for the first time, ratings of the performance of companies and products were provided based upon environmental criteria.

Concern over the environment manifested itself in consumer behaviour, in various ways, in different countries. In Britain, there was a virtual consumer boycott of aerosols that contained chloro-fluorocarbons (CFCs), after the media and environmental pressure groups alerted consumers to the role of CFCs in ozone depletion. In America, consumers' primary concern was with waste and excessive packaging on products, and German consumers' concerns also rested with packaging and the plastics used to make drink bottles.

Market research at the end of the 1980s supported the observation that concern over the environment was high. Martin (1997) comments on the results of a survey conducted in 1989, of a representation of the British public by the Market Opinion Research Institute (MORI), a leading British market research company.

When asked the question: 'What would you say is the most important issue facing Britain today?', 35 per cent of the respondents identified environmental issues, a higher percentage than for health care, unemployment, and inflation. However, as Martin points out, just sixteen months later when the survey was repeated, only 10 per cent of the sample identified the environment as being the most important issue and in subsequent surveys this would seem to be a consistent rating. This 'outbreak' of green consumerism forced companies to begin to respond to the environmental concerns of an affluent and sizeable minority of the market.

Not only did this influence the retail side of the market but also the supply side of the market as a few retailers began to check the environmental practices of their suppliers.

For instance, B&Q a British hardware chain, questioned their suppliers about the quality of their environmental management of the peat bogs from which the peat sold as fertilizer in their shops came from, and one supplier was subsequently discontinued for having insufficient environmental standards.

In America, the three leading tuna canners, controlling 70 per cent of the market, decided to ensure that their fish were caught only in 'friendly ways' which were not harmful to other types of fish.

Other new companies emerged into the consumer market, based upon a philosophy of selling ethically sound and environmentally friendly products. One of the most notable business success stories in the British market was the Body Shop, which now has hundreds of stores worldwide. The Body Shop's primary concerns are with skin and hair care, and it has emphasised from its foundation that environmental and social considerations have been at the forefront of its decision making.

The view of the Body Shop is made clear in their policy document: 'The Body Shop has always had a clear, top-level commitment to environmental and social excellence. Because of this, we make sure we include environmental issues in every area of our operations'. As part of this policy, the company does not carry out any animal experiments to test its cosmetics and also emphasises 'fair trade' practices with its suppliers, based upon buying from businesses who wish to protect their culture and practise traditional and sustainable land use.

There was also a growing consumer demand for ethical investment funds, which can be traced to the early 1980s and the desire of the universities and churches in America not to put money into companies trading with South Africa, whose government supported the system of apartheid at that time.

The consequences for companies that ignore consumers' environmental concerns are illustrated by the case of Royal Dutch Shell, the world's biggest oil company. In 1995, Shell intended to bury an obsolete oil rig called the Brent Spar, at the bottom of the North Sea. Concerns raised by Greenpeace, the non-governmental organisation, over the possibilities that toxic sludge released from the rig would contaminate the sea floor, led to a great deal of controversy over the plan.

Activists encouraged boycotts of Shell service stations in Germany and motorists also began to shun Shell garages in Denmark and Holland. In Germany, service station income fell 30 per cent and the financial losses and adverse publicity led Shell to cancel the sinking of the oil rig.

At the beginning of the twenty-first century, 'green consumerism' seems to have established itself as an integral part of the consumer market. Although it is difficult to define exactly what green consumerism is, and therefore measure it, consumer surveys of behaviour patterns, based upon environmental attitudes, lend support to the feeling that environmental concern will play an increasing part in consumer behaviour in the future.

For instance, when a sample of 2,000 people in Britain were asked if they had 'Selected one product over another because of environmentally friendly packaging/ formulation/ advertising', 36 per cent said they had in 1996 compared to 19 per cent in 1988. Market research results in America also support evidence of a trend towards green consumerism. A survey by Michael Peters (MPG) of Americans in the summer of 1989, found that 53 per cent of the public had decided not to buy a product during the previous year, owing to concerns over the effects of the product or the packaging upon the environment.

A survey carried out by the same firm in Canada found that approximately 66 per cent of the Canadian public would be more likely to buy a product that is recyclable or biodegradable, and approximately 60 per cent said they would be willing to pay more for such products. The growth in demand for organic farm products since the mid-1990s in Britain, associated with scares over salmonella poisoning in chickens and bovine spongiform encephalopathy (BSE) in cattle, also support the notion that people want to consume in a healthier, less environmentally damaging and more ethical way. The relatively high prices charged for organic farm produce in comparison to other produce reflect the willingness of a sizeable part of the consumer market, to pay premium prices for 'environmentally sound' produce.

The willingness of people to pay more for products and services that are advertised as being environmentally sensitive does, however, offer the opportunity for consumer exploitation by companies. Claims that a company operates in an 'environmentally friendly way' are often difficult to substantiate, and many people remain sceptical that a company's claim of employing green practices and acting in an environmentally conscious way, is little more than a public relations exercise.

According to Cairncross (1991), a market survey carried out by Environmental Research Associates of Princeton, New Jersey, found that 47 per cent of consumers thought that environmental claims made by many companies were 'mere gimmickry'.

Consumers may often be confused about which products are genuinely environmentally friendly, given the lack of, or misleading, information that is sometimes presented. There is a necessity for the regulation of environmental claims made by companies through independent bodies.

For example, organisations such as the Organic Soil Association in Britain who verify farmer's claims of organic farming have been influential in implementing standards set by the European Commission on organic farming and reassuring the public that claims are genuine. Thus, although certification by the association is voluntary, it has become virtually necessary for any UK farmer wishing to sell organic produce to have certification, especially to sell their produce in supermarket chains.

In the tourism sector, besides the 'International Standards Organisation' (ISO) logo that is available to companies who implement 'environmental management systems', other green labels emphasising green credibility have appeared over recent years. One such scheme is the 'Green Globe', which was originally launched by the World Travel and Tourism Council (WTTC) in 1994.

The WTTC is a trade association which incorporates many of the leading multinational travel and tourism corporations. In 1999, 'Green Globe 21

Certification' became established as an organisation independent of the WTTC, concerned with verifying the environmental standards of companies and destinations operating in the tourism market.

The Green Globe 21 logo is applicable to many of the different elements of the tourism system, including tour operators, transport services, visitor attractions, hotels, local communities and destinations. Any travel and tourism company can apply to become a Green Globe 21 member as long as they want to be involved in sustainable tourism development. Green Globe 21 provide information and advice on the ways companies can modify their business practices to improve the environmental quality of their operations.

After six months the company must decide whether to pursue formal certification from Green Globe 21, which involves establishing environmental management systems (EMS), necessitating the formulation of an environmental policy for the company, and environmental auditing of their business practices. Once the company decides to pursue certification they must pay a fee to Green Globe 21, which in 2000 varied from US $750 for local companies to US $15,000 for companies operating internationally, after which they can use the Green Globe 21 logo.

The verification that standards are being met is undertaken by Societe Generale de Surveillance (SGS), an international verification body, and an International Advisory Council of industry, government, and NGO experts. This is a direct attempt to overcome the earlier criticism of the scheme, which was that as environmental monitoring was carried out on a self-assessment basis by the company rather than by independent verifiers, there was no real guarantee of standards and it was open to bias. However, a major criticism of the present scheme is that a company can use the logo after electing to follow the certification scheme, without having actually put an environmental management system into place.

Once the company has implemented an EMS system and met the necessary criteria, a new logo is given to the company with a tick in it, though the ability of the consumer to understand the difference is very uncertain. Indeed, at present the level of awareness of the logo in the consumer market is probably low, and its meaning uncertain.

Consequently, the scheme remains open to criticism about its standards, and to suspicion over the degree to which it represents a true desire to improve the environmental standards of the tourism industry, or an attempt to make money on the premise of voluntary environmental regulation.

Consumers are also encouraged to become members of Green Globe 21 by registering on their web page, for which there is no charge, but customers will find environmental information about companies and destinations. The third part of the system is the inclusion of communities into the award scheme. The basic cost of membership for communities is US $50,000 and thereafter the fee will be adjusted to reflect the complexity and scale of the EMS. The scheme is innovative, both in the idea of certifying the operations of the tourism sector, and in its holistic approach which recognises tourism as a system, incorporating consumers, the industry, and the destination community.

However, the scheme is very market-driven and its success will be dependent upon a growing number of consumers being interested in the green credentials of tourism companies and destinations, and having faith in the environmental integrity of the logo.

Another symbol of environmental standards in the tourism sector is the kitemark awarded by the 'Campaign for Environmentally Responsible Tourism' (CERT). Established in 1994, CERT is currently located in the United Kingdom and unfortunately is currently only accessible to UK tour-operating companies, although there are plans to expand the scheme into other countries and other companies in the sector.

Tour operators can be awarded the CERT logo if they make a commitment to:

- Develop and publish an environmental policy statement which is relevant to the business needs and destinations of operation;
- Ensure that staff are aware of this environmental policy and trained in its implementation;
- Distribute a lively, upbeat leaflet to clients which provides advice about how they can reduce the environmental impact of their holiday;
- Include some questions about their environmental performance in their customer evaluation form. These are passed on to CERT and provide independent verification of the status and effectiveness of their environmental programme;
- Help raise funds for environmental projects which will bring benefits to the environment, local people and the travel industry.

The effectiveness of the company in meeting the above criteria is verified by a CERT specialist who also gives specialist advice to help the company. However, as for Green Globe 21, the success of this scheme will be dependent upon its recognition by consumers, and an understanding of and belief in the environmental quality that is portrayed in the logo.

CONSUMER TRENDS AND GREEN TOURISM

The influence of green consumerism upon the tourism market is not easy to discern. As Swarbrooke and Horner (1999:198) comment: 'One thing is clear - as the debate has developed, the term "green tourist" has not achieved the acceptance that the phrase "green consumer" has in general.' This does not mean that consumers do not have concerns about the activities of the tourism industry.

The interests of consumers in the environmental aspects of tourism were reflected as early as 1991 with the publishing of the book, *The Good Tourist*, which advised tourists how to act in a more environmentally responsible way. As Wood and House (1991) comment on the back cover:

Thankfully now, the mistakes of the past are being recognised and a new breed of tourist is emerging. Travelling independently or in small groups, living as locals caring for the country they are visiting and its peoples, the Good Tourists take a long-term look at travelling and the world we live in.

Empirical research also supports the view that consumers are aware of the environmental impacts of the tourism industry. Martin (1997) cites a survey carried out by MORI in the summer of 1995 in Britain, in which when asked 'how much damage to the environment do you think travel and tourism causes?', 64 per cent of the respondents were found to think that tourism caused some degree of damage to the environment.

However, in the same survey, when asked about the damage to the environment caused by tourism in comparison to other industries, tourism ranked fourteenth out of seventeen possible choices behind other services such as road transport and domestic waste disposal.

The opinion of the public about the efforts of the tourism industry to mitigate any of the harmful environmental impacts caused by it, in comparison to the efforts of other industries to reduce the negative environmental impacts their operations may be causing, is not reassuring for the sector. When presented with the statement, 'I'd like you to tell me how much you feel each industry is doing to reduce any harmful effects its activities might have on the environment', tourism ranked sixteenth out of seventeen industries behind 'nuclear fuel manufacturing and reprocessing' and 'oil exploration and production'.

Yet, as for other consumer goods and services, there does seem to be a market opportunity for tourism companies to increase their revenues through environmental improvements. In the 1995 MORI survey, 30 per cent of the respondents stated they would be prepared to pay an extra premium on top of their holiday price, to ensure that tourism companies were committed to environmental protection. In reality, there is always a difference between people's willingness to say they would pay more for environmental care, and the likelihood of them actually doing it, as was discussed within the context of charging admission fees to visit national parks. Nevertheless, the results suggest that a sizeable minority of the market is willing to pay more for environmental quality.

Although concerns over the environmental effects of tourism are unlikely to stop the vast majority of people taking some kind of holiday, for a part of the market, the type of holiday they choose may be increasingly influenced by their environmental attitudes. The development of green consumerism in the 1980s coincided with the development of a range of holiday types that inferred a greater level of awareness of the environment than is associated with mass tourism.

Many terms have subsequently been used, often interchangeably, to describe these new forms of tourism including 'alternative', 'green', 'nature', 'sustainable', 'responsible', and 'ecotourism'. Mowforth and Munt (1998) extend this list to include other forms of new tourism such as academic tourism, agro-tourism, appropriate tourism, contact tourism, and wildlife tourism. A common theme of these labels is that they are indicative of a more caring approach to how tourism should be developed in the future.

As Shackley (1996:12) comments on new approaches to tourism: 'Terms such as environmentally friendly tourism, sustainable tourism, ecotourism, responsible tourism, low impact tourism are just a few among many in common use.... These designate low impact tourism programmes which might result in some form of sustainable benefits to the destination area.'

Certainly, the idea of alternative types of tourism to mass tourism seems to have found favour with a significant segment of the tourist market. Besides the growth in environmental consciousness since the late 1980s, the development of alternative forms of tourism can also be associated with consumer over familiarity with mass tourism, and a subsequent desire for new types of holidays. This latter point means that the concept of 'alternative tourism' can be interpreted in at least two ways: alternative tourism as a form of more environmentally aware tourism; or alternative tourism as types of tourism that are different to mainstream tourism without necessarily being any less environmentally damaging.

For example, 'activity holidays' have become a segment of the tourism market that is growing, attracts high income groups, and is a component of a healthy lifestyle for many. Concerning changes in the market and the growth of the activity holiday market in Scotland, Scottish Enterprise (1995:2) comment:

Changes in consumer behaviour and values are a driving force for tourism. Today's tourist is becoming more experienced, more quality conscious, more independent, more discerning, and is therefore more difficult to please.... However, not only is the tourist becoming more sophisticated, experienced and quality conscious but also more active on holiday, reflecting the general growing awareness of healthy lifestyles and the increasing importance of active relaxation.

Yet it would be mistaken to think that a sports-based activity holiday would necessarily be compatible with the surrounding environment. For example, mountain biking, downhill skiing, and even hiking have all caused soil erosion, disturbance of wildlife, and problems of aesthetic pollution in mountain areas.

So what are the criteria of alternative tourism? Whilst there is no universal agreement on a definition of what alternative tourism actually is, the differences of alternative tourism to mass tourism are highlighted by Cater (1993:85) as follows: 'Activities are likely to be small scale, locally owned with consequentially low impact, leakages and a high proportion of profits retained locally.

These contrast with large-scale multinational concerns typified by high leakages which characterise mass tourism.' Utilising this definition it is possible to highlight the characteristics of alternative tourism which differentiate it from mainstream tourism.

Characteristics of alternative tourism:

- Small scale of development with high rates of local ownership
- Minimised negative environmental and social impacts
- Maximised linkages to other sectors of the local economy, such as agriculture, reducing a reliance upon imports
- Retention of the majority of the economic expenditure from tourism by local people
- Localised power sharing and involvement of people in the decision-making process
- Pace of development directed and controlled by local people rather than external influences

Using these criteria, alternative tourism surpasses purely a concern for the physical environment which typifies green tourism, to include economic, social, and cultural considerations. If the physical, environmental and cultural dimensions of the environment are considered in an integrated fashion, and tourism is developed with the characteristics displayed, then alternative tourism can be viewed as being synonymous with the concept of sustainable tourism development.

A kind of tourism that is often associated with the characteristics of alternative tourism outlined above is 'ecotourism'. According to Shackley (1996) it is a term invented by conservationists in the 1970s, whilst according to Fennell (1999) the term can be traced back as far as 1965 to the work of Hetzer, who used it to explain the interaction between tourists and the environments that they come into contact with.

However, like the concept of alternative tourism, there is no consensus about the meaning of ecotourism. The difficulty of trying to define ecotourism is referred to by Cater (1994:3) thus: 'In particular, the term ecotourism is surrounded by confusion. Is it a form of 'alternative tourism' (furthermore, what is "alternative tourism?")? Is it responsible (defined in terms of environmental, socio-cultural, moral or practical terms)? Is it sustainable (however defined)?' Waldeback (1995) recognises different dimensions and interpretations of what ecotourism can be.

Dimensions of ecotourism:

- *Activity*: Tourism which is based upon experiencing natural and cultural resources

- *Business*: Tour operators who provide ecotourism tours
- *Philosophy*: A respect for land, nature, people and cultures
- *Strategy*: A tool for conservation, economic development and cultural revival
- *Marketing device*: For promoting tourism products with an environmental emphasis
- *Handle*: Convenient umbrella name for a number of tourism related concepts such as 'responsible or ethical travel', 'low-impact tourism', 'educational travel', 'green tourism' and so on
- *Symbol*: Of the debate about the relationship between tourism and the environment
- *Principles and goals*: Defining the symbiotic and sustainable relationship between tourism and the environment

Evidence of the confusion over the term can be seen in the continued attempts to define what it is. For example, McLaren (1998:97) comments:

Ecotravel involves activities in the great outdoors - nature tourism, adventure travel, birding, camping, skiing, whale watching, and archeological digs that take place in marine, mountain, island and desert ecosystems. Much of the travel is now called ecotourism, although critics argue that the definition of 'ecotourism' is so broad that almost any travel would qualify, as long as something green was seen along the way.

The danger of ecotourism being used as a marketing term in a disingenuous fashion to promote unsustainable forms of tourism is highlighted by Goodwin (1996), who comments upon its opportunist usage by the tourism industry, where the tag 'eco' has become synonymous with responsible consumerism. Hall and Kinnaird (1994) also make the point about the problematic nature of defining ecotourism, stating that there is no consistent definition. They comment that: this term [author's note: ecotourism] is used in a generic sense to cover tourism development which is sympathetic to, complements and/or is employed as a vehicle for, conserving and sustaining natural and cultural environments and their resources and which may encompass the domain of such terms as 'sustainable', 'green', 'soft', and 'alternative' tourism.

Holden and Kealy (1996:60) add an explicit economic component in their definition:

Implicit in all the definitions is respect or friendliness for the physical and cultural environment, *i.e.* developing a form of tourism that is non-damaging and non-degrading; subject to adequate and appropriate management controls; and that offers financial contributions for the protection of indigenous cultures and environments.

Goodwin (1996:288) links this economic dimension directly to conservation of resources in his definition of ecotourism as:

Low impact nature tourism which contributes to the maintenance of species and habitats either directly through a contribution to conservation and/or indirectly by providing revenue to the local community sufficient for local people to value, and therefore protect, their wildlife heritage area as a source of income.

Both these latter definitions emphasise the economic aspect of ecotourism in conservation, and the involvement, instead of the exclusion of local communities in the conservation process. A comprehensive list of guiding principles for the development of ecotourism is set out from Wight (1994:40).The direct relevance of ecotourism to sustainability following the principles of Wight (1994) is highlighted by Shackley (1996:13) stating: Ecotourism projects should meet the following criteria.

They must:

- Be sustainable (defined as meeting present needs without compromising the ability to meet future needs)
- Give the visitor a unique and outstanding experience
- Maintain the quality of the environment.

Guiding principles for ecotourism:

- It should not degrade the resource and should be developed in an environmentally sound manner
- It should provide long-term benefits to the resource, to the local community and industry (benefits may be conservation, scientific, social, cultural, or economic)
- It should provide first-hand, participatory and enlightening experiences
- It should involve education amongst all parties - local communities, government, non-governmental organisations, industry and tourists (before, during and after the trip)
- It should encourage all-party recognition of the intrinsic values of the resource
- It should involve acceptance of the resource on its own terms, and in recognition of its limits, which involves supply-oriented management
- It should promote understanding and involve partnerships between many players, which could include government, non-governmental organisations, industry, scientists and locals (both before and during operations)
- It should promote moral and ethical responsibilities and behaviour towards the natural and cultural environment by all players
- Sustainable use
- Resource conservation
- Cultural revival and decolonisation
- Economic development and diversification
- Life enhancement and personal growth

- Maximum benefits and minimal costs/impacts
- Learning about the natural culture and environment.

Who are the 'ecotourists'?

Based upon the principles and goals of ecotourism described by Wight (1994), Waldeback (1995) and Shackley (1996), it is evident that ecotourism places a much heavier emphasis upon conservation, education and ethics than mass tourism. The emergence of a form of tourism that is based upon the premise of an ethical relationship with the environment is reflective of changes that are occurring in the consumer market for tourism. Poon's (1993) concept of the 'new tourist' was referred.

According to Poon 'new tourists' display a 'see and enjoy but do not destroy' attitude and do not assert that the 'west is best'. Other labels have also been given to the tourists who constitute this emerging environmentally conscious market segment, including the 'ethical tourist', 'environmentally responsible tourist', 'good tourist' and 'ecotourist'.

So who are the ecotourists? Just as there is no definitive definition of ecotourism, similarly there are different opinions on the characteristics of ecotourists, and who ecotourists actually are. Given the difficulty in defining ecotourism, it is unsurprising that it is subsequently difficult to categorise the 'ecotourist', which leads to confusion over the type of behaviour that ecotourists could be expected to display.

As Cater comments: 'There is an inherent risk in assuming that the ecotourist is automatically an environmentally sensitive breed. Although small, specialist, guided groups of ecotourists may attempt to conform to this identity, the net has now been cast sufficiently wide to include less responsible behaviour.'

It would therefore be mistaken to think that being labelled an 'ecotourist' will necessarily mean that a tourist will particularly desire to be environmentally educated and have a minimal impact upon the environment. According to Mackay (1994), the tourist industry divides ecotourists into three distinct categories, of the big 'E', little 'E' and soft adventure types.

The most popular group is the little 'E', in which tourists' environmental concerns are characterised by a wish to know that the hotel, airline or tour operator they intend to use has acceptable environmental standards. Big 'E' travellers are willing to travel into new, 'undiscovered' areas, and accept the standards of accommodation and services offered by local people or camp in the wilderness.

The 'soft adventurer' also wishes to visit wilderness areas, but wishes to visit them in comfort, however, without a sense of feeling that the nature or culture of the area they are visiting is being 'exploited' through tourism.

A further categorisation of tourists into different types relating to their level of interest in the environment, based upon the work of Cleverdon

(1999).The level of demand for each typology is reflected in the width of the base of each segment, that is, demand decreases upwards from the base of the pyramid to its apex. The model suggests that the largest segment of the tourist market, the 'loungers', has a low level of interest in the environment beyond its providing pleasant surroundings.

The focus of the holiday of this typology is likely to be based upon relaxing and enjoyment. The second typology of tourist, 'the users', is interested in the environment having the special features that are required for the type of holiday they wish to pursue.

The types of environment required for this typology are therefore specialised and limited. For example, typical activities associated with this group would include wildlife watching and downhill skiing, each of which need environments that possess specialised features.

The next typology, the 'eco-aware' show an increasing interest in the environment, not for how they can use it but for its own sake. They have an interest in environmental issues connected with tourism, and would look for evidence of environmental commitment, and perhaps certification of a high level of environmental practice from the tourism companies and suppliers they use.

Typical types of holiday activity will reflect an interest in knowing more about the nature and the culture of the destination they are visiting. The last group, the 'specialist ecotourist' has a high level of commitment to the environment, to the extent that they want to actively protect it. This is reflected in the kinds of holiday they participate in, such as conservation holidays or scientific research.

Just as it as incorrect to talk about tourists as being one homogeneous group, Swarbrooke and Horner (1999) suggest that it is not possible to talk about the 'green tourist' as if they were one homogeneous group, preferring to refer to 'shades of green'.

They suggest that the environmental commitment of tourists will be influenced by an amalgam of different factors, including: their awareness and knowledge of the issues associated with tourism and the environment; attitudes towards the environment in general; and the degree of fulfilment of other commitments in their life such as employment, housing and family needs. The different categories of green tourist and their associated environmental attitudes and actions are shown.

Empirical studies of ecotourists are limited, however research based upon demographic (age, gender, occupation, income) characteristics and psychographic (values, attitudes and motivation) characteristics has been attempted. According to Wearing and Neil (1999) research conducted in the USA suggests that ecotourists have higher than average incomes and levels of education, and are also willing to spend more than the normal tourists. In terms of their psychographic characteristics, Wearing and Neil report that they possess an environmental ethic, and are biocentric rather than anthropocentric in orientation.

ECOTOURISM: PRODUCT OR PRINCIPLE

The title 'ecotourism: product or principle?' is a question that was raised by Cater and Lowman (1994) to illustrate the different interpretations of the term 'ecotourism'. Although the preceding part of this chapter has illustrated how ecotourism may be defined using a set of principles which reflect very closely those of the concept of sustainable tourism, as previously stated, there is also a distinct danger that ecotourism may be interpreted purely as another tourism 'product' to be sold into the market-place.

This may involve putting landscapes, that have had little or no human interference with them, directly into the market-place for tourism. As Baroness Chalker, then Minister for Overseas Development for the United Kingdom government commented, one of the characteristics of ecotourism is 'attracting tourists to natural environments which are unique and accessible' (1994:90). Given that many of the most beautiful natural environments are located in rural areas of less developed countries, where often there are problems of underdevelopment and poverty, the economic incentives to be gained from ecotourism mean that there is a possible threat to the conservation of these areas.

This is a theme developed by Butler (1990) who questions, profoundly, the idea that forms of 'alternative' tourism offer an alternative approach to mass tourism. As he points out, the idea of 'alternative tourism' sounds good to everyone and is hard to disagree with, but is so vague in its meaning that like sustainable development, it can mean almost anything to anyone.

Further, he continues to say that although mass tourism maybe criticised a lot, many people still like to be mass tourists. It is therefore highly improbable that low-scale alternative tourism will ever replace the mass tourism market. Butler is especially critical of the idea that one form of tourism can be promoted as the panacea to problems that have resulted from extensive and long-term tourism development, commenting: 'Mass tourism need not be uncontrolled, unplanned, short-term or unstable'.

Harrison (1996) also questions the extent to which ecotourism and 'good tourists' are genuinely alternatives to mass tourism or whether they merely represent stages towards it. The danger of being complacent over ecotourism is also highlighted by De Alwis (1998:232), who cites Robertson Collins the tourism veteran and conservationist as saying:

Most of those who tag tourism 'ecotourism', after a while begin to believe that all they do is ecologically and people friendly. The customer who buys into an ecotourism labelled product also satisfies his or her conscience that they are not causing any damage to the nature or people that they visit.... Ecotourism today, is big business.

Products with an eco label are able to command higher prices in the market place. Similarly, there is also substantial funding for 'ecotourism' proponents by donors and well meaning agencies, making it a lucrative consultancy based business as well. This situation has unfortunately led to the creation of the popular perception that 'tourism is bad' and 'ecotourism is good'.

De Alwis (1998) also makes the point that demand for ecotourism is market driven, as more people express an interest in nature, and the desire for independent travel has become stronger. The dangers of ecotourism are also elaborated by Shackley (1996) who suggests that the introduction of visitors into ecosystems that we barely understand can instigate long-term changes. Rogers and Aitchison (1998) draw attention to the point that, although the definitions of ecotourism sound attractive in theory, they do not address the more problematic issue of how to develop and promote ecotourism.

They point out that ecotourism is often subject to the same market forces that led to the environmental problems associated with mass tourism, and that there are many different players involved in both the public and private sectors, leading to problems of coordination and planning of development. They add that ecotourism sites are diverse and at early stages of development, which limits the opportunities for comparative study, and that models of 'good practice' are lacking.

The ability to make financial profit from ecotourism is also emphasised by Mowforth and Munt (1998). In their view not only does 'ecotourism' signal an interest in the 'environment' (*eco*logy) but it also indicates the ability to pay the high prices that such holidays command (*eco*nomic capital). Ecotourism is, as has been explained, a form of tourism that relies upon being alternative to the mainstream, and is therefore in one sense exclusive.

The association of ecotourism with exclusivity is a theme emphasised by Wheeller in his extensively quoted work, in which he renames ecotourism as 'egotourism'. Mowforth and Munt (1998) link the idea of 'egotourism' to being in a competition for distinction, uniqueness and differentiation, alternatively expressed as another form of 'conspicuous consumption'.

Given the seeming willingness of ecotourists to pay premium rates to visit 'unspoilt' nature, there are therefore strong economic and financial incentives for governments and business entrepreneurs to facilitate the use of the environment for ecotourism.

One of the great dangers in opening up new areas of the environment to ecotourism relates to the issue that unless development is strictly controlled, there is little reason to assume the development cycle should be any different than for other forms of tourism. There has been and perhaps still is an inability to accept that ecotourists are a form of 'trail-blazer', opening up new areas to the hordes they disdain, unless there are strict development and planning controls.

The application of planning controls limiting the number of ecotourists to a particular area may in reality prove difficult to implement and maintain, and may fluctuate in response to a country's economic situation and the policy of the government in power. This latter point concerning the development of ecotourism in Belize.

ECOTOURISM IN BELIZE

One of the first countries to promote itself as an ecotourism destination was Belize in Central America, which is less than two hours' flying time from Miami in the USA. The country has a small land area of 23,000 square kilometres but contains a wide variety of vegetation types, including mangrove swamps, wetland savanna, mountain pine forests, and tropical rainforests. Additionally, the coral reef off Belize's coast is the second longest in the world, after the Australian Barrier Reef. There are also several notable archaeological sites of the Mayan civilization.

The attraction of ecotourism for the Belize government is to earn foreign exchange, and the government committed itself to balanced and environmentally sound tourism in the 1980s. The typical advertising slogans to promote Belize are 'Belize so natural', 'friendly and unspoilt', 'naturally yours'. The majority of tourists who come to Belize do not arrive on package tours, but their travel and accommodation is organised by foreign tour operators, and subsequently the economic leakage factor is likely to be high. The financial opportunities to be gained from ecotourism have led to rapid property inflation around the coastline and it is now estimated that 90 per cent of the coast line is under foreign ownership. United States based developers are building luxury resorts, with golf courses and marinas, and it is estimated that 65 per cent of the members of the Belize Tourism Industry Association are expatriots mainly from the USA.

However, the government has no plans to restrict foreign ownership of land as it requires the foreign investment. The arrival of tourists at approximately 200,000 per annum is also beginning to have environmental consequences. Some of the coral in the Hol Chan Marine Reserve established in 1987 has become infected with black band disease, a form of algae which kills the coral, when it has already been broken. There has also been a decline in the numbers of conch and lobster owing to overfishing, partly to satisfy tourism demands.

Other examples of the impacts of tourism are more dramatic. In 1992, 'Eco-terrorism at Hatchet Cay' was the headline, in reference to a US resort owner who had attempted to blow up part of the coral reef to make his resort more accessible to visiting boats.

Unfortunately, it would seem that ecotourism development in Belize has become characterised by the problems of mass tourism, including foreign exchange leakages, a high degree of foreign ownership of prime coastal land and tourism facilities, and environmental degradation. The government's desire for foreign exchange, combined with global market forces and trade liberalisation, means that the environment is becoming little more than a selling point for a form of mass ecotourism.

Other criticisms have also been made of alternative forms of tourism like ecotourism, such as that they cannot provide a viable level of income and employment, and that education of the tourist into a form of behaviour that is respectful of the environment is a long-term process for which the financing and logistics have not been thought through properly.

It is evident that alternative forms of tourism will not necessarily lead to tourism that is culturally and environmentally friendly. In a neo-liberal global economy, the regulation of market forces to allow a balanced use of environmental resources will be critical in determining the success of any alternative tourism policy. However, this may not be that easy to achieve, especially for countries who are in need of foreign investment and foreign exchange.

This means that for many less developed countries, the global political economy, which incorporates international debt repayment and the domination of transnational corporations, places their environments under threat of exploitation for short-term need and profits. The use of environmental resources for ecotourism may, in terms of negative environmental consequences, prove to be little different to that of mass tourism, in fact perhaps even more detrimental as ecotourism environments are likely to be rich in biodiversity and highly susceptible to damage.

THE FUTURE RELATIONSHIP BETWEEN TOURISM AND THE ENVIRONMENT

A central theme of this book has been that understanding the relationship that exists between tourism and the environment is concerned not just with the destinations that tourists go to but also the societies which they come from. It would seem that as societies become more economically developed, wealthier and urbanised, then the propensity to consume through tourism increases. The projected levels of tourism demand of 1,600 million international tourist arrivals by 2020 suggest that tourism will become an even more significant feature of society and the global economy than it is at present.

This projected growth in tourism will provide both opportunities and threats to the environments and societies it interacts with. The economic opportunities offered by tourism mean it is increasingly likely to feature as a key part of many governments' economic policies, especially in less developed countries.

Importantly, by encouraging development and helping to eliminate poverty, tourism can assist in building a more sustainable future by meeting human needs and helping to conserve environments and wildlife, protecting them from threats such as poaching or potentially destructive forms of economic activity such as mining or logging.

However, the achievement of this relies upon government policy reflecting a stronger commitment to an environmental ethic and a long-term perspective, than has historically been the case. The significant lesson of tourism development in the second half of the twentieth century was that although tourism can bring economic benefits, it can also contribute to the destruction of the natural environment.

It can also be a cause of cultural changes, for instance changing the value systems of traditional societies by propagating consumerism and associated materialist values, and also displacing people from their traditional lands and denying them access to resources they require to meet their needs.

Many of the negative effects of tourism have resulted from a *laissez-faire* approach to development, determined by free market forces, in which the full social costs of tourism development have failed to be reflected.

Government policy and planning for tourism in the future is essential. Policy and planning need to reflect a balanced approach to how natural resources are used and include local communities in the development process. For want of a better word, a more 'sustainable' approach to tourism development is required.

As a key stakeholder and the catalyst to tourism development, the tourism industry will also need to increasingly address its role and responsibilities to the environment.

The tourism industry continues to display increasing signs of market maturity, with the acquisition and merging of companies into larger multinational conglomerates, which are increasingly being floated on stock-exchanges as public shareholding companies. This trend is likely to continue as the market demand for tourism continues to increase.

These multinational companies will subsequently have increasing influence in many destinations and markets around the world, and interact with the many locally owned small and medium-sized enterprises, which continue to constitute the major part of the supply market in most tourism destinations.

In an increasingly global business environment and market-place, which facilitates the movement of international capital and the establishment of business operations in different countries, it can be argued that major international companies have an increasing responsibility to address ethical issues of their operations.

Such issues will include their interaction with local communities, indigenous cultures, and the natural environment. Practical initiatives could include actions such as strengthening supply linkages to locally owned businesses, helping to reduce the level of economic leakages and increase the economic benefits of tourism for members of the local community, and developing environmental management systems to cover all aspects of their operations.

However, there is no one model that can act as blueprint of how tourism, the natural environment and local communities can interact in the most beneficial fashion in the future.

Different destinations will have differing degrees of tolerance to tourism, based upon their own environmental characteristics, and the extent to which the natural and cultural environments have already been subjected to change by outside influences.

Some tourism destinations, such as many of those on the western Mediterranean coastline, are already in a mature stage of development. For these areas, the major physical and cultural changes that tourism can bring have already been experienced, and in many of these areas efforts are being made to redress the negative effects of tourism. Other environments have yet to be 'discovered' by tourism, subsequently different environments will have different tolerance levels to tourism. This is not to say that destinations in a mature stage of development are free from any further environmental damage from tourism, as continued expansion may push them past a further threshold level, where environmental management and technological measures cannot redress the balance.

However, it is particularly in areas of the world where tourism is developing, or has yet to develop, that there is the potential for many environmental problems. As the pressure grows for kinds of tourism that are increasingly based upon the natural environment, including special ecosystems, wildlife and indigenous cultures, there is a requirement for strict planning controls to avoid unacceptable levels of environmental change.

A further issue in defining tourism's future relationship with the environment is that ultimately what is an acceptable level or unacceptable level of environmental change and development will not be quantitatively fixed but determined by decision makers in society.

Tourism development and economic growth cannot take place without some degree of trade-off between the use of the environment and economic benefits. Ultimately the extent of this trade-off, and the amount of environmental change incurred and whom it benefits, will be a reflection of decision makers' value systems and environmental philosophy.

There is therefore a danger that where decisions are made by a small elite, there will be an inability to hear a wide range of views across the political and philosophical spectrums, and decisions will not be made on a consensual basis. Subsequently, there are likely to be clashes over the use of natural resources for tourism, particularly in situations where local people are denied access to resources that they have traditionally used to meet their needs.

Tourism thus becomes viewed by many local people not as a constructive force for development but as a propagator of inequality. It is therefore necessary that the process of tourism development incorporates community participation, a principle agreed to by the majority of the world's governments when they became signatories of Agenda 21 in 1992.

Yet the future of tourism's relationship with the environment lies not only in what is happening in the tourism destination. Mass participation in international tourism is a feature of economically advanced countries, reflecting privilege, and is now an integral part of a postmodern consumer lifestyle. Whatever the motivations for participation in tourism, whether as consequence of anomie and the need for ego-enhancement or the desire for escapism *vis-à-vis* the search for the authentic, tourism is a function of economically advanced and urbanised societies.

The desire for tourism is a reflection of the quality of life experience of many people living in western society. Empirical evidence would suggest that, whilst material wealth is higher than ever before in western countries, the quality of life in many of them has begun to decrease.

For example Carley and Spapens (1998) point out that according to the Index of Social Health published by Fordham University in New York which measures well-being, America's social health declined from 73.8 out of a possible 100 in 1970 to 40.6 in 1993 as homicides, suicides, the gap between the rich and the poor and drug use all increased.

Likewise, the pressures of the consuming life are also evident in Britain. Under the title 'Britain in 2010: rich but far too stressed to enjoy it', the point is made that the pressure of modern working patterns and the desire for wealth are fuelling family breakdowns, drug and alcohol dependency. At the end of the twentieth century nearly a quarter of all men and women in Britain believed that they had sacrificed seeing their children grow up because of the pressures of work.

Taking the view that tourism is representative of a wish to escape from societies, at least periodically, it can be interpreted as a symptom of postmodern society.

It is likely that within the time-constrained framework of modern life, tourism will, for the majority of the population, be an experience to be consumed in a highly packaged format.

Under these circumstances, the extent to which tourism can act as an educational medium, involving constructive and meaningful exchanges with foreign cultures and environments, is doubtful. Tourism's function for many in society will be to act as a reward for the stresses of day-to-day living, during the rest of the year.

As the world becomes increasingly urbanised and economically developed, and more people seek to consume the experiences and rewards of tourism, a major question facing tourism planners is where the predicted extra 1 billion tourists in the next twenty years are going to be accommodated. This question of course oversimplifies the issue, as within that figure of 1 billion lies a complex market pattern, including issues such as types of tourism, repeat visitations, and low and high seasons.

Nevertheless, this rapid increase in the level of international tourism during the next twenty years will pose a strain on environmental and cultural resources. Many of these extra tourists will be travelling by air transport with the subsequent effects upon the atmosphere from the emissions of carbon and nitrogen oxides. Yet it is particularly in tourism destinations where the pressures on the environment will be most intense, as this is where tourism is most concentrated.

Of particular concern is the increasing demand for nature tourism, which potentially could take tourists to some of the most ecologically fragile areas of the earth. As already mentioned, alternative tourism such as ecotourism may in reality represent little more than the first stage of mass tourism. If tourists can go to space, which will probably happen in the next five years, no part of the earth's environment can be considered to be inaccessible to tourism.

The relationship between tourism and the environment therefore faces many challenges over the next twenty years. Economic development and the social conditions of postmodern societies are a fertile breeding ground for tourism demand. The answer to a harmonious relationship in the future between tourism and the environment thus lies as much within the holistic philosophy of society and environmental attitudes as it does with a reductionist approach of finding technical solutions to environmental problems caused by tourism.

The emergence of green consumerism since the late 1980s points to a realisation, at least by a part of the population, that present rates of consumption cannot continue without adverse environmental effects. At the beginning of the twenty-first century, we are aware that many adverse environmental effects are the consequence of human actions, such as ozone depletion, global warming, pollution of rivers and acid rain.

There is increasingly a realisation, judging by the demand for more environmentally friendly products and ethical investment funds, that individual action can make a difference to environmental issues such as pollution and fair trade.

Some people are also increasingly disenchanted with the 'rat race' associated with 'comparative consumption', in which we work harder to buy more goods and services, to keep pace with our neighbours.

The idea of 'downsizing' to a more simple lifestyle is an option a few people have decided to take in the western world, perhaps indicative of wider changes to come in the twenty-first century. However, for the majority in the next twenty years, tourism is probably going to be increasingly viewed as an essential component of having a better quality life. During the next twenty years tourism will bring changes to many environments around the world. In 2020, the extent to which these changes will be determined as positive or negative will be a reflection of the values held in society at that time and who is doing the judging.

4

The Importance of Agritourism for Rural Development and the Environment

In a fundamental change of approach in recent years, it is now recognised more clearly that the efforts of developing countries and societies to help themselves have been the main ingredients in their success, and that people must be at the centre of all relevant policies. The role of aid donors is to work in partnership with countries and their people, to help increase their ability to do things for themselves.

If countries are to develop in a sustainable way, they must have the capacity to manage their natural resources effectively, to address environmental issues and to tackle environmental problems. In recent years, OECD donor countries have re-assessed their approaches to aid and consulted closely with partner countries to develop co-operation programmes aimed at enabling developing countries to improve their management of human resources in this area and expand their technological and institutional capabilities.

At a workshop organised recently by the OECD Development Assistance Committee (DAC), participants from 20 donor countries and 25 developing countries examined whether the theory behind capacity development of the environment is working in practice. They reviewed 46 cases drawn from around the world, aimed at working in partnership to increase environmental capacity within the principles of sustainable, participatory and people-centred development. One of these partnership projects is the Kenyan Green Towns project. Kenya's urban population has increased eightfold since 1962; today, more than 5.5 million people live in towns or cities, a figure that is predicted to double by 2010. As a result, the number of urban centres has jumped from 34 to 177. This rate of expansion has far exceeded financial planning and management capabilities in the new towns, and produced unhealthy living conditions and severe environmental degradation.

In 1986, Kenya asked the Netherlands government to help it deal with these problems by carrying out a series of pilot studies to see how local communities could plan for environmental management. In 1990 Kenya again asked the Netherlands for help in training Kenyans from central and local government, universities and other organisations, to prepare themselves to become trainers in participatory environmental planning.

Armed with these new skills, the Kenyan trainers, working with local authorities, ran a series of public workshops in different towns. The idea was to generate awareness, encourage people to take responsibility for the state of their environment, and show them how to do so. The programme resulted in many urban communities developing action plans, which eventually brought real benefits — drainage and sanitation improvements, 'clean-up days', distribution of dustbins, waste recycling and tree planting. The towns involved are now noticeably cleaner, and there has been a measurable drop in diseases such as malaria.

Over the same period, the Kenyan government has also established a soil- and water-conservation programme that has earned an international reputation for effectiveness and innovation. In 1987, with backing from Sweden, the Kenyan Ministry of Agriculture began to bring together a wide range of interest groups, including national, provincial and district governments, and farming communities. Under this programme, the number of farms practising soil conservation has increased in less than ten years from 600,000 to 1.3 million, and a network of farming participation groups has taken shape. Again, the benefits have been tangible for people's livelihoods as well as for conservation.

Another successful partnership project was developed in India, where — with help from Germany — the drought-prone Indian state of Maharashtra has adopted a new, participatory approach to watershed management. Small selfhelp groups have successfully planned, implemented and administered their own watershed development projects.

These groups have subsequently grown into independent organisations, Co-operation in environmental planning helped Kenyan trainers to encourage people to take responsibility for scenes like this. The resulting 'action plans' brought real benefits, including improvements in drainage and sanitation, leading to a drop in diseases such as malaria.

ENVIRONMENT AND POVERTY

Pakistan's North West Frontier Province is another area where environmental capacity is steadily being developed with donor support. The Province faces a multitude of environmental problems, with steady deforestation, excessive use of rangelands, and related soil erosion all-diminishing the natural-resource base and worsening floods during the rainy season.

Extreme poverty in the region is both an effect and a cause of the over-exploitation of natural resources, as people seek to maintain their existence in any way they can. To help address the two closely linked issues of environment and poverty, the government of the Province, working with Switzerland and a locally staffed non-governmental organisation, IUCN-Pakistan, has devised its own provincial conservation strategy and boosted the institutional capacity of its Environment Protection Agency.

A NEW DEVELOPMENT PARADIGM

These examples illustrate a new underlying philosophy. A fundamental change of approach has occurred: a shift away from older, paternalistic attitudes towards a recognition that countries must assume more responsibility for their own development, and that people must be at the centre of these policies. In this new model, the role of aid donors is to work in partnership with countries and their people, to help increase their ability to do things for themselves. This should lead to locally controlled strategies, which will have a far better chance of long-term success.

FOCUS

Aide Agencies Adapt to Meet Agenda 21 Requirements

Since 1992 and the UN Conference on Environment and Development (UNCED), OECD aid agencies have responded strongly to the challenges of Agenda 21. Sustainable development has been incorporated as a guiding principle, and the environment firmly established as an overall priority. Much of this has been achieved through innovative measures, and many agencies have contributed to the international debate on environment and development in the wake of UNCED. At the same time, there has been a steady commitment to funding for the environment.

A strong political commitment underscores these trends, confirmed in a recent OECD study, and has made it possible for even smaller-sized aid programmes to show substantial and innovative progress in the integration of environmental goals.

New instruments employed to this end include strategic environmental assessment, programming tools for developing environmental capacity, and initiatives related to economic environmental analysis and sustainability indicators. Training is also being increasingly recognised as a means of improving agency commitment to environmental of goals.

The OECD survey equally suggested that aid agencies strengthen their understanding of the complex interlinkages of sustainal 2 development and the implications for overall agency priorities. Another source of concern is growing capacity strains on environment units; it should be addressed so that e ronmental priorities and objectives may continue to be met.

Countries must actively plan for sustainable development, and have the capacity to do this for themselves. Environmental capacity must be complemented by other kinds of capabilities — social, political, institutional, economic and technical. But in many ways, environment has become the natural flagship for change, since it is all-encompassing and affects — and is affected by — all other areas. In addition, many environmental issues can only be addressed among communities themselves, because it is the community that directly uses natural resources such as forests, fisheries, water and wildlife. Building a community's capacities is central to the notion of sustainable development — and a considerable challenge to donors as pressure on the environment increases.

Developing environmental capacity is a process, not a product. It could even be said that the process is the product. It involves multidimensional changes which take into account all of a society's values, norms and interacting elements. The benefits of the process may take time, and may not always be easily measurable. Nevertheless, enduring results can emerge.

FLEXIBLE DONOR FUNDING

Flexible donor funding is also important for developing capacity. More experimentation is required to see what kind of funding produces the best results. For example, more frequent use of trust funds, or of small project funds administered locally may be beneficial. Another effective solution may be for a recipient government to agree upon broad objectives for programme funding in a particular sector and then make its own decisions about how and over what period the funds are employed.

To allow developing countries to proceed at their own pace, donors should be less prescriptive about the length of time projects take, and about the reporting and accountability they require for their funding. The Green Towns project, for example, began in 1986 and is currently projected to run until 1999. The success of the Kenyan government's soil- and water-conservation programme is ascribable in part to Sweden's flexible approach over a period of eight years; funding and advice were given only when required.

LOCAL CONTROL OF STRATEGIES

An essential condition for developing capacity and local control is that all groups likely to be affected have the opportunity to participate in decision-making, including indigenous peoples, religious groups, advocacy groups, private entrepreneurs, non-governmental organisations, the media and, especially, women. Women and children suffer most from poor environmental conditions — women because they have to put disproportionate efforts into finding food, clean water or firewood, and children because they are the first to contract diseases in unclean environments.

In the Green Towns project, 14 per cent of the participants in the environmental-planning workshop were women, and women's clubs continue to be used as a vehicle for community awareness. The other participants in the workshops also had a stake in the urban environment: local councillors, heads of schools, youth and women's groups, church leaders and members of the business community.

Doing the work as close to the ground as is practical is equally important. This means not only decentralisation of development co-operation decisions from the donor country to the aid office in the field, but also going beyond government-to-government co-operation to working with lower tiers of administration such as sub-national regions, districts or municipalities. This approach can be seen in a Canadian-supported project in Costa Rica to strengthen ecological management in the Arenal Lake conservation area.

In co-operation with the local government, academic institutions, non-governmental organisations and community groups, particular emphasis was placed on devising socially acceptable and productive alternatives to directly consuming the area's natural resources.

An eco-tourism programme was launched in co-operation with the local tourism industry, and research and information programmes were established. Any process of change takes time, and the changes necessary to develop sound capacity are very demanding. Not all of the cases examined at the workshop fully adhered to the principles of capacity development, and it was clear that the approach is not yet universally understood or embraced. In addition, the process oriented characteristics of capacity development, and the longer-term and less easily measurable results, can be difficult to reconcile with the domestic pressure on most aid budgets to come up with quick, tangible results.

A climate of public-spending constraints and staff cuts does not help, nor does the fact that aid often becomes linked to trade or political objectives that have little to do with capacity development. And yet the success or failure of developing countries in making their way in an interdependent world will have a profound influence in shaping the 21st century.

In recognition of this, OECD development ministers have set targets for future co-operation in three broad, interrelated categories: economic well-being, social development, and environment regeneration and sustainability. Developing adequate capacity will underpin work towards all of these goals evaluating tourism and its impacts.

The World Travel and Tourism Council [Gatty 1993] projected that in 1994 travel and tourism would generate direct and indirect employment for more than 200 million people - one of every nine workers in the world economy. In the United States, the projection was that travel and tourism supported one of every 10 workers directly and indirectly.

It was estimated in the same year that global travel and tourism would:

- Generate US$3.4 trillion in gross output.
- Produce 10.1 pre cent of direct and indirect gross domestic product.

- Result in 10.7 pre cent of total capital investment - $693 billion.
- Contribute more than $655 million of tax revenue, 11.7 pre cent of total indirect taxes.
- Account for 10.9 pre cent of all consumer expenditures and 6.9 pre cent of government spending.

Domestically, the U.S. Trade Data Centre [Mashatt and Cronin 1990] observed that by the late 1980s the tourism industry in the United States was the second largest employer and the third largest earner of sales receipts, accounting for 6.4 pre cent of GDP and an estimated $37 billion in federal, state, and local tax generation. Internationally, the World Tourism Organization estimated that in 1994 tourism accounted for 12 pre cent of the world's gross product and was responsible for an estimated 7 pre cent of global capital expenditure.

On a local scale, tourism possesses many attractive features for communities. It provides a practical economic alternative to the intense competition for manufacturing plants - a competition that is most likely to increase with the gradual decline of manufacturing and manufacturing employment in industrialized countries. Second, tourism is considered to be reasonably attainable even for communities with minimal public resources.

All that is required is public investment in improved roads, downtown cleanup and rehabilitation, and marketing, and private-sector investment in hotels, motels, restaurants, and other tourist facilities. Additionally, such private-sector provisions frequently consist of many small and diffused enterprises, with relatively low individual capital requirements, allowing for considerable ease of entry.

Since tourism is easily understood and builds on existing characteristics or amenities of the area, public support for it can be readily generated. An overriding benefit is that the resources that will attract tourists are often perceived as essentially "free" while providing the opportunity for derivation of surplus and generation of much-needed income in otherwise poor areas.

Finally, tourism is favorably viewed as a clean industry as well as a labour-intensive one, with the latter being a decidedly beneficial characteristic in economies consisting largely of poorly educated or unskilled workers, a characteristic of many rural areas.

In spite of its conspicuous growth in the last few decades, the tourist industry has not received much attention from economists because it is "also a collection of service based activities spread across a variety of industrial classifications and consumer expenditure categories not generally grouped together". Given the attractiveness and growing reliance on tourism as a means of overcoming underdevelopment, it is, however, increasingly important that we better understand the limitations and strengths the industry has in achieving the desired goals. One argument of this paper is that the most common analytical techniques used to study tourism limit perspective and can yield misleading conclusions and policy prescriptions.

This most common approach to the study of tourism is to consider the overall impact of growth of the sector. Total income generated, total job creation, and attendant multipliers are estimated and evaluated. Using this method, gross, first-order economic impacts are used to determine the benefit to the economy at large.

A second framework for analysis is provided by a destination life-cycle approach whereby differential impacts of evolutionary stages of tourist development can be identified. Here, second- and third-order economic impacts are emphasized, and tourism is examined for its effect on the human component of the economy writ small.

Fundamental to the latter approach is the recognition that tourism is not a static industry. Rather, it changes, and it changes the economic landscape with it. Based on patterns observed in the transformations of some popular tourist destinations, models have been suggested to identify crucial components of the evolutionary process. Rationales for both the standard, aggregate approach to tourism and the alternative life-cycle and social-indicator based perspectives exist. The ability of the economy to generate profit, savings, investment, tax receipts, and growing GDP are legitimate concerns.

Questions about gross job growth and reduction of unemployment can also be addressed by use of the aggregate method. Essentially, this is a top-down approach, which adopts the perspective of the economically and politically dominant - those most likely to influence the future course of development. This view is also reminiscent of older development approaches that emphasize rapid economic growth through capital accumulation. These models project that the benefits of tourism will be widely dispersed in the economy.

An alternative perspective that can be integrated with the life-cycle approach focuses on the employees and laborers - those that Michal Smith [1989] refers to as the backbone of the industry. This is a bottom-up approach that not only emphasizes the condition of the economically and politically marginal, but also considers how their situation changes as tourism evolve over time.

This method can be extended to consider the effects on other pertinent aspects of the locality such as culture and environment.

Ultimately, it can also be integrated with more recent development approaches that stress distribution and sustainability. These are based on the recognition that economic growth per se is not inevitably beneficial (and may be detrimental) to large segments of the socio-environmental system. Complex consequences of growth need to be evaluated and considered both before and during its pursuit. Another tenet of this perspective is that development does not necessarily mean growth.

Clearly the choice of perspective is an all-important first step leading to the selection of evaluative methods. Is the researcher interested in aggregate, top-down, first-order effects or in factor-oriented, bottom-up, second-and-third-order effects? The choice corresponds in some ways to the difference between the neo-classical and institutionalist approaches to economics. Multiplier analysis entails static enquiry; it buries normative considerations and ultimately proceeds from a belief that more is always better - more total income, more production, more growth, etc.

Conversely, the life-cycle approach addresses historical processes, path dependence, and evolutionary change. It also obligates regard for normative considerations; all identifiable consequences have to be subjectively weighed in the course of evaluation for policy recommendations.

A modification of the life-cycle approach will be suggested, one that incorporates indicators of effects on the local population and gives social welfare indicators highest priority. In the concluding section, the implications of the respective approaches will be compared and summarized.

MULTIPLIER ANALYSIS

The quantification of total incomes and job creation is reasonably straightforward and is done by tourist boards and government agencies from the local to the national levels. The resulting statistics allow comparisons of per capita incomes such as those cited by Somerset Waters [1990], which showed that some tourist areas had higher income levels than some manufacturing regions (*e.g.* Hawaii, \$14,886 and Bermuda, \$18,000 versus Ohio, \$13,933: Indiana, \$13,136; and North Carolina, \$12,438 per capita in 1986).

A much more complex and rigorous approach to incomes and jobs is by use of multiplier analysis. The goal of multiplier analysis is to determine the impact generated in a tourist destination for every dollar that is spent on the tourist product itself. The greater the mount of local/regional resource utilization, and the lower the proportion of imported goods that enter into local consumption and production expenditures, the higher the multiplier [Eadington and Redman 1991].

According to Alister Mathieson and Geoffrey Wall [1982, 64-68], the calculation is influenced by three levels of expenditure. First, an initial expenditure creates direct income for the industry. Second, a significant portion of this income is used to pay salaries and wages, to replenish stocks, and to purchase services necessary for continued production - indirect expenditure. Third, the income that is generated results in greater consumption and a higher local level of economic activity - induced expenditure. The principal difficulty with this analysis is to accurately incorporate all leakages.

The formal specification of the multiplier is provided by Marion Clawson and Jack Knetsch [1966, 241]:

$$\text{Multiplier} = \text{total income increase} = A * [1/(1 - BC)]$$

where A equals the proportion of income remaining in an area from the first round of expenditures (how much stays versus how much is paid out for imports immediately), B equals the proportion of income that local people spend on local goods and services (the propensity to spend locally), and C equals the proportion of local income versus imports that accrue as a result of subsequent rounds of local expenditure.

William Eadington and Milton Redman [1991] provide a simplified model to arrive at a "quick and dirty," first approximation of an employment multiplier:

$$\text{Multiplier} = (Nb + Nn)/ Nb$$

where Nb equals basic employment for export, and Nn equals non-basic employment for regional consumption.

Francois Vellas and Lionell Becherel [1995] specify four possible types of multiplier analysis - sales, production, income, and employment - and agree with Fleming and Toepper [1990] that these involve business expenditure only and do not include wages paid to employees. Based on this definition, a multiplier of 1.5 does not indicate that for every dollar of expenditure, another 50 cents is created. 'Instead, a multiplier of 1.5 implies that in order to meet a dollar of output demand, 50 cents in business activity in the area is stimulated".

Multiplier analysis can be seriously limited by the fact that the data necessary for accuracy may be unavailable. Thus, as Mathieson and Wall [1982, 64-68] and Eadington and Redman [1991] observe, efforts at multiplier analysis are clearly problematic. Disregarding difficulties in obtaining reliable data, even an accurate multiplier will have serious shortcomings.

Use of the multiplier gives apparently rigorous and quantitative information that is of significant interest to some industry participants, but this is information that is superficial and of little consequence to other participants. It provides only a point-in-time impression of the general state of linkages versus leakages.

Furthermore, the multiplier is heavily influenced by the size of the study area; the larger the study area, the higher the multiplier; "leakage from a local economy often creates additional demand and income in the regional economy'. While studies have been conducted to calculate the multiplier for an entire tourist destination and also for separate sectors within a destination (hotels, bed and breakfasts, restaurants, gas stations, etc.), the result is a number or numbers that taken by themselves provide little guidance or direction for planning or improvement.

The comparison of linkages to leakages, or imports to local production, is not insignificant, but reliance on a single, point-in-time number to indicate economic impact is an oversimplification.

A substantial portion of the total economic impact of the tourist industry is not addressed by multiplier analysis. While multiplier analysis gives an indication of total income that can be derived from tourist expenditure, the benefits and costs that arise from this activity are unlikely to be evenly distributed in the local economy. Both the facility owners and the employees will benefit from increased income, but benefits will also vary widely.

Further, the local population may have to bear some of the burden of increased costs required to support the growing industry: increased waste disposal, improvements to roads, enlargements to water and sewage systems, increased fire and police protection, and perhaps increased welfare funds. This will be especially burdensome if the increases in government revenues generated by tourism do not cover the added costs of necessary government services. Non-quantifiable costs that might be borne by the local population include: crowding, noise, traffic, possible loss of indigenous culture, and potential degradation of the resource assets that attracted tourists in the first place. While multiplier analysis suffers from a lack of attention to relevant detail, it can provide some insight by evaluating different segments of a given component of the tourist product.

An example of this would be to compare the income-generating as poets of substitute products within the lodging sector, such as hotels, campgrounds, or bed and breakfast establishments. According to Donald Lundberg and Peter Murphy, people who stay in hotels or motels are likely to spend several times more money than those passing through or staying in self-catering facilities such as campgrounds. According to studies cited by Mathieson and Wall and Murphy, however, bed and breakfasts have higher multipliers than hotels because the hotels are more likely to import goods, services, seasonal labour, and capital from outside the area.

Another possible comparison would be between various segments of the amusement sector. For example, golf and ski resorts tend to attract a clientele with greater purchasing power than do family-oriented amusements. Also, studies by Thomas Rogers [1973] and the Mountain Outdoor Recreation Alliance [1991] show that these upscale attractions not only generate substantial income, but have considerable job-creating ability. Once again, though, imports are likely to be prominent, especially given the probable need for outside financing.

These comparisons also demonstrate the dichotomous nature of tourism. It can be an industry typified by small businesses in a location dominated by locally run bed and breakfasts, inns, specialty shops, and restaurants, or the development can be of the large resort variety described by Rogers [1973]. In this latter scenario, one set of investors will buy up a very large tract of land, quickly build a recreation facility and infrastructure, and then attract second-home buyers and retirees to purchase lots. This type of tourist development is very rapid and involves large-scale, planned resort communities.

The intention of the investors is not only to build a recreation site, such as ski runs or a golf course that will attract people and generate profits, but also to buy up all the adjacent property so as to capitalize on the increasing land values. The advantage (at least conceptually) to local governments is that all of the infrastructure is financed as part of the development.

With infrastructure already in place and an upscale attraction close by, second homes and retirement homes become very attractive, and the developers have land and construction crews ready to accommodate the demand. Consequently though, speed of development and magnitude of capital requirements suggest that imports will be high and local linkages will be low.

In contrast, tourist development might take the form of small-scale businesses, very likely locally owned and family run. If this type of tourist development is coupled with slow growth, then theoretically there should be more time for local linkages to be established, thus decreasing imports or leakages and augmenting local income.

Between these two extremes, we can find popular destinations that exhibit some features of both. In such locations, single business investment can run from small to large (*e.g.*, motels and local craft shops alongside hotels, factory-outlet malls, and theme parks). Under these circumstances, we might expect that rapid growth, coupled with increasingly larger capital requirements, could lead to more imports (including capital), less likelihood of local linkages, and possibly a declining multiplier over time.

When considered from an inter-temporal perspective, multiplier analysis could be used to provide greater understanding of economic impact and indicate which forms of tourist development might be more beneficial. But, since accuracy is difficult to achieve in analysis of the present, it is all the more likely to be difficult over time.

Murphy [1985, 95] notes that the static nature of the multiplier model "restricts its application to the base year of data collection and the cost of updating the information can be almost as great as the original study." Difficulties aside, any total income approach fails to address the distributional aspects of tourism. It is simply not possible to determine whether development with a low level of new spending generated, but a large multiplier, versus one with a high level of new spending, but a small multiplier, would be more desirable. Without further research, we do not know which is preferable because the distributional aspects will vary considerably.

DESTINATION LIFE-CYCLE ANALYSIS

One method with which to evaluate the uneven distribution of costs and benefits is through the framework provided by a destination life-cycle model. The evolutionary nature of the tourist industry is marked by distinct stages of development, and the changing characteristics of tourism in the diverse stages leads to anticipation of varying economic and social impacts. Although several life-cycle models have been offered to explain tourism's evolutionary nature, the one most referenced and discussed is that of Butler [1980]. This model consists of six stages of development and essentially involves the familiar "S-shaped" curve typical of life-cycle representations, which demonstrate the birth, growth, decline (and possible rejuvenation) of the product or industry in question.

Although the application of this model is not without controversy, it does provide a framework for analysis. Charles Stansfield [1978] notes how closely the model fits the experience of Atlantic City even though the first two stages were bypassed. After a conspicuous decline stage, the resort experienced a rejuvenation with the introduction of gambling. David Weaver [1990] also observed a reasonably close fit in the Cayman Islands, although the development and involvement stages seem to have been transposed, followed by what is best described as a period of stable maturity due to the placement of limitations on growth and the protection of "foundation" assets.

Gary Hovinen [1981] finds that the model does not apply in all respects, although his study of Pennsylvania clearly reflects an involvement and development stage. In Lancaster County, there was a significant decrease in tourism that did not arise from changes in the destination itself. This particular decrease was a result of exogenous forces: a publicized outbreak of polio among the Amish population, the Three Mile Island accident nearby, and the second oil shock of the 1970s, which caused gas shortages for travelers. The model suggests the inevitability of stagnation and decline that cannot be demonstrated in this case.

A possible alternative is offered by Donald Getz [1992] in whose study of Niagara Falls, the elements of consolidation, stagnation, decline, and rejuvenation are observed to occur simultaneously as the industry participants react to changing market conditions. In such instances, a multifaceted "maturity" stage more correctly describes a destination with a unique natural attraction that lends permanence to the viability of that tourist market.

Although the model lacks certainty of outcome, it offers a framework from which the evolutionary nature of tourism can be observed or anticipated. An exploration stage may be difficult to perceive, and decline may not be inevitable, but involvement and development stages were observed in all of the previous examples. These and the consolidation stage clearly emphasize the significance of tourism growth rates and the degree to which the industry can dominate an economy. Further, the transition to stagnation highlights the importance of capacity limitations as a consideration.

Once thresholds of capacity begin to be approached or exceeded, then the visitor experience and tourist industry become potentially less viable, resulting in the inability to sustain growth or even in declining rates of growth. Carrying capacity is therefore a significant concern requiring planning and management of growth and resource allocation so that the negative aspects of tourism can be minimized while the economic, social, and natural health of the resort can be maintained.

Thresholds or capacities can exist in different forms. One is physical capacity or tangible resource limits.

These can represent:

- Obstacles to be overcome, such as limited facilities or services;
- Obstacles that cannot be reasonably overcome given current levels of input (financial or technological) such as new transportation links; and
- Natural resources that might be destroyed or degraded unless limits to use are imposed [Getz 1983].

Another threshold to be considered is the perceptions (psychological capacity) of the visitors. At what point are they no longer comfortable? One cause of discontent is congestion (although some leisure activities are not diminished by the presence of crowds). A similar problem is social capacity. When will the tolerance for tourism by the host population be exceeded? After a certain point, locals may no longer want tourism because they have been crowded out of local activities, their culture may have been damaged, or their environment has been degraded [Getz 1983].

Despite the difficulty in defining and measuring these thresholds, there is an interrelationship between them and the various stages of the life cycle. By means of planning and control at each stage, a desired position can either be maintained or an unacceptable one could be improved. Whenever one of these capacities has been exceeded, regardless of the stage, a measure of decline will have occurred. The destination life-cycle approach, therefore, offers some insight into the probable course of change and the knowledge that different stages require different methods of control.

INTEGRATING SOCIAL WELFARE INDICATORS AND THE BUTLER MODEL

The strength of the Butler model is in its ability to convey the evolutionary nature of the tourist industry. As a framework for economic analysis, the model allows consideration of the impacts of tourism that will vary as the industry evolves. Second- and third-order effects on the local population, not the first-order effects evaluated under multiplier analysis, can be used as a means of observing the changing impact of this evolutionary process. With the variation of social welfare indicators (both quantitative and qualitative) over time, some general patterns can be anticipated.

During an involvement stage, lower levels of capital availability and visitation yield low levels of income growth and new capitalization and slower growth than later. However, this stage also represents high levels of local participation and greater economic diversity as tourism becomes an export component of the local economy by bringing in "new" money.

As an involvement stage gives way to development, local participation is displaced by outside interests due to their ability to quickly mobilize much higher levels of capital. Total income levels rise, and the rate of economic growth increases significantly, but most of this benefit is realized by the new investors who take profits out of the local economy. Accelerated expansion means that the local economy will probably be unable to accommodate many of the input demands of the new industry or to penetrate the external linkages once they are established. The continued displacement of local businesses will leave low-income employment as the primary means of participation for the resident population.

The growing popularity of the destination will also result in high returns from resource ownership, which will drive up the price of land, making housing less affordable for tourism employees. A concurrent effect is that alternative uses of the resources become less attractive, resulting in fewer alternative sources of employment.

During a consolidation stage, outside investors will have not only displaced most locally run tourist businesses, but also other components of a more diverse economy as tourism becomes the dominant industry. In its initial stages, tourism is typically welcomed as a means of bringing additional income to an underdeveloped agricultural region. A possible consequence of tourist evolution, however, is that much higher incomes can be generated but at the expense of the local economy and not in service to it.

When local participation is accomplished in the form of business ownership and/or supplemental income in conjunction with other forms of employment, then an involvement stage should result in improving social welfare, even if total income levels are low and growth rates are modest. When development and consolidation stages result in displaced local businesses, then tourism can only offer low-wage and frequently part-time or seasonal employment.

The further reduction of economic diversity confines the workers to the tourist industry, which now must be utilized for primary income since alternative sources have been extensively reduced or eliminated. The effects on a local population from these changes should result in non-improving or possibly declining social welfare.

During this process, capacity limitations can impose constraints on further growth. If constraints are ignored until a crisis point is reached, then further growth will be restricted, and the attractiveness of the destination may be compromised. In an extreme case, this could leave a locality destitute from the loss of an industry that has obliterated all other sources of income. More likely, the destination will become somewhat less desirable, leaving the native population with varying degrees of unacceptable crowds, a degraded natural environment, or a debased culture to coincide with economic marginalization. The greatest likelihood that such an outcome could occur is through unrestricted growth.

Without planning or controls, a laissez-faire approach to tourism, with rapidly mobilized external capital and emphasis on short-term returns, could quickly bring a destination to capacity thresholds. Also, with a laissez-faire approach, as long as the discounted private returns exceed internal costs, long-term consequences and social costs are largely irrelevant.

The potential disparity in outcomes was noted by Weaver [1990] in his comparison of tourist development in the Cayman Islands and Antigua. The former case involved controlling growth, encouraging local participation and protecting the "foundation" assets which provided the natural attraction to visitors. The latter case involved unrestricted growth that created excessive duality in the economy and considerable resentment on the part of the native population.

Branson, Missouri, represents another example of the problems related to uncontrolled growth. There, the local authorities are forced to respond to the burgeoning demands of growth that consistently outpace the provision of infrastructure and municipal services. The difficulties in Branson also extend to housing for tourism employees. With available resources being rapidly deployed for tourism, too little affordable housing exists for many of the workers employed by the industry. Consequently, hundreds of workers are living out of their vehicles, trailers, tents, or homeless shelters in the neighbouring town of Springfield.

Another potential advantage of the involvement stage, therefore, is that the slower growth associated with this stage allows greater time to recognize and evaluate capacity limits, determine priorities, and enact measures to protect valuable resources and economic diversity. The effectiveness of these efforts will depend on the farsightedness of those involved and on the willingness to have generalized, equitable participation.

If successful, this will produce widespread vested interest in the long-term health of the local economy and collective wealth. The importance of this wealth is that a significant portion of the derived surplus may come from pre-existing natural, historical, or cultural assets. These assets are not produced by the market for its own use, but can provide considerable positive externalities to those offering tourist facilities.

In opposition to this is the desire for resource owners to capitalize quickly on the gains derivable from rapid tourism development. This tends to attract outside capital, and once ownership of wealth is largely external, then decision makers become significantly less interested in local considerations. The probability that dispersed managers in distant board rooms are going to multilaterally incorporate external costs in their investment decisions is particularly remote; the lure of capturing the short-term gains is too great. Further, if the source of that profit is degraded in the course of utilization, its future revenue stream has been effectively discounted to zero.

Consequently, the further into a development or consolidation stage that a destination finds itself, the more difficult it becomes to ameliorate or reverse the effects created by unrestrained growth. As before, when these effects are realized by the local population, then social welfare indicators should demonstrate a lack of improvement or decline.

AN APPLICATION OF THE MODEL

Empirically, involvement stages were observed to have been beneficial in the Smoky Mountain region - a region of substantial tourism - for Gatlinburg (Sevier County), Tennessee, from 1930 to 1970 and Asheville (Buncombe County), North Carolina, particularly from 1882 to 1930. In Gatlinburg, Tennessee, the involvement stage was preceded by a recognizable exploration stage that occurred in the 1920s. In the 1930s, the Great Smoky Mountain National Park was created, and from then until the early 1970s tourism expanded, but local ownership continued to predominate. While a few families were able to invest in tourism facilities, others supplemented their meagre agricultural incomes through employment therein.

Of particular importance to the local farmers' incomes, however, was their production for the rapidly expanding home handicraft industry that supplied local shops. This not only permitted participation in tourism for virtually every family, but also included local women among income earners for the first time.

In Asheville, North Carolina, the completion of the railroad in 1882 significantly improved accessibility to the city, which then blossomed into a resort area. By the early 1920s, up to 250,000 visitors arrived annually. In the city, numerous hotels and many boarding houses offered accommodations, while in the surrounding countryside farmers also offered boarding facilities and grew produce to feed the throngs of tourists. A handicraft industry was developed as well to promote income generation among poor farming families and particularly women.

In both destinations (although especially in Asheville), the involvement stages created previously unavailable economic opportunities as linkages with the local economies became well developed. Consequently, social welfare improved because tourism enhanced the diversity of those economies and permitted increasing supplemental income generation thereto. In Sevier County, the heart of Smoky Mountain tourism in Tennessee, this was followed by a development stage with much higher levels of total tourism income but social welfare that did not demonstrate corresponding improvement.

The state officially recognized this by designating Sevier as a depressed county in spite of its growth of tourism revenues from $169 million in 1980 to

$662 million in 1992. In addition to the influx of outside investment, tourism grew to dominate the local economy and minimize economic diversity. The effect of this is to leave part-time and seasonal employment as the principal means of local participation with little alternative primary employment.

Conversely, in Asheville (Buncombe County), North Carolina, a development stage occurred subsequent to 1970 in an economy that was too large for tourism to overwhelm. There, a diverse economy allowed tourism to provide considerable supplemental income so that social welfare indicators were consistently high or superior when compared to those of its Western North Carolina neighbours and state averages.

As a representation of tourist development, the life-cycle model is useful as a framework for understanding the evolutionary nature of the industry and the need for implementing planning and controls towards acceptable levels of growth. The model, however, must be applied with recognition that reality is complex. In the Smoky Mountain region of East Tennessee and Western North Carolina, characteristics from several stages were observed to occur simultaneously.

In this case, both Swam County, North Carolina, and Sevier County, Tennessee, which are the gateways to the Great Smoky Mountains National Park, have economies dominated by tourism (a principal characteristic of the consolidation stage) while they are still experiencing what otherwise appeared to be involvement and development stages respectively.

The importance of this is illustrated by the case of Swam County's tourist industry, which is dominated by the presence of a Cherokee Indian Reservation. Here the benefits of an involvement stage with high levels of local ownership seem to have been offset by other structural characteristics. In addition to the region having been a particularly poor one since well before tourism began to develop, the county, because of the reservation and extensive federally owned forest land, has very little land available for development, which also restricts the influx of more affluent residents.

Further, Swain's involvement stage has occurred more recently than Sevier's or Buncombe's, when local linkages tend to be more fragile, or do not develop, due to more widespread integration - nationally and globally - of modern economies. Finally, as mentioned above, although the involvement stage has persisted, tourism has concurrently grown to dominate the local economy.

These factors are significant in explaining why Swain's social welfare indicators remain chronically below those of Sevier. Swain, however, compares more favorably to adjacent Graham County, North Carolina, which has had very little tourism development. Thus, tourism is seen to provide some benefits but also has limitations in its ability to overcome underdevelopment. What further does the life-cycle model have to offer in this example? The recognition that tourism is not a static condition.

The Cherokee Tribe concluded a pact with the State of North Carolina in 1994 to allow gambling on the reservation. Large increases in visitation were expected from this new attraction, which could boost the area into a development stage. This, in turn, not only raises the question of how social welfare indicators will respond, but also what capacity limitations will be approached or exceeded and with what consequences. Such considerations are inherent to the life-cycle approach but are not requisite in use of multiplier analysis.

Tourism is a multifaceted industry with a diversity of long-term consequences, one that is being pursued on a global basis as a remedy for underdevelopment. Under the circumstances, it is prudent to evaluate its potential and complexities from a variety of methods and perspectives. Neither technique discussed in this paper is singularly informative. The life-cycle approach introduces concepts that necessitate circumspect deliberation. Since the model is a simplification, it requires additional understanding and analysis. This can easily include multiplier analysis.

Of primary importance is that the limitations of each tool be recognized along with the need to acknowledge the significance of perspective in formulating discussion and research.

There is a real danger that governments and local residents in their zeal to get a share of tourism dollars will be persuaded by the numbers generated through multiplier analysis and fail to give sufficient consideration to distribution of costs and benefits. If they also ignore the changing nature of tourism, there is a danger that they will be left worse off than when they started, with hard-to-fill facilities and no- longer attractive sites. If ever there was an industry that required non-static and holistic analysis, it is surely the tourist industry.

THE PATH TO SUSTAINABLE DEVELOPMENT

There has been growing awareness in recent months in international political circles of the urgency of steering the world economy, and particularly that of the OECD countries, towards 'sustainable development'. What does this mean in concrete terms? And how can it be achieved? 'Sustainable development'—the concept, if not the expression— springs from the very roots of modern economics. Malthus and Ricardo had already foreseen 'natural' limits to economic growth. The work of the Club of Rome, nearly twenty years ago, sparked off an acute awareness of these problems.

This way of thinking has become more common since then and the expression 'sustainable development' has recently come to be used again internationally following the report by the World Conference on Environment and Development (WCED), known as the Bruntland Commission, which defines it as 'a process of change in which the exploitation of resources, the direction of investments, the orientation of technological development, and institutional change are all in harmony and enhance both current and future potential to meet human needs and aspirations'.

In truth, economic literature of the last ten years abounds with definitions of sustainable growth or development; the WCED Report itself contains several.

THE GLOBAL ECONOMIC APPROACH

This plethora of definitions results from the fact that the concept of sustainable development can refer to many aspects of economic reality. The picture might become more clearer if one distinguishes between two types of approach to sustainable development: a global economic approach and an 'environmental' or 'ecological' approach.

Some authors define sustainable development very generally, meaning the entire combination of conditions and factors contributing to the maintenance or growth of income, improved standards of living and well-being.

The promotion of such development consequently involves many aspects of economic activity, and in particular:

- Control of population growth
- Encouragement of technical change
- The optimal increase in the stock of factors contributing to the production of wellbeing
- Pricing of resources reflecting their relative scarcity
- A change in the pattern of production and consumption in order to maintain the stock of scarce resources.

Many authors emphasise that the 'sustainability' of development implies the transmission or handing-down of growth potential to future generations, and in particular the maintenance of a stock of capital, a resource base necessary for the 'production' of well-being. Others underline the importance, not of conserving this base as such, but of maintaining its productivity.

The exhaustion of resources will therefore have to be offset by the accumulation of capital and by technical progress. Yet, in view of the many forms of interdependence between the economy and ecology, the maintenance of a fund of resources would be inconceivable on a limited national scale. This is why many authors stress the international, or worldwide, dimension of sustainable development. The WCED, the World Bank and the United Nations Environment Programme (UNEP), in particular, lay weight on their interdependence and solidarity with the Third World countries.

THE 'ECOLOGICAL' APPROACH

The stock of capital with which it should be possible to maintain the potential for growth of well-being and which must be transmitted to future generations comprises two different elements: the stock of 'artificial' capital, or all the goods and factors of production created by man; and 'natural' capital, or natural, renewable or non-renewable, resources. According to the 'ecological' approach to sustainable development, the maintenance and transmission of a potential for growth and wellbeing require the application of management principles specific to each of these components of the overall capital, each of which makes its own contribution to wellbeing.

Thus 'artificial' capital has a special function; 'natural' capital (water, soil, fauna, flora, mineral resources, and so on) has another indispensable and, indeed, irreplaceable function.

The production of 'artificial' goods by economic activity would not be sufficient in itself to ensure at least a constant flow of income unless those goods could fulfil the same functions as natural resources, or be substitutes for them (for example, wood might be replaced by plastics, natural substances by synthetic chemical products), always supposing that there were no technical limits to such substitutability.

Several authors emphasise that for many natural resources there is in truth no 'artificial' substitute4 (for example, essential ecosystems such as tropical forests, marshland, oceans, animal and plant species, many of which become extinct each year).

Sustainable development should therefore ensure that this natural capital is safeguarded and transmitted to future generations, and for several reasons:

- Certain resources are not renewable, and are exhausted or lost immediately, as, for example, when an animal or plant species or a natural site disappears. We are faced, therefore, with the irreversibility of certain actions, or an extreme form of non-substitutability.
- Natural capital constitutes the very substratum of economic growth to which it contributes directly.
- Natural resources are themselves a source of well-being by virtue of the amenities they provide: the beauty of a site, leisure, factors for health, etc.
- The existence: of many uncertainties, and in particular: the possibilities for substitution; irreversibility; the risks and thresholds of deterioration or exhaustion of resources; technical progress which would make it possible to compensate for the disappearance of certain natural resources; the tastes and preferences of future generations.

This approach places the emphasis on conservation of natural capital as a factor of production for which there is still no substitute.

COMMON GROUND

Indeed, the supporters of the global economic approach and those of the environmental approach are agreed on the final objective of sustainable development, namely, the preservation of a growth potential for well-being. In this case it is hardly worthwhile trying at all costs to work out a definition on which there could be general consensus, probably introducing a good dose of ambiguity and lack of clarity.

It seems more realistic and more profitable to look at the practical consequences of certain aspects of sustainable development on which agreement exists, i.e.:

- Sustainable development means improving the well-being of present generations as well as preserving the patrimony of future ones, including man-made capital in the form of productive assets; the stock of scientific and technological knowledge; natural capital constituted by natural resources, ecosystems, and so on.
- Because of the specificity of certain features of natural capital (non-substitutability, irreversibility, uncertainty, etc.), it should be made the subject of particular attention.
- Sustainable development must be seen against a background of international interdependence, particularly with the Third World countries.

To determine strategies to launch a process of sustainable development, it is essential to forge measurement instruments, devise valuation methods and perfect policy instruments.

FORGING INSTRUMENTS OF MEASUREMENT

As the conservation of the stock of national capital constitutes a vital factor for sustainable development, one has to be able to measure its composition and any changes in it. Several complementary approaches may be envisaged. The most immediate method is to use environmental indicators: 'flow indicators,'—the quantity of pollutants released into the atmosphere, water or soil; 'quality indicators'—the concentration of pollutant substances in the atmosphere, water and soil; 'resource indicators'—wooded areas, fresh water resources, inventory of certain animal species, land use, and so on.

The OECD prepares such indicators more particularly by the publication every two years of an *OECD Environmental Data: Compendium* and about every five years a report on *The State of the Environment*. But a large quantity of data is difficult to consolidate.

This is why it is necessary to develop, urgently, composite indicators which would provide an overall view of changes in the quality of the environment. A second line of study at present being followed by the OECD is the development of 'sectoral' indicators (transport, agriculture, energy, etc.) to assess the impact of these sectors on the environment and determining the policies to be introduced in order to reduce this impact.

To take the example of transport, three categories of sectoral indicators could be developed: indicators of sectoral trends significant for the environment (the motor vehicle stock, average number kilometres per vehicle, road network, etc.); indicators of impact on the environment (emission of pollutants, noise, etc.); sectoral indicators of structural and economic change which can serve as a lever to improve integration with environment policy (pricing, taxation, subsidies, etc.). The essential objective of this approach is to establish a relationship between the main characteristics of a sector of activity and the environment to ensure effective integration between the policies applicable in the sector involved (here, transport policies) and environmental policy. Such integration constitutes a central element in sustainable development.

Another approach consists of establishing a genuine system of resource accounting, since the conservation of natural capital calls for knowledge of the available stock and changes in it, an activity in which France and Norway in particular make substantial efforts. There are, for example, 'forest accounts' or 'water accounts' showing available stocks, according to their type (for instance, volumes of standing coniferous or hardwood forest, surface and ground water), and annual flows (for example, any Increase in stock of standing wood, or reductions because of natural losses and exploitation, withdrawal and replacement of water). Unfortunately, as there is no monetary valuation of the magnitudes measured, different cases are difficult to compare in the national accounts system.

Finally, a study is currently being made of the construction of 'satellite accounts' in national accounts which would make it possible to quantify consumption, deterioration or exhaustion of natural resources in the calculation of economic aggregates.

This has been tried out in Indonesia for forest, oil and land resources. The inclusion of a debit item for the exhaustion of these resources has made possible the calculation of an adjusted GDP, a 'net domestic product', which in 1984 was 4 per cent lower than the 'traditional' GDP if one takes into account forest and land.

Other satellite accounts should make it possible to identify expenditure by households and by government to combat pollution and other forms of damage to the environment ('defensive expenditure'). Treating this expenditure in the accounts, not as final consumption but as intermediate consumption, would lead to a downward adjustment in GDP. The value of this approach lies, perhaps, less in the actual adjustment of GDP than in the explicit identification and entry in the accounts of 'defensive' expenditure, damage and consumption of natural capital. If GDP is shown to be reduced by a few percentage points, what is most useful is to be able to determine why and how this has happened. It is for that reason that the establishment of satellite accounts would seem particularly promising.

DEVISING VALUATION METHODS

Sustainable development is possible only if all the projects and operations that constitute economic development (industrial investment, construction of transport and tourism infrastructures, agricultural development, etc.) are themselves planned and carried out in accordance with the criteria of sustainability. To that end a consistent set of methods has to be developed to make it possible, for each product, to set a monetary value on damage to the environment, and the consumption or destruction of natural resources, and to take into account irreversible effects and the well-being of future generations.

Certain methods already exist, in particular for damage (monetary valuation of morbidity and mortality due to air pollution, losses to fisheries and agriculture due to pollution of water and air); but these methods must be refined and grouped together coherently, for example, in the form of a manual on project evaluation.

The problem of assessing of all the consequences of a project is all the more complex in that sustainable development has a marked international dimension: through direct or indirect physical links between ecosystems (acid rain, climatic change, and so on); and also through economic links. Massive imports by the industrialised countries of rough timber, for example, lead to excessive felling of forests in the developing countries; low taxes on rough timber combined with high duties on wood manufactures, will lead to similar effects; agricultural policies in the industrialised countries have obvious repercussions in the developing countries.

Can the accumulation of environmental policies, conducted separately in different states, ensure sustainable development throughout the world? The international dimension raises the question of whether assessment of the impact of the policies of a particular country must take account of the overall impact on the rest of the world, assuming that it is possible.

Some analysts point out that this question is all the more complex in that there may be substitution between different forms of capital: for example, a country which exports 'natural capital' (raw materials, timber) could, in theory, re-invest its in come in order to ensure a certain longterm sustainability for its development. But is this really possible?

PERFECTING POLICY INSTRUMENTS

Instruments of measurement and methods of valuation must lead the way to the establishment of policy instruments for economic and environmental management that are capable of ensuring sustainable development. Three types of instruments are essential. The first instrument is the pricing of environmental resources. It is not surprising that the emphasis should be placed on this management instrument—a basic principle in environmental economics—as one of the major ways of securing sustainable development.

This is pricing resources in the strict sense, to ensure that their price reflects both utility and scarcity. Thus the price of a natural resource (forest, for example) should include three elements: the marginal cost of extraction or working; the marginal cost of damage caused thereby (for example, deterioration of the ecological or climatic functions of the forest); the marginal cost of the loss of non-renewable resources for future generations (the user cost).

It is also important to include in the price of goods and services the social cost related to their production and use (in particular, the cost of damage caused by pollution).Indeed, this was the origin of the Polluter Pays Principle in 1972, the most recent principle of pricing resources, and the 'economic instruments' approach studied and advocated though the conceptual foundations and certain practical aspects of pricing resources and economic' instruments are now well established, the practice is still far from being consistent and widely applied.

Nonetheless, this recourse to market mechanisms to protect and manage environmental resources is at present arousing very considerable interest in most countries. The second instrument is the integration of economic policies with policies for the management of the environment and natural resources.

A process of sustainable development can be maintained only by making good a *posteriori* the damage and deterioration resulting from economic activity. Thus practices and policies applied in the different sectors of activity (transport, agriculture, energy, and so on) have to take environmental constraints into account at the planning stage. For example, transport pricing and taxation should be planned in such a way as to avoid expansion and structural changes harmful to the environment. The same applies to agricultural policies (taxation* and subsidies, for example), forestry, energy policies, etc. There is enormous scope here for investigation and innovation, and considerable potential for adjustment, that have barely been explored.

The third instrument requires the working out, internationally, of principles for action and machinery that can take into account these global aspects of sustainable development. These might include arrangements for financial transfers between industrialised and developing countries, allowing the developing countries to take measures which not only ensure the protection of their own natural and environmental capital, but also contribute to the solution of such world problems as climatic change or the disappearance of natural resources.

Alongside economic interdependence there is now ecological interdependence. And as well international solidarity there is now solidarity between the generations. This calls not only for new analytical and management tools but also, and more basically, a new look at the process of development, and wider responsibilities— in short, stronger political will. Some say that in the long run it is a question of survival. It is certainly a matter of common sense.

TOURIST IMPACT IN THE HISTORIC CENTRE OF PRAGUE

Prague, known as 'The City of a Hundred Spires', has a historic built environment which is internationally renowned for its quality and unique ambience. The central area comprises four towns. Hradcany, the castle district, is located at the top of a hill on the western side of the River Vltava which runs through the heart of the city. Maler Strana, the Lesser Quarter, which was established during the earliest years of growth of Prague, spreads downhill from Hradcany to the banks of the Vitava. Further south of Mala Strana, the tree-covered Petrin hill overlooks the Vltava, its open aspect contrasting with the medieval close-knit street pattern of the adjacent built up area.

Stare Mesto, the Old Town, which lies across from Mala Strana on the eastern bank of the Vltava, is the largest of the four historic towns. Staromestske namesti forms its centre, where the Old Town Hall and the astronomical clock are the focus of tourist attention. Josefov, the Jewish Quarter, although officially within Stare Mesto, maintains a history and identity of its own despite comprehensive redevelopment having been carried out at the end of the nineteenth century.

The Charles Bridge links the streets which make up 'Karlova' (the Kings' Way) to form a central route linking the castle in Hradcany with the Municipal House in Stare Mesto. This route provides a focus of tourist activity and is widely considered a compulsory part of any visit to Prague. In short, there is clearly a definable historic core which has long been the overwhelming focus of tourist activity in the city.

Since the collapse of communism at the end of the 1980s, cities in the countries of Central and Eastern Europe have undergone a process of rapid transition.

With the opening up of these countries to the influence of mass international tourism, related land-use change in historic city centres has emerged as a key aspect of post-socialist urban restructuring. Whilst sharing common themes, the impact of tourism in historic cities is inherently place specific. Prague's historic environment is imbued with significant social, political and cultural meanings, which have become all the more important as the Czech Republic struggles to maintain its cultural identity within the processes of globalization and European integration.

The complex interplay of tourism and historic preservation lies at the centre of the management of urban conflict in historic European cities. In the first instance, tourism can be regarded as a threat to the historic fabric. Conversely, however, the economic gains incurred by tourism's accompanying development can directly and indirectly finance the required conservation measures. Tourist impact is emerging as one of the clearest indicators of the new pressures facing post-socialist cities, as they embrace the free market. This paper, therefore, explores perceptions of tourism in Prague, in forming an insight into how mass tourism has impacted on the meaning of historic cities for both their residents and visitors in the post-socialist countries of the 1990s.

TOURIST CONSUMPTION OF THE HISTORIC BUILT ENVIRONMENT

A key ideological question raised by tourist consumption of the historic environment lies in ascertaining to whom the past 'belongs', linking values in the conservation process with the influence of its consumers. Recognition of the uneasy relationship between tourism and the historic environment in this sense is well established in the literature, and relates not only to tangible negative impacts, but also to the erosion of the sense of place which can arise as a result of incremental internationalization.

For instance, Chamberlin (1979) undertook interviews with tourists returning from European holidays who recollected superficial descriptions of historic sights and little else about their context or meaning. He described the tourists as 'the innocent enemy of the past' and went on to discuss entrepreneurial selling and profiting from the 'quick sale' of heritage to tourists whose impacts were often highly destructive. Hubbard (1993: 368) also discusses the way in which the public are less concerned with actual historic and architectural integrity than they are about the actual meaning of the buildings and the history they convey.

In emphasizing the role of capital cities in post-socialist Europe, the wider re-establishment of national identity as a by-product of closer European integration is also important. This is occurring in many areas of Central and Eastern Europe as countries have increasingly rejected the collective labelling associated with the Soviet 'Bloc'. When combined with the assertion of the critics and advocates of conservation alike, that historicism is used to stabilize society's perception of itself in times of hardship and change, a further dimension is added to a review of perceptions of the historic centre of Prague.

This is confirmed by many researching the influence of tourism in the post-socialist context with tourist images and the meanings and history contained within overall tourist experiences becoming in themselves a component of the new international identities of each of the countries in the region. At the same time the complex nature of heritage in the post-socialist context must also be taken into account within a study of this type.

History has often been defined by social selectivity, with the recent period of communist rule for instance having widely been rejected as a legitimate period within national development worthy of recognition through conservation of its relics.

The complex nature of historic cities in this context is compounded by the ambiguity which also existed prior to 1989. Conservation in Prague is presented with a distinctly more complex and problematic set of circumstances than in many comparable European cities, particularly in Western Europe. The ideological discussions relating to the meaning of the historic environment clarifies, to a certain extent, the contentious nature of conservation during the communist regime. The historic built fabric, not least in capital cities, represents past fives of a society and is often inherently nationalistic and at times religious.

Commonly a historic area is characterized at least in part by monuments commemorating battles, symbols of past monarchies and statues of patron saints. Prague is no exception, with monuments of the city's important and turbulent religious past and references to former ruling monarchies being manifest. Under communism conservation in this sense was at odds with the ruling state, owing to the apparent endorsement of Czech national identity, and its being imbued with reminders of pre-communist times. Indeed, given that the state sought to deny the past through promotion of a progressive communist future, conservation and any opportunities to relate to a non-sanitized history were often supported by 'ordinary' people, becoming a form of passive opposition to the political doctrine of the time.

In post-socialist times the historic centre of Prague continues to be an especial focus for contested meanings of national identity, with Vaclav Havel's entry into the castle, for instance, representing the overthrow of the old regime. The historic centre has shifted from representing the antithesis of the communist regime, to expressing civic and national identity which, in these difficult times, is crucial for the social well-being of the country.

However, it is important to recognize that such meanings can themselves be dynamic, and may not be universally shared, with visitors and residents often experiencing and hence perceiving the same place in very different ways. In particular, tourism has been repeatedly identified as a threat to the expression of national identity within the built environment, as destinations take on international characteristics which are not specific to the locality or history of place in which they define change.

In short, the meanings of the historic environment in Prague are complex, and at the same time fundamentally important to the emerging Czech nation. Underlying this, the contested meanings assigned to the historic built environment during communism as a result of Soviet ideals of urban form, and more recently as a result of the conflicting land use and process of internationalization, point towards a need to understand the perceived meanings of the environment as it changes. Assessing user perceptions should, therefore, form an important part of policy and decision-making in the area.

The concept that each place has a certain capacity - a level to which development is acceptable, but beyond which it is likely to have negative effects, is relatively longstanding within tourism planning literature. Tourism impact studies and the setting and regulation of carrying capacities of attractions which are under pressure, are both tools which have been extensively used and are well documented in the literature. Capacity analysis theory relates to a wider field than that of tourism alone, but the concept is being increasingly applied to improve regulation and management of tourism in times when sustainability and concern for the environment are receiving attention. In turn, recreation and tourism have been primary elements in the development of urban capacity analysis both in theory and practice.

The key methodological problem which pervades planning for tourism in any form is the highly diffuse and complex nature of its constituent features and their impacts. Tourism is difficult to isolate in the simplest of analysis, but within the concept of capacity analysis the task is compounded by the need for a holistic view of the area being examined, in order for a fully informed assessment to be made. Despite this, the assessment of the carrying capacity of tourist destinations is a longstanding part of the literature relating to tourism planning and is sufficiently robust and multi-faceted as to take into account tourist impact in a relatively comprehensive manner.

The level at which the use of a destination detracts from its original attraction is a crucial element to be assessed within research focusing on the dynamics of tourism and the environment. Glasson et al. (1995) describe the difficulties which have arisen in the application of the concept to tourism, as a result of its traditional association with scientific values. They suggest that this has led to the exclusion of considerably more complex features relating to tourism, including economic, cultural and socio-political dimensions. For tourism, perception studies within the capacity analysis process could be seen as providing an important qualitative contribution to an otherwise technical style of assessment.

Perceptions would on first examination appear relatively straightforward to gauge, given that tourism is often the subject of popular debate and its impacts are often visually prominent, directly touching the lives of both residents and visitors to a city. Despite this, attaining a sensitive and accurate understanding of the underlying views is a more difficult task than it might appear.

As a result, the manner in which perception studies are implemented has often been included within methodological debates in this field. Grigson (c. 1994) for instance, criticizes the use of 'interested parties' and 'lobbying' in a key study in capacity analysis carried out in Chester and other capacity analysis studies which have been carried out as part of the development planning process in the UK.

Grigson goes on to urge caution in utilizing 'opinions' as part of what should be as objective an assessment as possible. Similarly, Lock (1996: 44) warns against basing policy-making on a professional as opposed to wider public assessment of conditions.

APPLICATION OF PERCEPTION STUDY METHODOLOGY IN PRAGUE

On the basis of the above debate relating to the need for a measured and sensitive approach to perception studies of this type, questionnaires were set up to gauge the perceptions of the residents and visitors to the historic city centre of Prague, with direct comparability of results being a central aim. The resident survey aimed to assess the degree to which the lives of the local population were influenced by tourism, whilst the visitor questionnaire aimed to examine levels of visitor satisfaction for cross-comparison with the views of residents.

Whilst the questions posed were essentially confined to a single point in time, developing in effect a 'snapshot view' of perceptions, the responses can be interpreted as being representative of the post-socialist as opposed to pre-Velvet revolutionary period. Tourism numbers have risen sharply in the city since 1989, and the current level of commercial development and related urban change has not been experienced in the city centre since the pre-communist years.

The tourist interviews were conducted aurally, with the use of translated versions where the interviewee was willing to complete it him/herself. The same questionnaire was sent to residents in the historic city centre. The data were not intended to provide an objective or definitive assessment of the environmental characteristics of the historic core, but were used as an integral part of the assessment of levels of capacity in contrast to the more peripheral role which they have been afforded in similar studies of this type.

For the resident survey, in order to ensure that the full case study area was covered but that the sample remained relatively random, ten streets were randomly drawn from lists of all the streets in Stare Mesto (excluding Josefov) and Mala Strana. Five streets in Hradcany and Josefov were also picked using the same process, providing a total of thirty streets in all. Within these streets ten questionnaires were delivered randomly to those buildings in residential use which had names on doors (signifying that they were likely to be occupied) or to which access to postboxes could be made.

Delivery was 'random' only in terms of contingent circumstances such as access to postal boxes being possible through open doors/or on street locations etc.; distribution also sought not to be overly concentrated in a single tenement building, utilizing as wide a spread within each street as available at the time of delivery. Clearly this was not a strictly scientific random sample, but it was considered the best practical and systematic course of action in the circumstances.

The visitor questionnaire was carried out at pre-identified places in the case study area, which together reflected a diverse range of environmental conditions.

Interviews were conducted at the key tourist focal points:

- The Charles Bridge (including the adjacent streets of Krizovnicke namesti and Mostecka);
- Outside the castle gates in Hradcanske namesti;

- In Staromestske namesti; and
- At the exit gates of the Old Jewish cemetery.

For the purposes of maintaining a balance in perceptions interviews were also carried out in the more peripheral locations:

- The quieter square of Uhelny trh in Stare Mesto;
- Southward from Karlova along Ujezd in Mala Strana; and
- On Pohorelec in Hradcany.

Seventy-one of the 300 resident questionnaires were returned - a rate of 23.66 per cent. Given a number of difficulties, including the lack of familiarity of Prague residents with such questionnaires, the level of response was acceptable.

Despite the complexities involved in implementing the questionnaires, the resident sample was found to be broadly in line with the overall population of the historic centre, in terms of demographic characteristics and tenure of residence. In particular the maturity of the population of the historic centre was reflected in the sample.

In total 185 visitors were interviewed using the standard questionnaire. The respondents originated from a wide range of countries, with a high number from Western Europe, the UK and the USA. The reported accommodation related directly to the supply of facilities in the city, with a high number staying in budget accommodation such as youth hostels, and a similarly high proportion staying in private rooms. The popularity of the city for short breaks was also reflected, with just over a quarter of the sample (26.5 per cent) staying for two nights.

The differences and similarities in the views of residents and visitors provide an insight into how the changes in land use and place identity are influencing both everyday life in the area and the tourism product being offered. In addition, the linkages between perceptions of change and the views about potential methods of mediating these changes add a further dimension to the socio-cultural attitudes to planning and land-use change which are evolving as Prague undergoes the process of transformation.

In the analysis and comparison of visitor and resident perceptions, three key themes of: aesthetic aspects of the townscape quality; 2 levels of pedestrian activity; and 3 provision of retail facilities illustrate most clearly the complex relationship between contextual change, the cultural environment and their influence on changing perceptions of place in the post-socialist historic city.

Perceptions of aesthetic aspects of townscape quality The attraction of Prague, like many other European historic cities, lies in the overall townscape environment and atmosphere of the city, with visits to the centre being the general focus as opposed to there being one or two definable attractions to which visits are exclusively orientated. Although not easily quantifiable, street character is, therefore, an important element within the capacity of Prague to attract visitors.

Difficulties with acute overcrowding arise partly as a result of the 'human scale' of the historic core of Prague - a feature which in turn is a crucial part of the attraction of the city. Positive responses were made by both visitors and residents when ranking the characteristics of the area according to importance. 74.3 per cent of residents and 90.8 per cent of visitors considered street ambience to either be an important or very important element of the character of the area.

Similarly, the actual medieval street pattern and cobbled streets were repeatedly underlined in terms of their importance to the character of the area, with 84.3 per cent and 55.7 per cent of residents and visitors respectively stating that they contributed 'a lot' to the historic centre's identity. Despite both groups attributing great importance to the historicism of the built environment, there was widespread recognition by the area's residents of the erosion of the quality of the townscape.

However, few of the residents with negative perceptions of the townscape support greater intervention on the part of planning. This reflects a key issue identified by many researching the changes since 1989. Planning has not enjoyed public support, at least in part as a result of the rejection of what is perceived as controlling elements of public authorities in the city in countering the shackles of the totalitarian regime prior to the revolution. Public participation and accountability of the planning system remain limited, the system requiring considerable revision before a more inclusive approach to policy-making can be established.

A key question arising from this is, therefore, how quickly the Czech Republic and other former Eastern Bloc countries will return to supporting planning intervention, and what form such planning intervention might take. It is possible that aspirations towards EU membership may bring about a wider return to planning values, particularly in response to the notorious environmental degradation in northern Bohemia which will need extensive assistance to be remedied.

This increasing recognition of the value of planning and environmental management has already begun to filter through to the local level, with the development of a new Strategic Plan for the city and strengthening of the institutional context of planning.

However, planners in Prague dealing with developers are only now learning the dynamics of a free property market, and in the light of considerable international interest in development, the resulting position of planning has been weakened considerably.

Perceptions of levels of pedestrian activity Observation of street use confirmed that tourism was an important element of pedestrian capacity levels, not least as a result of the plethora of guided tours operating, mainly on foot, on almost identical routes through the area. To assess the legitimacy of the concerns expressed within the perception studies and the extent to which problems were attributable to tourism, observation was undertaken of selected streets in the historic city centre to assess levels of use and types of user.

Observation was based on numbers of pedestrians relative to pavement space available at each location. Times of observation were also monitored to take into account external factors such as weather and special events, within each of the ascribed weightings. Street activity was found to be (predictably) concentrated, with a distinct correlation between congestion and high levels of tourist use emerging. In addition to the streets observed in more general terms throughout the historic centre, the main tourist attractions and the Karlova route dictated the spread of the network of primary tourist streets.

There were relatively few instances of tourists using routes in the more peripheral areas away from attractions. Public transport was additionally an important influence on the level of use, with access to metro stations precipitating a high level of usage by tourists and non-tourists alike. The most important contributing factor to overcrowding was the guided tours operating on foot in the area, which had the effect of keeping large numbers of slow-moving people together, exacerbating their impact on pedestrian flows.

When questioned about the perceived levels of pedestrian comfort in the historic centre, further negative perceptions were identified. Whilst 23.9 per cent of visitors classified the streets as 'overcrowded', 60.0 per cent of residents were of the same view. Cross tabulation of the results highlighted the greatest sensitivity to overcrowding being expressed by residents who also stated that they would 'definitely not' be living in the area in the future. As before, perceptions of the situation and support for possible solutions to the problems did not correspond.

The potential improvement of the area through a reduction in the number of tourist users was more strongly supported by visitors (77.2 per cent) than by residents (34.3 per cent). This cross-over between perceptions of crowding being viewed more negatively by residents, to visitors advocating reduction in the numbers more strongly than their counterparts, could be attributed to the high concentration of tourist street use, focus areas being confined to a small number of streets in the area.

Alternatively, visitors may have felt that they are not experiencing the 'real' city and/or integrating with residents and everyday life, the concentration of tourists leading to the streets becoming a more artificial environment.

At the same time, however, despite tourism exacerbating if not entirely causing pedestrian crowding in the area through walking tours and group visits, residents maintained support for tourism, perhaps as a result of its clear economic benefits.

Perceptions of retail provision A third area of interest which provides a further insight into the repercussions of the changes taking place in the area, is the reaction of residents and visitors to the range and type of retail outlets.

A retail survey of Prague's historic core reveals the pressure for land use relating to tourism which has arisen over the past decade. All of the retail units within the historic city centre were categorized according to the classification system proposed by the Institute of Retail Studies (IRS) and according to observation of the units' respective user origins.

The retail sector of activity has been an important catalyst for regeneration of the city centre, but has also instigated considerable land-use change, having positive and negative implications for the character of the area (Plate IV). Analysis illustrates the high degree of tourist dominance in retail outlets in the city, with very few units catering for resident or resident-tourist use, and a similarly low number catering for household or essential shopping. The spatial distribution of tourist outlets is relatively widespread throughout the centre, although there are also patterns of extreme clustering around tourist attractions.

Many of the non-tourist outlets, and those selling non-luxury goods are located within Josefov, reflecting the relatively higher level of residential use and continuing sense of community which remain relatively identifiable characteristics within the area. Non-tourist outlets can also be found in the most peripheral streets, where there are relatively low tourist user numbers. As a result, the consideration of this sector of economic development illustrates the rapid progress of the area towards tourist domination, and within overall trends, the high degree of concentration of tourist activity within the area.

Whilst visitors were consistently happy with the range of units provided, residents were clearly considerably less satisfied - 23.9 per cent of visitors as compared to 42.2 per cent of residents felt that there were too many souvenir shops in the historic core. This corresponds with the increasing supply of outlets catering for tourists, as compared to the substantial decline in shops selling everyday goods.

The extent to which this is leading to the depopulation of the area is difficult to ascertain in terms of directly-related cause and effect, particularly in light of the myriad of alternative reasons for relocation. However, the most significant correlation of all the issues was identified between levels of dissatisfaction of residents with this aspect of the change, and the likelihood of relocation outside the historic core in the foreseeable future.

Comparison of visitor and resident perceptions illustrates the need to take into account the distinct agenda of each group in terms of their expectations of the historic city. In Prague, perceptions of residents as compared to those of visitors highlight the different meanings of the city which are expressed by people when questioned, and the way in which their use of the city has a direct influence on their perceptions of problems within the area. Undertaking such research adds a further dimension to more quantitative aspects of analysis, allowing important qualitative impacts to be explored, for example in relation to the genus loci or ambience of a place. Perception studies of residents and visitors can, in combination, go beyond a set of technically based (*i.e.* professionally perceived) values, incorporating the diversity of experiences and views of different groups and actors.

In Prague, the perception-based evidence indicates that there has been a substantial erosion of the sense of place and identity of the historic core. However, the extent to which this has occurred entirely as a result of the impact of tourism must be questioned.

Whilst tourism is undoubtedly the leading force in the changes which have occurred in the built environment, a range of other pressures for land-use change have also played an important role.

Whilst these are not comprehensively explored within this paper, the focus on perceptions of visitors and residents does illustrate that there is a need for wider consideration of the socio-cultural emphases influencing their views. For example, in the post-socialist context it is critical to note that tourism can instigate social change as local residents come into contact within visitors who have different values and perceptions.

In Prague, the influx of international visitors serves as a key part of the new cosmopolitan identity taken on by post-socialist cities as they have opened up to the West. The laissez faire attitudes of some of the residents of the historic core to continuing tourist activity could, therefore, be interpreted as going beyond a rejection of regulative planning regimes, being generated instead by a general positivity towards the opening up of cultural horizons and a welcoming of new social interaction. Further, more qualitative analysis of perceptions is clearly required to identify more deep-rooted socio-cultural views such as this.

Notwithstanding the need to view tourism as only one aspect of urban change, its importance in the historic centre of Prague cannot be overlooked. In revisiting the original literature relating to the meanings assigned to the historic built environment in the context of Prague, the research highlights the continuing complexity of place which has been compounded by land use and environmental change brought about by the rapid growth of tourism during the 1990s.

Whilst the historic centre represents a revitalization of national identity, the perception studies illustrate the extent to which its character is at risk of being eroded as a result of the changes which tourism has brought.

The impact of insensitively developed heritage tourism can lead to internationalization, creeping homogeneity and a shift away from 'true' history towards a more sanitized and popularized identity. Such changes must be avoided if the unique identity of the area is to be preserved. That uniqueness is best understood 'bottom up' *i.e.* from the local urban and national population; and it is that same uniqueness which ultimately is the key attraction for tourists.

The case remains that whilst visitors were repeatedly positive in their views about the historic centre, many residents are clearly dissatisfied, and this often reaches a level where their continued residence is directly affected by the tourist capacity of the area being breached. Tourism has not dominated Prague as a whole, but rather the city's small and densely-built historic core. The relatively non-regulative approach to development, particularly where it is considered of economic benefit, has already brought about considerable land-use change in the area.

Land use is being rapidly transformed (often from residential to commercial uses), the traditional resident population is being displaced and the overall atmosphere and congestion of the streets is being negatively influenced by the city's visitors. The research, therefore, illustrates a clear need to manage tourism-related activity within the historic core of Prague, if its quality of life for residents and the very character which attracted tourists in the first place are not to be eroded substantially.

REGIONAL TOURISM

Regional tourism within developing countries is a growing phenomenon. Yet this aspect has been largely neglected in social science research as well as tourism planning. This paper highlights the general nature, scale and economic significance of regional tourism in three leading regions in Asia, Africa and Latin America.

The topic is especially timely as economic self-reliance and cooperation are increasingly reiterated in the context of the emergence of regional groupings. A key question addressed is whether regional tourism development represents any new and viable prospects for regional economic improvement and partnership, especially compared to international tourism centred on attracting visitors from industrialized countries.

Based on a critical assessment of the experiences of three regional blocs (ASEAN - the Association of South-East Asian Nations; SADC - the Southern African Development Community; and Mercosur - a common market comprising Argentina, Brazil, Paraguay and Uruguay, with Chile being an associated member), the paper suggests that a basic appreciation of the prospects of regional tourism is not enough to produce perceptible benefits. Regional tourism development is occurring in a haphazard manner, with little attention to managing existing socio-economic inequalities and centre-periphery relations. The paper is based primarily on the review of secondary literature readily available to the author combined with a few documents obtained directly from different regional organizations or through Internet search. A small amount of material, especially concerning emerging tourism trends and outcomes, is drawn from a research project on national mass tourism in developing countries coordinated by the author at the United Nations Research Institute for Social Development, Geneva.

Tourism, like industry, transport and trade, has remained an integral part of development planning in developing countries. In some cases tourism has been seen as a 'saviour' to stagnant industries and traditional agriculture, creating new inter-sectoral linkages and demands. In particular, the different branches of the tourism industry, such as accommodation, catering, food and beverages, excursions, recreational activities and the entertainment industry, tour operating and transport, souvenir production and sale are considered to open vast prospects for employment and income to diverse population groups.

Governments, associated business groups and international financing institutions tended to regard tourism as a 'clean' industry (especially when compared to manufacturing). But in recent years, environmental problems associated with tourism, such as pollution, the waste problem, overconstruction, excessive use of water and wood, and degradation of other natural resources, have become clearly manifest.

Developing countries considered they had a 'comparative advantage' vis-a-vis the industrialized world as they possessed exceptional tourist resources and attractions, such as warm and sunny weather, attractive beaches, unique wildlife and tropical forests and exotic or authentic cultures. Indeed, in the 1950s and 1960s, newly-independent countries in Asia and Africa frequently inferred tourism development to be a means of 'resource transfer' from the North to the South.

As such, developing countries (usually with financial and technical assistance from bi- and multilateral agencies) sought to promote tourism through identification and development of new sites, promotion and marketing of diversified tourism products, enactment of favourable labour laws, provision of subsidized credits and tax exemptions to foreign investors. National and international tourism business groups gladly collaborated with governments when they saw possibilities for profit.

A thorny issue, however, was that the privileged tourist groups, coming mainly from the industrialized countries in the North, tended to respond more to the economic and political circumstances in their respective countries than to needs in Southern countries. In particular, developing countries possessed little capital, technology and know-how to develop tourism.

Instead, this situation reinforced 'dependency' relationships with industrialized countries. There is a vast amount of literature that indicates how this relationship has resulted in the repatriation of the bulk of tourism revenues to industrialized countries, while generating many enduring exploitative economic relations, human rights violations, and cultural and environmental problems in tourist destinations in developing countries.

It has thus become clear that tourism, based on the arrival of international tourists from Northern countries, was not such a reliable sector as initially perceived. At the same time, in several developing countries, the accompanying modernization processes and development of Westernized leisure ethic - in part stimulated by the arrival of Northern tourists - have fostered increased domestic tourism. Not only the privileged, but increasingly the middle and lower strata of the population groups are seeking to travel, and at times even abroad.

In fact, in a number of developing countries where one would usually imagine international tourism to be providing a substantial income, deficits have emerged between tourism receipts and expenditure by their nationals abroad. Recent examples include Brazil and Thailand.

Increasingly, in several developing countries, national tourism has become more important in terms of the total number of tourists and its contribution to national economy than international tourism (Ghimire 2001). In general, it can be said that national tourism is less sensitive to international political instability and economic stagnation, less detrimental to the country's balance of payments and should create substantial income and employment. But despite this potential, very few developing countries have a consistent policy on national tourism. When a significant number of tourists begin to take holidays, they demand facilities and services. Governments have tended to cope with this process in an ad hoc manner, with tourism policies being developed in a completely unplanned fashion.

Another characteristic of tourism is the rapid development of regional tourism within developing countries, with certain emerging prospects for economic development in the South, but also many impending problems similar to those associated with international tourism. This aspect is so far totally neglected in tourism literature, but a few policy measures are being undertaken at the level of regional institutions. This paper will explore this particular aspect of Southern regional tourism, especially looking at it as a possible way of strengthening South-South economic cooperation.

For several decades now, South-South collaboration has remained an important foreign policy agenda in developing countries. This issue has been especially articulated in the context of the work of the Non-Aligned Movement, Group of 1 5, Group of 77 and many other forums. South-South cooperation has been regarded as an essential mechanism for promoting economic development and self-reliance, increasing understanding and solidarity within the South and being able to negotiate its demands in world forums.

Trade, finance, industry and business, science and technology, transport and infrastructure have been considered as priority areas for collaboration. However, there are few tangible achievements. Many of the Southern initiatives are limited to designing appropriate strategies and mechanisms rather than implementing them. A South Centre report admitted in 1990 that... it has generally proved easier to co-operate in the political sphere, where important joint initiatives continued to be mounted and sustained. On economic issues there has been a wide gap between, on the one hand, the rhetoric of solidarity, the ambitious objectives in international resolutions, and the many programmes set out in intergovernmental agreements, and, on the other, the action that has ensued.

In recent years, the issue of South-South collaboration has been especially reiterated through regional organizations such as ASEAN (Association of South-East Asian Nations), SAARC (South Asian Association for Regional Cooperation), and SADC (Southern African Development Community). These organizations have sought to intensify regional economic and political cooperation.

In line with this rationale for regional cooperation, tourism is often seen as an exceptional means of revitalizing and diversifying the regional economic base, generating new employment and income possibilities for local communities and strengthening people-topeople contacts. And a few specific policy initiatives have been started along these lines in different regions. This paper attempts to discuss the principal features, magnitude and possible outcomes of some of these initiatives.

In particular, the paper will examine whether regional tourism development stands for a new economic dynamo for the region, especially compared to North-South tourism.

UNDERSTANDING THE GENERAL NATURE AND SCALE OF REGIONAL TOURISM

'Regional tourism' is identified here as activities of leisure travel by people within the same region, but outside their usual country of residence, such as South East Asia, Southern Africa, Central America and South America. Besides the close geographical proximity, countries in a given region may share many similar historical developments, ecological characteristics, standards of living, socio-economic structures, cultural features and population composition. Hence there are likely to be many distinct features in the composition of the principal tourist groups, their leisure interests and activities and their influence on the local economy, culture and so forth as compared to international tourists from the industrialized North. But information on many of these crucial aspects is totally lacking.

There is no coherent approach to regional tourism development. For example, the World Tourism Organization (WTO), a United Nations agency which has responsibilities for gathering data and elaborating plans on tourism, has primarily been concerned with the promotion of international tourism involving tourists from developed countries. It has paid trivial attention to the emergence of Southern regional tourism.

This is reflected in the lack of its treatment of core concepts, definitions and classifications of regional tourism, as well as in understanding the major tourist groups involved, their behaviour and interests. Looking at its past projects and publications' list, it becomes clear that the organization has undertaken no major projects in this area (WTO 2000). This is surprising knowing that in the past the WTO has remained keen to get involved in technical and managerial issues, while generally avoiding politics, power relations and socio-economic inequalities.

At the national level, there are only a small number of developing countries that have attempted to assess the potential gain (as well as harm) from regional tourism development. It is very recently - especially with the creation of regional cooperation bodies - that regional tourism has been considered as a phenomenon to be recognized and worth integrating into the regional planning process.

Regional travel patterns, based on the data provided by WTO, for ASEAN, SADC and Mercosur, are presented. They suggest that a substantial tourism flow occurs between developing countries in the respective regions. In 1998 about 55 per cent of tourists in the ASEAN countries came from Asian and Pacific developing countries. Some 73 per cent of the visitors to the SADC region originated from Africa. In the case of Mercosur, visitors from Latin America constituted over 70 per cent of regional arrivals. Indeed, not only is the number of tourists from developing countries in the region high, but WTO forecasts suggest a sustained growth of intraregional travel in most regions within developing countries in coming years.

Intraregional tourist arrivals in Africa, for example, will constitute 64 per cent of all tourist arrivals in 2020 (compared to 58 per cent in 1995). Similarly, 83 per cent of all the tourist arrivals in East Asia and the Pacific are to be from within the region in 2020 (compared to 79 per cent in 1995). In contrast, the WTO suggests a decrease for intraregional tourist arrivals to the Americas from 77 per cent in 1995 to 62 per cent in 2020 (WTO 1997).

Since national tourism authorities, the WTO and tourism business groups are keen to give optimistic figures on the current and future patterns of tourism expansion, they at times disregard the various complexities involved in defining and counting different tourist groups. In the case of regional tourism, in particular, it is possible that people frequently crossing borders to neighbouring countries for all kinds of purposes may be registered as tourists each time they pass the checkpoints. Despite these difficulties in the definition and counting of regional tourists, regional leisure travel today is undoubtedly a significant phenomenon in many regions in the South.

The importance of regional or Southern tourism appears especially evident when it is compared with the number of tourists coming from developed countries. For example, WTO data suggest that in 1998 within ASEAN, SADC and Mercosur blocs Northern tourists comprised only 39, 23 and 24 per cent respectively (WTO 2000a). Future expansion in tourism within developing countries is more than likely, given a changing leisure ethic that attaches importance to recreational and holiday activities, growing urbanization and the aspiration of city dwellers to escape to pleasure and holiday spots, and increased disposable incomes for leisure purposes among the middle classes as well as the aspiring low-income classes in many regions (Ghimire 1997).

Given this growth potential, and in the context of seeking to foster increased political, economic and cultural links, it would seem natural that different regional organizations would consider regional travel promotion to be an important policy issue. But how are concrete policy measures undertaken in different regional contexts? What are their political and economic settings? How consistent are these measures in terms of their general objectives and outcomes in practice? The underlying issue is to what extent regional tourism is integrated in the regional planning process as a means to enhance regional economic cooperation in order to take advantage of human, material and natural resources available in the region, or is it mainly induced by powerful regional business as well as national elite groups that are keen to maintain a closed, opportune tourism market for themselves? How are the rights of tourism workers protected?

Crucially, how would the ensuing income and benefits be distributed across different population groups in the country or region? Are there any regional policy specificities in these respects compared to the management of international tourism for example?

SPECIFIC EXPERIENCES IN REGIONAL TOURISM COOPERATION

The perceptions of collective regional self-reliance and economic cooperation are not new in developing countries. Nor is there any lack of formal regional groupings. Indeed, regional organizations of one type or another are now commonly found in all regions.

But much of the work of these regional organizations is limited to the level of political cooperation between governments and parliamentary bodies. Although close collaboration in trade, industry and business, transport and infrastructure, science, education and technology, information and communication, environment and so forth is commonly called for and some initiatives have been taken, in most contexts achievements in these areas are meagre. Nevertheless, the establishment of regional organizations has provided a political space to discuss collaboration and to seek implementation of a certain number of policies in these broad areas.

As far as the tourism sector goes, very few regional groups have paid specific attention to this area of activity. Tourism is understood to expand in parallel to growth in regional trade, industry and business, as well as to the development of transport and infrastructure. In some ways, this approach was more realistic than trying to promote travel and related business without cooperation within the broader issues of economy and commercial relations.

With a view to boosting tourism in the region, people-to-people contacts are perceived vital by removing visa and currency restrictions. In the case of certain regional blocs, tourism development committees and study groups have been created. In a very few cases, concrete regional tourism policy measures have also been undertaken. To elaborate on these developments and draw relevant conclusions on the role of regional tourism to promote South-South cooperation, the work of three regional blocs in Asia, Africa and Latin America are assessed.

ASEAN

An examination of the Association of South-East Asian Nations (ASEAN) is instructive for at least two reasons. First, it is one of the leading Southern regional blocs, with significant experience in regional economic cooperation extending over three decades. Second, tourism has received comprehensive consideration in the organization's work and strategic planning, especially as the region is one of the world's major tourism destinations. The organization sees tourism to be 'an important industry providing substantial foreign exchange receipts and employment opportunities'. Given this, it believes

...tourism has to keep pace with globalisation trends and market liberalization, to enhance the opportunity for travel business to expand and compete across national borders and attract investments and technology to sustain the long-term viability of the tourism industry.

ASEAN UNDATED A, 4

Regional visitors encompass a significant group of tourists in most ASEAN countries. In 1998, for example, in Thailand and Singapore, these tourists comprised 21.3 and 26.8 per cent of total incoming tourists. In Indonesia and Malaysia, they represented the substantially higher proportions of 45.2 and 69.3 per cent respectively.

Among the original members, only the Philippines has a relatively low number of regional tourists visiting the country, reflecting the lack of tourist security and infrastructures. Newly emerging tourism destinations, notably Laos and Cambodia, have also begun to attract a considerable number of regional tourists, especially since access by cars and coaches has become possible from Thailand.

A cheaper cost of living and relatively unspoiled natural and cultural traits provide further incentives to visit these countries. Furthermore, in recent years, the Mekong region has proved alluring for economic investment and tourism development projects, thereby attracting various grou ps of business people, government officials and tourism promoters.

Regional tourism collaboration was seen as an important sphere soon after the establishment of ASEAN in 1967. In the late 1960s and early 1970s, when trade and economic investment were the principal areas of regional cooperation, development in tourism was already recognized to be an important element in fostering these activities. In 1976, the organization created a Sub-Committee on Tourism for the development of coordinated tourism projects and their enhanced marketing.

In 1981, the ASEAN Tourism Forum was established as an annual event. Various aspects relating to tourism promotion, marketing, research and training are discussed and plans of action elaborated through this Forum. It designated 1992 a 'Visit ASEAN Year' with various measures to promote tourism in the region.

In 1998, ASEAN proposed to focus its tourism activities on the following five strategic themes:

- Marketing the ASEAN region as a single tourism destination;
- Encouraging tourism investments;
- Tourism manpower development;
- Environmentally-sustainable tourism; and
- Facilitation of intra-ASEAN travel (ASEAN undated b, 1).

In recent years, the ASEAN National Tourism Organizations (NTOs) have remained especially active in formulating national and regional tourism strategies and plans of action. They have served as a useful institutional mechanism for the exchange of vital information and experience, harmonization of tourism policies and programmes, marketing, training, research and information dissemination. Indeed, most of these activities have consistently been identified as core issues of regional tourism development since major collaboration efforts began to take place in the 1970s.

The NTOs have also sought to tackle problems such as epidemics (*e.g.* cholera), the haze originating from fires in Indonesia, negative media reports and other problems which affect tourist arrivals in the region. They thus attempted to reassure tourists as well as business partners that ASEAN NTOs were doing their best to address these issues jointly.

These organizations were also motivated to promote tourism more energetically in order to help to overcome the financial and currency crisis that the region faced in 1997. In order to improve the region's image and boost tourism, ASEAN designated 2002 the 'Visit ASEAN Millennium Year' under the leadership of the NTOs as well as the private sector (ASEAN undated b, 1).

Clearly, tourism is recognized as a vital element in regional economic development and cooperation. But most of the efforts have been put into the development of international tourism. Regional tourism development has tended to receive insignificant attention, despite the fact that regional tourists are clearly the largest tourist groups in most South East Asian countries. Indeed, the recent financial and economic instabilities have encouraged many South East Asian tourists previously travelling to North America and Europe to take their holidays in their own countries or the region, thereby providing further impulse to regional tourism development. Among the strategies developed to enhance regional tourism are improved transport links, steady removal of visa restrictions and the provision of easier currency exchange.

Economic links have continued to flourish among South East Asian countries in spite of national political instabilities or the establishment of authoritarian regimes (*e.g.* Myanmar). But the econ omic competition among countries and concern about rapid immigration from poorer neighbouring countries at times also tended to hold back development in regional travel and tourism.

In addition, a marked difference in standards of living between the poorer countries (Cambodia, Laos, Myanmar and Vietnam) and the relatively better-off ones (Malaysia, Singapore and Thailand) means that not all South East Asians have an equal capacity for leisure travel, although upper and upper-middle classes even in the poorer countries have always had sufficient economic means to travel in the region.

Attentive NGOs and academics have tended to point out how this division in the standard of living and national economic strength are allowing richer countries to take more advantage of regional economic and tourism collaboration. Business and tourism groups from the latter countries are encouraged to make investments in new destinations and products, with little control over their activities.

On the whole, in promoting this new or regional-level tourism initiative little attention is given to the undesirable social and economic hardships caused by tourism, human rights violations and environmental degradation. The Tourism Investigation and Monitoring team, an NGO designed to foster popular debate and action on tourism, development and environmental issues in the Mekong sub-region, for example, states that: Instead, people are seduced to increasingly consume glorified and distorted images of reality and spend money to enjoy the sights and pleasures on offer.

NEW FRONTIERS 1997, 3

Increasingly, the rise in Western-style leisure travel in the region is thought to trigger many negative consequences on traditional practices, customs, and family and community values (Pleumarom 1999).

SADC

Originally known as the Southern African Development Coordination Conference (SADCC) and established in 1980, the Southern African

Development Community (SADC) aims to bring accelerated economic growth, creating more jobs and reducing poverty in the region, in line with the achievements made by ASEAN countries. However, there have been few tangible accomplishments. One problem was that until 1994 South Africa, the largest regional economic power, was not the key player.

Following the end of the apartheid regime, the country has swiftly moved to hold 'centre stage' within the functioning of the organization. As the organization sees bright prospects for expansion in regional trade and investment, various institutions have been created and new protocols signed in these areas in recent years.

Tourism is important in most Southern African countries, especially international safari tourism. Regional tourism has also remained significant. In the past, regional tourism was geared towards meeting the leisure travel and vacation needs of a privileged group of white people and a few black elites and businessmen. But in recent years, sections of the middle and lower-middle strata of the population have shown interest in leisure travel, frequently combined with other activities (*e.g.* shopping, health treatment, business). Most of the tourists in the region come from the SADC countries.

In the context of regional cooperation, the development of tourism is considered to be a key policy objective. This is guided by the idea that tourism would be one of the main sectors benefiting from closer regional integration. The specific goal of tourism has been to maximize tourism's contribution to regional development through the generation and retention of foreign exchange earnings, employment creation, human resources development and rural development.

SADC UNDATED, 4

A five-year tourism development strategy was elaborated in 1994 which examined investment needs, development of visitor facilities and infrastructure, human resources development, research and data collection. It specifically identified the need to promote tourism on a regional scale bearing in mind many unique tourist attractions in the Southern African region.

A primary outcome of this strategy was the establishment of a Regional Tourism Organization of Southern Africa (RETOSA), in 1996, with the view of coordinating and implementing some of the above activities. But as the organization lacked both human and financial resources, its work became limited mainly to the promotion of tourism in the region. In particular, the organization has sought to increase the volume of tourism business by welcoming international tourists and by identifying and developing new market niches for the region.

Besides the creation of RETOSA, several initiatives have been taken to attract increased international tourism.

Some of the recent projects undertaken with the specific goal of expanding tourism-related physical and social infrastructure and facilities include the:

- Trans Africa Coast2Coast Spatial Development;
- Maputo Development Corridor;
- Lubombo Spatial Development; and
- Okavango Upper Zambezi International tourism zone (de Beer et al. 1999).

Another project includes the creation of trans-frontier parks between South Africa, Mozambique and Zimbabwe, thereby facilitating easy travel and improved accommodation facilities for tourists. But progress in the execution of many of these projects has been slow due primarily to the lack of necessary funds, especially as the implementation of most projects is left to the individual countries which have to deal with many competing needs.

The above initiatives have nevertheless provided increased institutional space for tourism officials in the region to exchange their points of view and organize protocol meetings. One such meeting, in September 1998, proposed the creation of a single tourist visa for the entire region to ease border restrictions and formalities for international tourists, and the issue has since been discussed by immigration authorities in the different member countries (SADC undated).

As far as regional tourism involving travel by citizens of SADC countries is concerned, few — if any — concrete measures have to date been undertaken, although a number of countries, such as South Africa, have noted the importance of this sector. Despite the overwhelming number of regional tourists, most tourism promotion activities are targeted towards international tourists from the North. Tourist products too are heavily biased to servicing this group of tourists, focusing mainly on nature tourism.

Regional tourists, on the other hand, are mainly interested in holiday recreation involving visits to cities and historical monuments, shopping and entertainment. On the whole government investments in accommodation and other visitor facilities do not reflect the interests and motivations of the bulk of regional visitors. The participation of the private sector, which is seen as crucial to tourism development in the region, has also tended to concentrate on the international tourism niche market, as much of the investment in tourism has tended to come from foreign groups.

In many countries, national and local investors remain merely as subordinate partners of foreign investment groups and the limited government attempts to encourage domestic or community entrepreneurship has produced few tangible results; this has been, for example, the case in South Africa. Visa and currency regulations for regional visitors are frequently intractable. And there is still a widespread cultural preconception which considers 'tourism to be an exclusive privilege of whites', thereby making many blacks feel uneasy about visiting Westernized tourism destinations. Little attention is given to many of these critical issues at the SADC level.

MERCOSUR

Mercosur (meaning 'southern market' in Spanish; and in Portuguese it is called Mercosul) is comprised of Argentina, Brazil, Paraguay and Uruguay, with Chile being an associated member. Bolivia, Peru and other Andean countries have also entered into various cooperation agreements with the group.

Established in 1991, Mercosur has two objectives:

- Free trade between member countries; and
- A common external trade policy.

It aims at full liberalization and expansion of trade within VVTO regulations, its target being to achieve a free single market in four member countries by January 2002. However, progress is limited.

Although various strategies have been elaborated, their implementation has been extremely slow owing to the lack of coordination in monetary and fiscal policies, financial and political instabilities and the dominance of Brazilian national interests to promote its automobile, manufacturing and agricultural sectors. Unlike ASEAN and SADC, tourism has received little attention within the institutional structure and working of Mercosur. Most of its decisions are taken under 11 working subgroups that extend from tax and customs matters to transport, industrial and agricultural policies. Tourism is not included in these subgroups, although harmonization of customs, common taxation and investment policies and development of transport would have an indirect influence in the expansion of tourism in the region.

This is not to suggest that the tourism sector is totally disregarded by the Mercosur group of countries. At the national level Brazil and Argentina, in particular, have active tourism policies. This has somewhat influenced the Mercosur secretariat to recognize the economic potential of regional tourism. It has looked at ways of facilitating regional tourism by easing border restrictions.

Also, the development and improvement in cross-border infrastructure has remained a constant concern (The Economist 12 October 1996; The Financial Times 1 September 2000). These issues were considered by the Specialist Meeting on Tourism and the Technical Committee No. 2 on Custom Affairs (OAS 1995). The organization has also sought to launch a more coordinated marketing strategy on the Internet by seeking to promote leading tourism sites and facilities in the region.

Regional tourism is a well-established phenomenon in South America and recent policy measures to improve infrastructure and visitor facilities as well as to reduce frontier formalities have produced several positive results in terms of increasing the number of tourists in various countries.

In Brazil, for example, regional tourists came mainly from Argentina and Uruguay before the 1 970s, but in recent decades the number of incoming tourists from other neighbouring countries has increased significantly as a result of the improvement in roads and communication systems, with regional tourists comprising nearly half of the total incoming tourists. In Chile, 54 per cent of the tourists come from neighbouring countries. In Argentina, Paraguay and Uruguay, this group comprises between two-thirds and three-quarters of total tourists.

Visa and custom restrictions still remain complex, especially for tourists from poorer countries. No specific policy measures have been adopted towards creating a single currency or facilitating currency exchange for regional tourists. Despite much discussion, there has been no noteworthy investment in major infrastructure projects and the costs involved are gigantic. Also, the lack of a coherent regional tourism development policy results in investments taking place in a highly haphazard manner. Research, data collection and analysis on tourism potential, as well as its unintended negative impacts on the environment, local economies and livelihood systems are completely absent.

What is evident from the above discussion is that regional tourism is significant in all three regional blocs. In ASEAN countries regional tourists comprised 36 per cent of the total. The percentage of regional tourists in ASEAN countries stands somewhat low, partly because there is a substantial international transit of tourists through Singapore and Thailand. Also, the large number of Japanese tourists who come to the region lessen the figure for regional tourists. In SADC and Mercosur, regional tourists added up to 59 and 69 per cent of total tourists respectively.

In actual numbers, in the mid-1990s ASEAN regional tourists comprised annually 10.7 million; and SADC and Mercosur respectively had 7.9 and 7.2 million regional visitors (WTO 2000a). Given this, regional tourism held a certain degree of economic potential for increased investment and entrepreneurship, thereby creating new employment and income prospects for various sections of the population. Clearly, it was important to give impetus to regional tourism development, especially as most of the earnings from regional tourism should in principle remain in the region itself. However much of this has remained purely hypothetical.

The ASEAN bloc has extended experience in regional tourism cooperation. The central secretariat bodies and national tourism organizations are mobilized to foster tourism in the region. In SADC, a regional tourism organization has been set up to coordinate tourism development activities.

In Mercosur, too, attempts have been made to promote tourism in the region, although on a considerably lesser scale. However, most of these institutional structures and activities concerning tourism were geared towards marketing the region more effectively in order to attract an increased number of tourists from developed countries; regional tourism development involving the nationals of member countries received little or no attention.

Few concrete policy measures have been undertaken favouring regional tourists. In the first place, there is little understanding of who the regional tourists are, their aspirations and interests, and the economic potential as well as the socio-environmental problems they represent. Tourism research, data collection and analysis are heavily biased towards international tourism.

The economic capacity and specific recreation and entertainment interests of regional tourists are scarcely taken into account with regard to funding tourism projects, and there are no particular attempts to broaden those targeting regional tourists. Also, since the latter remain more or less invisible in tourism policies, no tourism-awareness raising measures are developed targeting these regional groups of tourists.

A simple recognition of the potential of regional tourism is hardly sufficient to produce tangible economic results. Also, the lack of government investment in regional tourism and tourism policies, mean that in the majority of cases they are not integrated in national or regional economic policies. There has been little assessment of the specific role of regional tourism in regional economic development, as well as in rural and urban development in specific national contexts. As such, it is not surprising that there are no concrete measures to promote community entrepreneurship and shareholding in tourism, and employment and income-sharing policies.

The crucial question is whether regional tourism is likely to help to change existing economic relations more in favour of poorer or weaker groups and areas, and what supplementary policy measures could be envisaged when this was not the case? This requires a continual process of policy monitoring and critical evaluation, which remain totally absent in present regional tourism strategies.

One major problem in regional economic cooperation is the handling of existing centre-periphery relations. In any attempt to foster regional political integration, create free trading zones, simplify customs and tax regulations and increase public financing of common industrial programmes, transport, energy and telecommunication there is actually; little guarantee that accrued benefits as well as associated costs will be equally shared by member countries.

Tourism is likely to reinforce the situation since the countries which have political weight, relatively large GDP and dominance over regional trade are most likely to take the lead in tourism investment in the region. This has been the case, for example, with Thailand within the Mekong-belt, where powerful Thai politicians, business groups, the army, and the like, often team up with the government in regional efforts to boost tourism.

Some of these groups are involved in shady projects involving the creation of environmentally damaging golf courses and casinos, and the rapid exploitation of unspoiled historical and ecotourism sites. In any event, as these groups commonly control the entire chain of tourism development, including the formulation of tourism plans, promotion, training, development of road links and investment in other tourism activities, their dominant role is guaranteed. In some ways, this regional domination of Thailand is quite expected as in 1999 its economy accounted for over 72 per cent of the Mekong region's (Cambodia, Laos, Myanmar, Thailand and Vietnam) GDP (World Bank 2000; UNDP 2000).

Brazil and South Africa are equally striking cases in their respective regions. In 1 999, Brazil retained nearly 60 per cent of Mercosur's GDP (50 per cent if Chile is included); the South African economy had a lion's share of 69 per cent of the total GDP of 13 SADC countries (World Bank 2000; UNDP 2000).

Given their overwhelming political and economic command, national economic interests (*i.e.* the interests of national business groups) tend to be reflected in the making and functioning of regional blocs in general and tourism investment, promotion and marketing, as well as the benefits derived from it, in particular.

Travel formalities, currency exchange, immigration, refugee issues and so forth, which frequently remain key barriers to regional integration, heavily reflect the interests of these countries. In short, in the absence of any institutional arrangements to share the costs and benefits of tourism in a more egalitarian manner among member countries, present tourism cooperation policies in these three regional blocs are simply likely to reinforce the prevailing centre-periphery relations.

Another dilemma is that since these regional blocs state their global policy framework to include firm adherence to economic liberalization policies and strong private sector involvement within the policies established by the World Trade Organization, it becomes very difficult to differentiate regional tourism investment groups from multinational corporations.

In any event, there is no guarantee that regional business groups would be more concerned with promoting regional economic development, improving community livelihood systems, protecting workers' rights and conserving the environment.

The trend is towards a rather close collaboration between multinational corporations and regional tourism conglomerates to exploit readily marketable regional features, products, tax incentives and cheap labour for generating hefty, short-term profits.

Indeed, most of the tourism promotion activities sponsored by regional blocs facilitated this alliance and produced many unintended socio-economic and ecological impacts at the local level. But research and debate are lacking on many of these critical issues.

In conclusion, it can be said that, although in principle regional tourism represents a useful instrument in regional economic self-reliance and progress, including a level of community welfare at the local level, this needs careful planning, taking into account political and economic realities and constraints.

Although the establishment of regional blocs has helped to bring to the fore some of the rationale and importance of regional cooperation in tourism, so far there have been few sustained outcomes.

Most activities remained limited at the level of a declaration of good intentions and elaboration of policy strategies, while the measures implemented thus far have tended to encourage unequal relations among member countries and support the interests of business groups. These results are not unique to the tourism sector, but are common to many other sectors, such as trade and investment; they reflect a structural weakness in South-South collaboration.

5

The Role of Marketing Philosophy in Rural Tourism Development

INTRODUCTION

Modern tourism, like many other business areas started to "branch" and has become a significant source of growth and development of companies, destinations, and entire national economies. All the effects of globalization and world economic trends can be integrated and analyzed through it. The last decade of the twentieth century brought significant changes in tourism, especially in regard to the behaviour of tourists as consumers. Accordingly, a strategic shift was carried out – from mass tourism towards the development of alternative forms of tourism such as eco-tourism, cultural tourism, rural tourism, congress tourism and others which are completely devoted to the individual and his specific needs.

In this regard, special attention is directed towards the development of the rural tourism. Rural tourism as a sustainable, multi-functional activity based on local resources and related traditional agriculture, culture and natural resources, is recommended for rural areas because of its multiple uses, and it is proved by numerous positive experiences of European countries.

On the other hand, there are many rural areas which are exposed to continuous processes of depopulation, economic decline and complete marginalization due to the intense process of industrialization, urbanization and electrification.

The village is declining, and takes away the authentic way of life and overall culture of the village, because people as carriers and transmitters of such values are leaving. Further depopulation, with the introduction of new non-agricultural activities and re-routing of mass tourism, cause the rural areas to squeeze traditional farming and rural life.

Above mentioned leads to the need that the rural tourism as an instrument of revitalization deserves more attention, and to make an analysis of those factors that are essential and/or critical for initiating rural tourism business.

Among them the application of marketing concepts in all stages of development of rural tourism takes a special place. Accordingly, this paper aims to provide insight into the role of marketing philosophy in the development of rural tourism. With regards to this, the structure of work consists of three interrelated parts. The first part gives the definition of rural tourism and analyzes the specifics of this selective form of tourism. Fundamental concepts of marketing in tourism are analyzed in the second section. The third section argues the necessity of implementing marketing and its peculiarities in rural tourism.

DEFINITION AND CONTENT

According to the World Tourism Organization, "rural tourism is a term used when rural culture is a key component of the product". In order to realize this concept, a tourist needs to provide personalized contact and the experience of a specific rural environment. In addition, the tourists should be given, as far as possible, the opportunity to actively participate in certain agricultural activities and other activities, traditions and lifestyle of local residents.

It certainly provides a whole new experience, which is almost impossible to achieve in destination of so-called mass tourism. Kušen considers it necessary to insist on a complex definition of rural tourism because it needs to include all its elements.

Thus, as tourism that takes place in rural areas, activities such as walking, biking, horseback riding, extreme sports (*e.g.* climbing), farm visits, tasting local food, hunting and fishing are also integral elements of integrated rural tourism product. Therefore, depending on the presence of such elements in the total supply, we can talk about agro tourism, green tourism, gastronomic tourism, nautical tourism, hunting tourism, cultural-historical tourism, different types of sports and recreational tourism (*e.g.* riding) and more.

The above suggests that this is a very complex type of tourism. That is why the division of rural tourism is very rich and very committed to the characteristics of the area in which tourist activity takes place. In other words, the boundaries and content of rural tourism are determined by the specific characteristics and limits of rural area in which to develop. If there are opportunities for the development of several forms or types of tourism in certain rural areas, then they all belong to the broader concept, which collectively are called rural tourism.

In any case, preserved rural area is an essential resource for rural tourism. Especially interesting are the areas where poor production, smaller quantities and maintaining the traditional way of life are carried out because they are so attractive to tourists from industrialized and suburban areas that have lost the key features of recognition as a rural area. The above is especially important for Montenegro and its rural areas of exceptional natural beauty and rich culture and tradition.

Authors Hall, Roberts and Mitchell highlight the sensitivity of tourism as an economic activity in the development of rural areas in the following segments:

- Generating new business and jobs is often limited due to small size and dispersed activity and low rates of return on investments;
- It requires more skill to achieve success, and the same is not possible to combine in one person;
- The development is in the hands of rural entrepreneurs, such as farmers and local municipal officials who often lack the necessary skills and knowledge in the field of tourism;
- It anticipates great number of micro enterprises;
- Sources of investment are often scarce;
- The duration of the tourist season is short;

In accordance with the preceding, it is possible pick out a few specifics for the tourist offer in rural destinations. Tourist offer is extremely fragmented, and consists of a large number of small, regionally dispersed bidders.

These are mostly small family businesses, which offer warm welcome and personalized contact with tourists. However, there is often a great lack of inconsistency with regard to the quality of services provided, which can vary to a greater or lesser extent. In addition, holders of such positions are limited with staff and finances, which directs them to join forces for more efficient implementation of destination management and marketing programmes.

In the examples of rural tourism development in Central and Eastern Europe risk factors that can affect the development of rural tourism are identified:

- Lack of understanding and/ or misunderstanding of the concept of rural tourism, coupled with the wrong initial assumptions about the simple and easy generation market, income and employment, which often leads to failure and the creation of a given image of negative rural areas and the whole country as a tourist destination;
- Low level of quality accommodation, associated with the poor resources of investment and lack of planning for further development;
- Lack of information about the needs and desires of tourists as a result of insufficient or poor quality of marketing research;
- Lack of funds for starting and/ or continuation of business as a result of insufficient understanding and support from the banking and other financial institutions;
- Low level of infrastructure in rural areas, but noting that this deficiency can be an advantage in terms of eco-rural tourism;
- Lack of information on the possibilities and opportunities of further development of tourism, leading to disconnection of villages in a unique tourist product and lack of support of local and regional, governmental entities;
- Non-compliance with the development objectives of local governments

and development agencies, and as a result of inadequate communication, lack of confidence, and lack of shared vision of development.

It is noteworthy that in many cases in rural tourist destinations, tourism is an additional activity that provides significant support to the traditional rural economy, made up primarily of agriculture, forestry, crafts and other activities. Therefore, the holders of such positions are farmers, and not tourist entrepreneurs with all necessary supporting knowledge and marketing skills. Thus, as one of the key limiting factors in the success of rural tourism are planning, organization and implementation of effective marketing.

Many rural areas face a lack of their own tourism image, as a result of insufficient application of marketing concept to create a tourism product. In this way, rural destinations cannot be successfully positioned in the market or they work in difficult circumstances, and it is their main limiting factor for further progress. The cause is less attention focused on the so-called "Soft" elements of rural tourism development such as knowledge and skills in the field of marketing, management, modern computer technology, foreign languages and more.

CONCEPTUAL BASICS OF MARKETING IN TOURISM

THE FUNDAMENTAL TENET OF MARKETING PHILOSOPHY

Contemporary needs of people as consumers, families, groups and the community at large are changing rapidly. Thus the enterprises need to inputs different contents. The basic assumption to meet their need is appropriate offer, which should coincide with them. Supply bidders realize their business goals in adequate exchange with market demand. The business philosophy, which helps bidders to timely focus on the potential demand, and achieve their own business objectives, is known as the "marketing". Applying its principles to create a supply helps managers to focus themselves on those market segments that may contain the expected demand in a timely manner.

Marketing is not just a need for manufacturing companies, but for all bidders regardless of whether it comes to material goods and/ or services. The newest concept of marketing is increasingly seen as *managing profitable relationships* with customers (Customer Relationship Management). Relationships with customers are the basic setting for the success of modern managers. Marketing concept is subject to change, like any other area of business economics. They occur in at least two directions: a) changes to the treatment of consumer and b) changes in area of specific applications of different businesses.

Today we can already distinguish and start a new concept of marketing. Previous (old) marketing concept based on several fundamental theses (1) Mass production, focused on economies of scale and low costs, (2) Mass and high standardization of products in response to requests of more picky customer, (3) "Mass marketing", based on a philosophy of maximizing the number of potential customers and based on appropriate media (TV, etc.) and the promotional mix and (4) "The average consumer", founded on the basis of standardized messaging to the company. Generally speaking, the old marketing concept is based on a stable demand, stable processes and stable product.

A new concept of marketing purposes, instead of the above, doesn't put an accent on customer *needs* any more but on the *value* he sees in the product, making the decision to purchase, along with the process of its consumption. Unlike the previous concept, which was based on creating and maintaining customers, the new concept is based on the respect of the previous, but adds "the development of connecting with the customer" (Develop Customer Relationship) as a new task management. It is based on a reconceptualization of marketing mix, especially some of its instruments. However, it is important to note that the changes that have taken place at the turn of the century in the field of marketing philosophy did not lead to changes of fundamental principles and settings.

THE OBJECTIVE NEEDS OF THE APPLICATION

As it is known, marketing appeared first in order to solve new problems in placements of a manufacturing enterprise. The phenomenon of marketing is to be understood as a reaction to the changing demands of enterprise environments and demand as most of its components. Expanding of the application of marketing to other areas is the logical flow from the increasing complexity of market and market relations with the other business areas. Today, the marketing concept and philosophy of business is just as important for industrial products and the service sector.

Tourism market is a special form of the market. Among the specifics of the service market and the appropriate application of marketing can be extracted:

1. The rapid growth of service markets,
2. The sensitivity of demand,
3. The exceptional competition,
4. Individuality of demand and consumption, and
5. Modern requirements for standardization.

These above mentioned specifics "dictate" the need and the specific application of marketing in tourism. In particular, we emphasize the need *for multiple layers of application of marketing* in tourism to the *destination* level. A modern tourist has in mind what is offered, but based on the destination as a global goal to meet specific travel needs.

That is why each bidder must bear in mind that his sale is under the "umbrella" of that destination with all its references which exist in the eyes of consumers.

Any changes that are rapidly taking place in the tourism market are a "challenge" for marketing managers. For the tourist market, apart from the extraordinary complexity of the phenomenon, its continuous expansion is one of the main characteristics. Specifics of the application of marketing in tourism, in principle, derived from "nature" of the tourist service itself.

It has three basic characteristics, namely:

- *The seasonal character of the demand.* Variations in demand are common in all sectors, but particularly pronounced in tourism. Demand is more pronounced in the season, which is different (summer, winter) depending on the type of travel needs. The role of marketing is to offer extended season and marketing tools to adapt to different intensity of demand. Seasonal demand is determined by the intensity of supply in all sectors of the tourism industry.
- *High fixed costs.* Tourist activity is characterized by high capital investment, because of the increasing of comfort that modern tourist demands. Equipment, airconditions, and other items cause high fixed costs which should be compensated from the income that tourists will spend. Therefore, the marketing managers should create that offer that will absorb enough income to cover these costs.
- *The interdependence of the tourism product.* Modern tourists are expected to be offered a combination of the tourism product or offer that will satisfy all his needs. In this conglomerate of products there are different types of services, as well as material goods, which constitute a whole offer.

Theory and Methodology of marketing is unique in its application of the fundamental determinants of tourism, and especially the following:

1. Consumer needs are fully the principle of economy,
2. The demand is unprecedented for the business success of the subjects in the tourism market,
3. The market logics is relevant to the enterprise in the field of tourism and tourist destination,
4. Profit is the motive of doing business (but not at any price) and
5. Increasingly prominent aspect of international business and upholding the principles of globalization.

In order to complete the implementation of the concept of tourism marketing in the above mentioned, a paragraph should be added that in this area its *integrity* is more represented than any other where the phenomenon of marketing is applied (1) and in addition to economic (narrow), the application of marketing in this sector expresses social values (2). In terms of treatment of tourism marketing, we should single out the wide application of achievements in other scientific fields. Therefore, marketing of tourism is associated with different (micro and macro) economic disciplines. We should primarily mention micro-economics (in the broadest sense), the organization, the science of consumer behaviour, and macroeconomic disciplines: monetary economics, economic development, international economics, various multipliers and other related fields.

Interdisciplinarity is especially required in the application of marketing in rural development. Globalization affects in the way that tourist enterprises increasingly characterise the concept of international business. So it is necessary to single out the increasing role of international marketing methods in tourism, or transfer its settings to a specific tourist area. This is understandable, since every company has a logic of the international tourism business.

Their business approach is logical from the domestic to global company. In all that, all the activities of modern enterprises in the tourism industry adapt to the market. At the same time there are major organizational changes in tourism businesses, through various forms of networking and cooperation, and the logic of international marketing is increasingly interpolated in tourism destinations and individual enterprises

NATURE OF RURAL MARKETS

Rural Markets are defined as those segments of overall market of any economy, which are distinct from the other types of markets like stock market, commodity markets or Labour economics. Rural Markets constitute an important segment of overall economy, for example, in the USA, out of about 3000 countries, around 2000 counties are rural, that is, non-urbanized, with population of 55 million. Typically, a rural market will represent a community in a rural area with a population of 2500 to 30000.

In recent years, rural markets have acquired significance in countries like China and India, as the overall growth of the economy has resulted into substantial increase in the purchasing power of the rural communities. On account of the green revolution in India, the rural areas are consuming a large quantity of industrial and urban manufactured products. In this context, a special marketing strategy, namely, rural marketing has taken shape. Sometimes, rural marketing is confused with agricultural marketing – the later denotes marketing of produce of the rural areas to the urban consumers or industrial consumers, whereas rural marketing involves delivering manufactured or processed inputs or services to rural producers or consumers. Also, when we consider the scenario of India and China huge market for the developed products as well as the labour support. This has led to the change in the mindset of the marketers to move to these parts of the world.

Also rural market is getting an importance because of the saturation of the urban market. As due to the competition in the urban market, the market is more or so saturated as most of the capacity of the purchasers have been targeted by the marketers.So the marketers are looking for extending their product categories to an unexplored market *i.e.* the rural market. This has also led to the CSR activities being done by the corporate to help the poor people attain some wealth to spend on their product categories. Here we can think of HLL initiatives in the rural India.

One of such project is the Project Shakti, which is not only helping their company attain some revenue but also helping the poor women of the village to attain some money which is surely going to increase their purchasing power. Also this will increase their brand loyalty as well as recognition in that area. Similarly we can think of the ITC E-Chaupal, which is helping the poor farmers get all the information about the weather as well as the market price of the food grains they are producing.In other view these activities are also helping the companies increase their brand value. So as it is given the significance of the rural market has increased due to the saturation of the urban market as well as in such conditions the company which will lead the way will be benefited as shown by the success of HUL and ITC initiatives.

SCOPE

The basic scope of this novel initiative will be the mutual benefits of the rural entrepreneurs and industries. The entrepreneurs – primary beneficiaries, SHGs – bridge with the community, participating companies/industries and rural consumers have befitted through a robust commercial relationship. These models of marketing linkages demonstrate a large corporation which can play a major role in reorganizing markets and increasing the efficiency of a rural product generation system.

While doing so it will benefit farmers and rural communities as well as shareholders. Moreover, the key role of information technology—provided and maintained by the industry/company for building linkages, and used by local farmers—brings about transparency, increased access to information, and rural transformation.

Besides, this strategy of market linkage, addresses the challenges faced by rural entrepreneurs due to institution voids, numerous intermediaries and infrastructure bottlenecks. Moreover, the prime scope of this model is the creation of opportunities for the rural entrepreneurs for product differentiation and innovation by offering them choices.

Because of this sustainable market linkages, rural producers can participate in the benefits of globalization and will also develop their capacity to maintain global quality standard. Nonetheless, it creates new stakeholders for the industry sector. And subsequently, they become part of the firms' core businesses. The involvement of the private/industry sector at the rural product and market development can also provide opportunities for the development of new services and values to the customers, which will find application in the developed markets. It will be worth mentioning that building a sustainable market linkage through industry's intervention will also empower the rural mass to cope with socio-economic problems in the rural society and will ensure economic self –reliance.

IMPORTANCE

In recent years, rural markets have gained prominence in countries such as China and India, the overall growth of the economy has resulted in a substantial increase in purchasing power of rural communities. Because of the green revolution in India, rural areas consume a large amount of industrial and urban. In this context, a specific strategy for marketing, ie marketing of agricultural products has taken shape. Sometimes rural markets coincides with the marketing of agricultural products, shows the first commercialization of rural areas for urban consumers or businesses, while the rural markets is to provide products or processed inputs or services, rural producers and consumers. Moreover, given the scenario of India and China huge market for products developed and supported employment. This has led to a change in the mentality of the operators to move to these parts of the world.

OPPORTUNITIES IN INDIAN RURAL MARKET

- More than 750 million people * Estimated annual size of the rural market

FMCG	₹ 70,000 Crore
Durables	₹ 5,500 Crore
Agricultural-Inputs	₹ 48,000 Crore
2/ 4 Wheelers	₹ 8,400 Crore

- In financial year 2001-02, LIC sold more than 50 per cent of its policies in rural market.
- 42 million rural households are availing banking services in comparison to 27 million urban HHs.
- Investment in formal savings instruments is 6.6 million HHs in rural and 6.7 million HHs in urban.
- In last 50 years, 45 per cent villages have been connected by road.
- More than 90 per cent villages are electrified, though only 44 per cent rural homes have electric connections.
- Government is providing subsidiaries to the villagers to use other source of energy like Solar System and is now being used in large amount.
- Number of "pucca" houses increasing day by day.
- Rural literacy level improved from 36 per cent to 59 per cent.
- Percentage of BPL families declined from 46 per cent to 25 per cent.
- Out of two million BSNL mobile connections, 50 per cent are in small towns/ villages.

- 41 million Kisan Credit Cards have been issued with cumulative credit of ₹ 977 billion resulting in tremendous liquidity.

CHALLENGES IN INDIAN RURAL MARKET

Rural markets, as part of any economy, have untouched potential. There are several difficulties confronting the effort to fully explore rural markets. The concept of rural markets in India is still in evolving shape, and the sector poses a variety of challenges. Distribution costs and non-availability of retail outlets are major problems faced by the marketers. The success of a brand in the Indian rural market is as unpredictable as rain. Many brands, which should have been successful, have failed miserably. This is because most firms try to extend marketing plans that they use in urban areas to the rural markets. The unique consumption patterns, tastes, and needs of the rural consumers should be analyzed at the product planning stage so that they match the needs of the rural people.

Therefore, marketers need to understand the social dynamics and attitude variations within each village though nationally it follows a consistent pattern.

The main problems in rural marketing are:

- Understanding the Rural Consumer
- Poor Infrastructure
- Physical Distribution
- Channel Management
- Promotion and Marketing Communication

Dynamics of rural markets differ from other market types, and similarly, rural marketing strategies are also significantly different from the marketing strategies aimed at an urban or industrial consumer. Strategies to be Followed in Indian Rural Market

MARKETING STRATEGY

Marketers need to understand the psychology of the rural consumers and then act consequently. Rural marketing involves more exhaustive personal selling efforts compared to urban marketing. Firms should abstain from designing goods for the urban markets and subsequently pushing them in the rural areas.

To effectively tap the rural market, a brand must associate it with the same things the rural folks do. This can be done by utilizing the various rural folk media to reach them in their own language and in large numbers so that the brand can be associated with the myriad rituals, celebrations, festivals, "melas", and other activities where they assemble.

DISTRIBUTION STRATEGY

One of the ways could be using company delivery van which can serve two purposes - it can take the products to the customers in every nook and corner of the market, and it also enables the firm to establish direct contact with them, and thereby facilitate sales promotion.

However, only the companies having excellent Infrastructure can adopt this channel. The companies with relatively fewer resources can go in for syndicated distribution where a tie-up between non-competitive marketers can be established to facilitate distribution. Annual "melas" organized are quite popular and provide a very good platform for distribution because people visit them to make several purchases.

According to the Indian Market Research Bureau, around 8000 such melas are held in rural India every year. Rural markets have the practice of fixing specific days in a week as Market Days called "Haats' when exchange of goods and services are carried out. This is another potential low cost distribution channel available to the marketers. Also, every region consisting of several villages is generally served by one satellite town termed as "Mandis" where people prefer to go to buy their durable commodities. If marketing managers use these feeder towns, they will easily be able to cover a large part of the rural population.

PROMOTIONAL STRATEGY

Marketers must be very careful while choosing the mediums to be used for communication. Only 16 per cent of the rural population has access to a vernacular newspaper. So, the audio visuals must be planned to convey a right message to the rural folk. The rich, traditional media forms like folk dances, puppet shows, etc., with which the rural consumers are familiar and comfortable, can be used for high impact product campaigns. Radio is also very popular source of information and Entertainment, Adds on radio can also be a helpful tool for marketers.

FACTORS INFLUENCING RURAL MARKETING

SOCIO-ECONOMIC POSITION

- Low purchasing power and per capita income
- Bounded by tradition, culture, religion and community
- 60 per cent of rural income is from Agriculture
- More than 50 per cent rural households have monthly income <₹ 25,000
- About 14 per cent have income >₹ 50,000
- In recent years, 70 per cent rural households have started saving/ investing their income
- Culturally a Diverse and Heterogeneous Market in terms of Religious, linguistic, social and cultural factors

- State to state variation in extent of development
- Average villages have 33 index points
- Literacy level: Rural India has a literacy rate of 28 per cent compared to 55 per cent of the whole country
- Lifestyle:
  - Conservative and tradition bound;
- There has been a change in the same over the years though with:
  - Increase in income;
  - Growth in education;
  - Greater media penetration;
  - Marketers efforts to reach and capture the rural market's
- Buying behaviour:
- literacy level;
- occupation;
- social and cultural factors;
- exposure to media;
- marketer's efforts
- The buying behaviour has undergone a major change. A huge population in rural areas has seen an increase in their income as a result of which they have the potential to buy expensive/luxury products

RURAL POPULATION

Table. Population of India

	Population In Crores	% to Total	Population In Crores	% to Total	Population In Crores	% to Total	Population In Crores	% to Total
Year	1971	1971	1981	1981	1991	1991	2001	2001
Rural	43.9	80	50.2	76.3	64.1	76	74	73
Urban	10.91	20	15.62	23.7	20.3	24	29	27
Total	54.8	100	65.82	100	84.4	100	103	100

OCCUPATION IN RURAL INDIA

Different kinds of occupation in Indian villages reflect the base of their socio-economic culture. Since the ancient period, the Indian villagers have been involved in various occupations out of which, agriculture is the principal one. Apart from agriculture, the villagers are also involved in other occupations like fishing, farming, cottage industry, pottery, business, various small, medium or large scale industries, carpentry, etc.

In the contemporary period, the evolution and advancement in different industrial and technological sectors in India have opened new job opportunities for the Indian villagers.

Agriculture, however, remains the principal occupation in Indian villages from the ancient period. The climatic conditions in most parts of India are suitable for agricultural activities and hence, India has become one of the leading producers of agricultural products in the world. In the changing time agriculture has been replaced by other occupations in different parts of India in the contemporary period. Other occupation in Indian villages includes the priests, carpenters, blacksmiths, barbers, weavers, potters, oil pressers, leatherworkers, sweepers, water bearers, toddy-tappers and many others.

However, most of the modern day Indian villages present a different scenario with villagers taking up the non-traditional occupations. They are involved in academics as teachers; truckers, clerks or getting engaged with various cottage industries, regardless of which caste or class they belong to. Different types of occupations are found in the modern Indian villages apart from agriculture or farming or the traditional occupations. The climate and location influence occupation in Indian villages to a large extent. In the villages of hilly areas, the principal occupations include agriculture and gardening. Several villagers in the South Indian states like Kerala, Andhra Pradesh, Tamil Nadu, Karnataka, etc. have taken fishing as the main source of income. This is mainly because of the coastal location of the states. However, agriculture is still the principal occupation in the northern and eastern Indian villages.

Another major occupation in Indian villages is the cottage industry. Cottage industry has emerged as a major source of employment in Indian villages over the period of time. Many villagers are involved in various kinds of art and crafts works. The villagers produce different types of handicrafts products and many of them are earning their livelihoods by marketing them. The occupations like artisan in pottery, wood, cloth, metal and leather have been in existence in Indian villages, since the ancient period and are found even in the modern times. Many Indian villagers are dependent on these occupations to earn their livelihoods.

The women in the rural areas, too are actively getting involved in different industries like matchbox and firework industries, Bidi making, agate and slate industries, coffee and tea industries, brick industry, construction industry, electronics industry, spice industries, etc. Among these, the Bidi, slate or brick making industries are the most well spread industries in Indian villages. Apart from these industries, the Indian villagers have also become sweepers and scavengers.

Tourism sector has emerged as one of the major occupations in Indian villages, in the contemporary period. Villages in most parts of India are endowed with natural beauty and have a rich tradition and cultural heritage. The rich cultural diversity in the villages attracts many tourists from all over the world every year. This has encouraged many villagers to get involved in various tourism related occupations. The villagers work as tourist guides or run different kinds of business in the famous tourist spots or even provide accommodation facilities to the tourists to earn their livelihoods.

The occupation scenario in Indian villages has changed mainly due to the changing economical scenario of the villages of India. The invention of new technologies has encouraged the Indian villagers to take up new occupations. Apart from that, decline in the fertility of lands in many villages has also forced many villagers to give up their traditional occupation of agriculture. Many of these villagers have moved to the nearby urban areas in search for alternative occupation.

Farming

Farming or agriculture has been the principal occupation for the people in Indian village since the ancient period. Farming in Indian villages is the mainstay for a majority of the total population, as they earn their livelihoods from agriculture. The people cultivate various types of crops throughout the year.

The climatic condition in India is perfectly suitable for agricultural activities and has been one of the major reasons behind people choosing farming as their principal occupation. In ancient India, farming in Indian villages was highly dependent on the monsoon condition and hence, most of the crops cultivated during that period were monsoon type crops. In the contemporary period, the dependency on weather has lessened with the advancement of irrigation technology and different types of crops are being cultivated in India.

People in Indian villages are involved with the agriculture sector in various ways. There are many people in Indian villages who cultivate crops independently in their own lands. They occasionally take help of others to do the farming. Another type of farmers in the Indian villages are those who do not have any land of their own. They help others to cultivate crops in their lands. In this way, these people are dependent on agriculture for earning their livelihoods. There are also many people in Indian villages who are involved in contract farming. In contract farming a person takes care of someone else‘s land and cultivates crops in the land. He gets a certain portion of the cultivated crops at the end of the season as his rewards. This is a very common practice in the Indian villages. In this way also, farming in Indian villages is providing occupation to many people.

Another form of farming in Indian villages that provides occupation to the villagers is organic farming. The organic farmers mostly rely on crop rotation, crop residues, animal organics and mechanical cultivation to maintain soil productivity and farmland. The main objective behind this is to supply plant nutrients and to control weeds, insects and other pests. More and more people in Indian villages are getting involved in organic farming, as this helps a lot to retain the productivity and fertility of the land for a long period.

Farming in Indian villages provides employment to more people than any other economic sector. The dependency of Indian villagers on agriculture and the suitable climatic condition has made India the largest producer of milk, cashew nuts, coconut, tea, ginger, turmeric and black pepper in the world. India is also the second highest producer of farm products in the world. As a whole, it can be said that farming in Indian villages is the backbone of the entire economical structure of India.

Teaching

Teaching has always been considered a noble profession in India. Many people in the cities and villages in India are engaged with this profession. They have taken the responsibility to build the backbone of India, as education is the most important aspect in every sphere of life. The rural population of India receives education from the governmental and non-governmental schools established in the villages. The educated people in the villages are usually involved with teaching in these schools. Teaching in Indian village schools is considered one of the most respectable occupations. The teachers usually hold a position of respect and honour in the villages of India.

In the ancient period, teaching in the Indian village schools was done by the Brahmins, who had the Vedic knowledge. They used to teach the children about the religious texts like Veda, Upanishads, Ayurveda, Sanskrit literature, etc. They used to teach the students by keeping them in their own houses. This was called the Gurukul System. With the inception of Muslim era in India during the medieval period, the teaching pattern in Indian villages changed a bit. The Madrashas came into existence during this period and the children started to get sessions about Islam religion and Arabic literature from the Moulanas. The British period saw the establishment of missionary schools in the Indian villages where the teachers gave sessions about Christianity and English literature.

In the contemporary period, there are numerous schools established in the Indian villages to provide education to the children. Both primary and secondary schools are established in the villages. While most of the schools are governmental, there are many that are run and managed by the private organisations. Many people are involved in teaching in Indian village schools. The teachers in the government schools are appointed by the governmental authorities, while the private school teachers are appointed by the schools' management committees. There are also a few schools in Indian villages that are run by only one person.

The children get sessions about many subjects including the science, arts and commerce subjects. The children are also given basic sessions about agricultural science and home science in the schools. Teaching is a good opportunity for the educated people of the village to further nurture their education and build a well-educated society for a better future.

India has a high rural literacy rate among all the countries in the world. The teachers in the village schools are to be given the credit for this impressive literacy rate. Teaching in Indian village schools is being given more and more importance by the governmental authorities in the recent years. The government is also sending the young educated people in the urban areas to the villages as volunteers to teach the underprivileged villagers. All these are being done to further improve the educational status of rural India.

Fishing

India is a land of water lands that include several rivers and seas. The rivers and seas flowing through and along with the border of India are home to a huge variety of fishes. Hence, fishing has been a major source of income for people living in the Indian villages for several centuries. Fishing in Indian villages is considered one of the major occupations for the villagers. People in the villages of the South Indian states like Kerala, Karnataka, Andhra Pradesh, etc. are mostly dependent on fishing to earn their livelihoods, as most of the villages are located along the coastal line.

Many people have taken to fishing in Indian villages as the primary occupation. They catch fish from the rivers or seas and then sell them in the local market. They earn their livelihoods in this way. Most of the fish caught in the Indian villages are sea fish. The major marine fish caught in Indian villages include mackerel, sardines, Bombay duck, shark, ray, perch, croaker, carangid, sole, ribbonfish, whitebait, tuna, silver belly, prawn, cuttlefish, etc. On the other hand, the major freshwater fishes caught in the Indian villages include carp and catfish; the main brackish-water fish are Hilsa and mullet. A majority of the fish is marketed abroad and it brings a huge amount of foreign exchange to India. Fish and their products account for a significant portion of the total export value in India.

Fishing can be of different kinds like deep-sea fishing, inland fishing, ocean fishing, etc. Though deep-sea fishing is not done in Indian villages on a large scale, inland fishing has developed mostly in the deltaic channels of Bengal. In the contemporary period, the Government of India is encouraging the Indian villagers to take up ocean fishing as their occupation. People get involved with fishing as both full timers and part timers. The occasional fishermen are mostly those, who are usually involved with agriculture.

Fishing in Indian villages has been providing employment to many people since the ancient period. It is still one of the major occupations for the people living along the coastal line. The number of people getting involved with fishing is increasing day by day, in the recent years.

Handicrafts

India is one of the richest countries in the world as far as arts and culture is concerned. The Indian people are often involved in making high quality handicraft products. Different types of handicrafts are made in India and have earned significant popularity in the international market. Handicraft in Indian villages is considered one of the major occupations, as many people earn their livelihoods by producing different types of handicrafts.

Handicrafts in Indian villages are of different kinds. The major types of handicrafts are pottery, metal craft, gold jewellery, wood craft, shell craft, cane craft, needle craft embroidery, ivory craft, comb craft, glass craft, paper craft, sholapitha craft, weaving, silver jewellery, etc. All these types of handicrafts are considered major sources of income for numerous people in the Indian villages. The artisans create these handicrafts either at homes or in a cooperative basis or on behalf of any big concern involved with the marketing of handicrafts products. The village fairs, melas and festivals are some of the best places for the Indian village artisans to sell their products.

Handicrafts in Indian villages are made for serving various purposes. While some of the handicrafts products are made for daily uses, there are a few that are made for decorative purposes. Villages in different parts of India are famous for producing different types of handicrafts. While the villages of West Bengal are famous for making the handicraft products like Terracotta, Sholapitha craft, etc., the villages of Gujarat are famous for the products like brass and iron items, clay items, wooden furniture, embroidery, silver jewellery, dhurries, carpets, blankets, rugs, etc. The villages in other parts of the country are also famous for making different types of handicrafts products.

Handicrafts in Indian villages are practised since the ancient period. Handicraft is also a major occupation for the villagers since the ancient period. The governmental authorities in India are encouraging people to take up handicrafts as their occupation in the recent years as the Indian handicrafts products bring a huge amount of foreign currency to the country.

Weaving

Weaving is an ancient art of making cloth and other fabrics and the Indians have been expert of weaving since the ancient period. Weaving is the process of making cloth, rugs, blankets and other products by crossing two sets of threads over and under each other. Weaving in Indian villages has been a hobby for several centuries now. Weaving has also become a major industry in the contemporary period. Weaving in Indian villages is done using threads spun from natural fibres like cotton, silk and wool and also using the synthetic fibres like nylon and Orlon.

The Indian hand woven fabrics have been famous all over the world since times immemorial. The ancient Indian cotton-fabric Muslin was considered one of the most unique creations of Indian weavers. India was also one of the major exporters of textiles to most parts of the civilised world in the ancient period. However, in contemporary India, weaving is not limited to cloth and textile products. It plays an important part in manufacture of screens, metal fences and rubber tire cord. Weaving in Indian villages is considered one of the largest cottage industries.

Several people are engaged in weaving cotton, silk and other natural fibres and not a single village can be found in India, where the weavers do not live. Various types of weaving are done in the villages of India. Some of the most popular types of weaving in Indian villages include cotton fabrics, patola weaving, ikat fabrics, phulkari, carpet weaving, embroidery, sanganeri prints, chindi dhurries, batik sarees, himroo, hand block printing, etc.

Different region of India is famous for different types of weaving. The villages of Tamil Nadu are famous for a special kind of weaving named Madras Checks. The ikat fabrics are the pride of the villages of Andhra Pradesh and Orissa and in the villages of Uttar Pradesh, the Brocades and jacquards are famous. The villages of West Bengal are famous for weaving the fabrics like Daccai, Jamdani, Taant, etc. and the villagers in Punjab are expert in weaving Phulkari. The other famous weaving styles found in the villages of India include Chanderi pattern in Madhya Pradesh, Baluchar, Surat tanchoi, Benarasi, etc. On the other hand, people in the villages of Jammu and Kashmir are involved in weaving the world famous Pashmina and Shahtoosh shawls. The villages of India are famous all over the world for producing the famous fabrics like mulberry silk, tasser, eri and muga as well.

Apart from weaving, people in the Indian villages are also involved in other occupations like dying, designing, etc. Weaving in Indian villages is one of those rare assets for which India can feel proud of.

LITERACY IN RURAL INDIA

Literacy in India is key for socio-economic progress, and the Indian literacy rate grew to 68 per cent in 2007 from 12 per cent at the end of British rule in 1947. According to the latest survey by the National Sample Survey Office in June 2008, the literacy rate among the population with age 7 and above was 72 per cent whereas the adult population had a literacy rate of 66 per cent. Although this was a greater than fivefold improvement, the level is well below the world average literacy rate of 84 per cent, and India currently has the largest illiterate population of any nation on earth.

Despite government programmes, India's literacy rate increased only "sluggishly," and a 1990 study estimated that it would take until 2060 for India to achieve universal literacy at then-current rate of progress. The 2001 census, however, indicated a 1991-2001 decadal literacy growth of 12.63 per cent, which is the fastest-ever on record.

There is a wide gender disparity in the literacy rate in India: adult literacy rates in 2009 were 76.9 per cent for men and 54.5 per cent for women. The low female literacy rate has had a dramatically negative impact on family planning and population stabilization efforts in India. Studies have indicated that female literacy is a strong predictor of the use of contraception among married Indian couples, even when women do not otherwise have economic independence. The 2001 census provided a positive indication that growth in female literacy rates was substantially faster than in male literacy rates in the 1991-2001 decadal period, which means the gender gap appears to be narrowing.

Functional Literacy in Rural India

Women in rural villages in India today tend to be treated as second class citizens. Their primary responsibilities are to look after the family and household and work in the rice fields. Little else is expected of them. It is against this background that Sinclair Community College in Dayton, Ohio, partnered with Stella Maris College in Chennai, India, to develop a functional literacy programme geared towards women in three rural villages outside Chennai, India, which ran from 1995 to 1999. Officials at Sinclair became aware of Stella Maris through a University Development Linkages Project managed by Sinclair in the early 1990s.

The purpose of this project was to create a Centre for Vocational Education in Chennai to deliver short-term technical training to early school leavers. Stella Maris College was on the advisory board for this project. At the time Stella Maris was active in the rural villages establishing self-help groups and conducting leadership and motivational workshops for women. Faculty and students would volunteer their time on weekends to accomplish these activities. The presence of Stella Maris in the villages enabled our two colleges to collaborate and take the village activities to a higher level. This project was funded by a College and University Affiliations grant from the United States Information Agency which has now become part of the United States State Department. Building upon the work done by Stella Maris College in the villages, a functional literacy programme was developed and targeted towards women in three rural villages. The project involved instructing local elementary school teachers to deliver the functional literacy training.

This functional literacy programme was timed to run during those periods when the women were not needed in the rice fields. Two crops are planted and harvested annually. If just a basic literacy programme were offered, participation tends to fade away in a relatively short period of time. The functional element was crucial as this was the key element in the programme. As the literacy programme progressed the women were also instructed in how to make products in their spare time to sell in the village market. The products were cleansing powder, tailoring and mat making. The village programme I observed taught the women how to make cleansing powder from ingredients available locally.

Women could make this product at home and sell it in their local market. The income they made helped improve the quality of life for their families and elevated their status socially and economically. A local bank was involved in the programme to provide the women with small loans to enable them to make the initial purchase of ingredients to make their product A by-product of the project was that the women began to learn some basic personal finance and business skills through their dealings with the bank. When this project was initially launched, the village men were very skeptical and they wondered what was happening to their women.

At the program's inauguration only the women were permitted in the small village meeting hall. The men watched through open doors and windows. It was a curious beginning to a programme that changed these women's lives. By the time this funded project ended, the word had spread and two more villages were asking to have this programme run for them. A video was made showing what life is like in these rural villages. Women who had participated in the functional literacy programme spoke of how their lives have been changed by this programme, and the literacy teachers spoke of the satisfaction they got by helping empower these village women. Even though the grant ended several years ago, Stella Maris College is still active today in providing functional literacy training in rural villages surrounding Chennai.

Illiteracy Problems in Rural Indian Areas

Illiteracy Problems in Rural Indian Areas "We are bumbling along with this outmodeled system of elementary education, which is a real shame." These are the words of Krishna Kumar, director of the Central Institute of Education in New Delhi, India. Unfortunately Kumars's views are shared with other educators concerning the state of India's deteriorating education system. Illiteracy rates in many third world countries are alarmingly high; nestled in the heart of Asia, India's education programme is falling behind other nations. It is a country where the population will reach one billion people by the next century, while only one-third of them will be able to read.

Due to various social and economic problems India's education programme continues to be undercut. Of the biggest victims of the educational system are those living in rural areas. The attitudes of the children and teachers also affect the quality of the schools. Allocation of government funds and the conditions of the destitute rural schools contribute to the low quality of education by rural children.

While there are many rural area school systems which are operating in poor conditions there is one in particular whose schools outperform most other rural schools and also those located in wealthy areas of India. Consequently, Kerala, a rural state of India remains a puzzle to many educators. Its illiteracy rate does not follow the trend of most rural schools.

Many children living in rural areas receive a level of education which is very poor. Overall enrollment in primary and middle schools are very low. Fifty per cent of children living in these areas leave school before the fifth grade These children leave school for variety of reasons: some leave because of lack of interest; most leave so that they can work in the fields, where the hours are long and the pay is low.

A large per cent of the dropouts are females. Forced by their parents, most girls perform chores and tend the family at home. These are some of the reasons why sixty per cent of all females in India are illiterate, a figure much higher than those of males. As these children grow into adults, many are still illiterate by the age of forty. These uneducated adults are also reluctant to send their own children to school because of their failure in the education system. This in turn creates a problem for the next generation.

While the children living in rural areas continue to be deprived of a quality education, part of the reason why is due to their teachers. A large number of teachers refuse to teach in rural areas and those that do are usually underqualified. In recent years the number of qualified teachers. has increased because of increased efforts by the government and private groups to improve the general education and professional training of teachers..

There is more of an emphasis on the training of rural teachers, whose educational backgrounds are generally not as sound as their urban counterparts. Those that refuse to teach in rural areas cite distance and lack of interest by students as problems. Many of the teachers also lack the enthusiasm to teach because of their meagre salary - less than one hundred dollars per month. Another obstacle faced by the schools is that obtaining more teachers for rural schools is difficult because of state guidelines that approve of high student-to-teacher ratios.

As the lack of teachers creates many obstacles for children in rural schools, another setback is the lack of resources which becomes detrimental to the learning process.

Lack of books and other reading materials seem to be a widespread problem.. The use of high-tech devices such as computers is very rare. Another condition of the schools are the inadequate facilities the classes are actually taught in. Some schools are located in warehouses while others in small houses. Many of the rural schools operate without electricity.

While many rural schools search for the proper resources, the distribution of government funds is major hindrance to the educational system. According to a recent study done by the World Bank, thirty per cent of the total educational funding goes towards higher educational institutions. This is an important issue because the number of students enrolled in these types of institutions represent such a small per cent of India's students. Other examples of the government's plans to undermine rural education can be found in the Constitution of India. In the Constitution it stated that the primary education of rural area children was a low priority in budget outlays.

Though rural children continue to be deprived of a formal education, the education system of Kerala, India is an exception. Located in the southern peninsula of the country, Kerala's illiteracy rates are lower than most other rural areas in India. Because of its immense population of twenty nine million and high unemployment rate, a large number of its inhabitants are forced to work outside of Kerala.

Many of the people of Kerala who work in a different country send lots of donations back to Kerala. These people believe that it is responsibility of them to donate back to their hometown. It is these donations which have funded many of the programmes that make Kerala stand out from other rural states. Coupled with the government and private donations the education system has been able to benefit.

More schools are being built and more teachers are willing to work there. The unusually low illiteracy rate is attributed to the planned education programmes. Although its economy is only growing slowly and unemployment rate is high, its illiteracy rates, mortality rates and life expectancy are comparable to richer regions of the country. Other rural areas can learn from Kerala so that its success can be duplicated. Receiving more private donations and government support is essential for those rural areas needing to improve the general lifestyle of its people.

High illiteracy rates in rural parts of India is an area of the Indian education system that cannot be overlooked. Hampered by the government and by other factors the quality of education in rural districts has been quite poor. High dropout rates and low enrollment by the children have contributed to the large illiteracy rate. Kerala, a rural state of India boasts many areas of progress and serves as a model for other rural areas and many of the wealthier parts of India. Without drastic changes by the government and by its citizens, India is well on its way to becoming the world's most illiterate nation.

DEVELOPMENT PROGRAMME

The rural economy, as much as urban economy, is an integrated part of the overall Indian economy. Any talk of overall development without rural development, particularly in a country where three-quarters of people below the poverty line reside in rural areas, is flawed. Poverty is indeed a global issue. Its eradication is considered integral to humanity's quest for sustainable development. Reduction of poverty in India, is, therefore, vital for the attainment of international goals.

Poverty alleviation has been one of the guiding principles of the planning process in India. This can be substantiated by the fact that anti-poverty programmes have been internalized in the five-year plan. This substance sheds light on the various "strategies and programmes" that form the instruments of the plan.

Integrated Rural Development Programme (IRBD)

First introduced in 1978-79, IRBD has provided assistance to rural poor in the form of subsidy and bank credit for productive employment opportunities through successive plan periods. Subsequently, Training of Rural Youth for Self Employment (TRYSEM), Development of Women and Children in Rural Areas (DWCRA), Supply of Improved Tool Kits to Rural Artisans (SITRA) and Ganga Kalyan Yojana (GKY) were introduced as sub-programmes of IRDP to take care of the specific needs of the rural population.

Wage Employment Programmes

Important components of the anti-poverty strategy, Wage Employment Programmes have sought to achieve multiple objectives. They not only provide employment opportunities during lean agricultural seasons but also in times of floods, droughts and other natural calamities. They create rural infrastructure which supports further economic activity. These programmes also put an upward pressure on market wage rates by attracting people to public works programmes, thereby reducing labour supply and pushing up demand for labour. It encompasses National Rural Employment Programme (NREP) and Rural Landless Employment Guarantee Programme (RLEGP) which were initially part of the Sixth and Seventh five year Plans.

Employment Assurance Scheme (EAS)

EAS was launched in October 1993 covering 1,778 drought-prone, desert, tribal and hill area blocks. It was later extended to all the blocks in 1997-98. The EAS was designed to provide employment in the form of manual work in the lean agricultural season. The works taken up under the programme were expected to lead to the creation of durable economic and social infrastructure and address the felt-needs of the people.

Food for Work Programme

The Food for Work programme was started in 2000-01 as a component of the EAS in eight notified drought-affected states of Chattisgarh, Gujarat, Himachal Pradesh, Madhya Pradesh, Orissa, Rajasthan, Maharastra and Uttaranchal. The programme aims at food provision through wage employment. Food grains are supplied to states free of cost. However, lifting of food grains for the scheme from Food Corporation of India (FCI) godowns has been slow.

Rural Housing

Initiated in 1985-86, the IAY is the core programme for providing free housing to families in rural areas, targets scheduled castes (SCs)/scheduled tribes (STs), households and freed bonded laborers. The rural housing programme has certainly enabled many BPL families to acquire pucca houses, the coverage of the beneficiaries is limited given the resource constraints. The Samagra Awas Yojana (SAY) was taken up in 25 blocks to ensure convergence of housing, provision of safe drinking water, sanitation and common drainage facilities. The Housing and Urban Development Corporation (HUDCO) has extended its activities to the rural areas, providing loans at a concessional rate of interest to economically weaker parts and low-income group households for construction of houses.

Social Security Programmes

Democratic decentralization and centrally supported Social Assistance Programmes were two major initiatives of the government in the 1990s. The National Social Assistance Programme (NSAP), launched in August 1995 marks a significant step towards fulfillment of the Directive Principles of State Policy. The NSAP has three components: a) National Old Age Pension Scheme (NOAPS); b) National Family Benefit Scheme (NFBS); c) National Maternity Benefit Scheme (NMBS). The NSAP is a centrally-sponsored programme that aims at ensuring a minimum national standard of social assistance over and above the assistance that states provide from their own resources. The NOAPS provides a monthly pension of ₹ 75 to destitute BPL persons above the age of 65. The NFBS is a scheme for BPL families who are given ₹ 10,000 in the event of the death of the breadwinner. The NMBS provides ₹ 500 to support nutritional intake for pregnant women. In addition to NSAP, the Annapurna scheme was launched from I April 2000 to provide food security to senior citizens who were eligible for pension under NOAPS but could not receive it due to budget constraints.

Land Reforms

In an agro-based economy of, the structure of land ownership is central to the wellbeing of the people. The government has strived to change the ownership pattern of cultivable land, the abolition of intermediaries, the abolition of zamindari, ceiling laws, security of tenure to tenants, consolidation of land holdings and banning of tenancy are a few measures undertaken. Furthermore, a land record management system is a pre-condition for an effective land reform programme. In 1987-88, a centrally-sponsored scheme for Strengthening of Revenue Administration and Updating of Land Records (SRA & ULR) was introduced in Orissa and Bihar.

Cease

Although these measures have been successful (to some extent) in curbing poverty, this model has a very basic flaw. Under this model resources are transferred from urban economy to rural economy just for short term political motives. This is affecting both areas, not letting rural economy develop on its own and hampering growth and investments in urban economy. An ideal approach should include the government, panchayats and key village personals, NGOs and private companies. This will not only help reduce this imbalance but will have a multiplier effect on the overall economy. By aligning the goals of the two parts we can convert this seemingly zero sum game into a win-win situation. It would be a very long drawn and difficult battle with conventions but the reward is worth the effort.

INFRASTRUCTURE

India's economic growth and development is predicated to a large extent upon the development of its 700-million strong rural population. Majority of the population lives in about 600,000 small villages and are engaged primarily in agriculture, directly or indirectly. A substantial portion of India's current agricultural labour force has to move to non-agriculture sectors for incomes in all sectors to go up. The challenge is to manage the transition of 80 per cent of the rural population from a village-centric agricultural-based economy to a industry based economy.

Grey areas of India Rural Infrastructure

- A set of basic facts define the constraints within which the economic growth and development of India's rural population must be addressed. Fundamentally, they relate to resource constraints, the nature of infrastructure, and the future trajectory of the geographical distribution of the population.
- These services includes, at a minimum market access, educational, health, financial, entertainment, transportation, and communications. Further, services depend on the availability of infrastructure.
- Infrastructure investment is irregular and inadequate to support 600,000 villages and the average cost of providing infrastructure is inversely related to the scale of the operation.
- Limitations on the financial and other resources available for providing infrastructure made it impossible to provide infrastructure at every village in India. Even if they were provided at every village, it will not be commercially sustainable.
- The basic geographical structure of population distribution will change once India shifts from being agriculture based country to industry based nation.

The Government has launched " Bharat Nirman" for the development of rural infrastructure.

Plans proposed for the development of India Rural Infrastructure are:

- Irrigation,
- Roads,

- Housing,
- Water Supply,
- Electrification,
- Telecommunication Connectivity.

The task ahead for the development of India Rural Infrastructure are:

- To connect 66,800 habitations with population over 1000 with all weather roads.
- To construct 1,46,000Km of new rural roads.
- To upgrade and modernize 1,94,000Km of existing rural roads.
- Total investment of ₹ 1,74,000 crore envisaged under "Bharat Nirman", investment on rural roads estimated to be at ₹ 48,000 crore.
- To provide corpus of ₹ 8000 crore to Rural Infrastructure Development Fund (RIDF).

COMMUNICATION MEDIA

"Development is neither a simple, nor straightforward linear process. It is a multi-dimensional exercise that seeks to transform society by addressing the entire complex of interwoven strands, living impulses, which are part of an organic whole".

Even now, rural development defies any clear definition as it has gone through a number of changes over a period of time. Hence, there is no comprehensive universally accepted definition of rural development. Earlier, we have taken rural development as commonly understood and expressed by political leaders, academics and a whole lot of UN bodies as an enabling force for improvement of the quality of life of rural people. Development, as a process meant to empower the poor, reduce exploitation, and oppression by those having economic, social, and political power.

It also means an equitable sharing of resources, improved health care and education for all. One of the major components and driving force of rural development is communication. Conventionally, communication includes electronic media, human communication and now information technology (IT). All forms of communications have dominated the development scene in which its persuasive role has been most dominant within the democratic political framework of the country.

Persuasive communication for rural development has been given highest priority for bringing about desirable social and behavioural change among the most vulnerable rural poor and women. Initially, the approach lacked gender sensitivity and empathy of the communicators and development agents who came from urban elite homes. Added to these constraints is political will that still influences the pace and progress of rural development. Technological changes further compounded the direction of rural development as information and communication technology (ICT) has been thought by communication and development workers as a panacea for other ills that obstructs the development process.

It has lead to indiscriminate applications and use of ICT in every aspect of information dissemination, manage-ment and governance of development. While there are few shining examples of achievements of ICT in development, there are a large number of failures and unauthenti-cated claims.

A view has also been advanced that "totalitarianism is latent in [information and communication] technology". Also communication technology is always expressions of socio-economic, geographical and political interests, partialities, alignments and commitments. In brief the will to technical knowledge is the will to technical power". To a large extent, my own view is that communication technology in more than one way reflects socio-cultural and political values of the society in which they were invented and nurtured. Earlier, I had postulated that the advent of satellite commu-nication in the country would lead to curbing of democracy. I am still inclined to postulate that the relationship between democracy and communication technology is quite tenuous and transient. In order to understand and appreciate the implications of communication technology for rural development, it would be essential to describe the current communi-cation scenario of the country.

Current Communication Scenario

The closing decade of twentieth century was the opening of historic information and communication technology interventions for development. This period has witnessed enormous and unprece-dented changes in every aspect of communications technologies, policies, infrastructure development and services. Political leaders of India have begun abandoning archaic government control over communication that has lately moved from government to national and international private players. Finally, airwaves and electronic signals have achieved their freedom from centuries old colonial bondage to reach out and connect people through a privately owned and operated communication network and infrastructure.

Both international and national private players have taken a dominant role in redefining, reshaping and providing tele-communication, broadcasting and information services for national development. It has initiated an era of partnership of public and private entrepreneurial skills and abilities to bring about unlimited connectivity. It has already started reshaping the life of a number of elites in India. But what about the rest? Little is known, though there is a trickle down communication effect in many areas of development including rural development. The role of communication technology for development must be viewed in this new and changed environment. How these ICT global and regional changes have influenced the access and use of ICT for development remains an issue of discussion and analysis.

Socio-Cultural Perspective

We are one of the world's oldest and ancient civilizations that evolved, matured and decayed over several millennia. After indepen-dence we have been experimenting and carving a path of revitalization for development through demo-cracy. The existing sharp divide between the small but economically, politically and socially "rich elite ruling class" and a very big but "economically poor and socially deprived" continue to persist as a legacy of the past. While the rich elite has had access to knowledge, both oral and written, the economically poor remained confined only to oral knowledge. The imposition of British educational system for over two centuries help add another layer of social barrier though on surface it gives an impression of equitable access to education.

Privatisation of education has further helped the rich elite to dominate the contemporary social and political scene at the cost of the poor who remain oblivious of communication technology for any improvement in their existing miserable life. Communication has been seen by a large number of development planners as a panacea for solving major social ills and problems. Apart from development, the introduction of communication in the educational process for open and distance learning is seen as step towards improving the quality of education and bridging the social and educational gap.

However, experience indicates that those rich who could afford to have access to private resources have hogged the advantage whether development or education. In this respect, it seems that communication technology has, in no way has helped the poor for improving their socio-economic condition. I shall try to support my observation by examining selected rural development projects. For discussion, communication tech-nology projects for rural development are divided into two categories. In the first category are those development projects which were implemented before 1992 economic liberalization. At that time the primary responsibility of rural development remained with the government.

These rural development projects broadly followed an "extension model" in which broadcast media were used to reach the large rural population or target groups. In the post economic liberalisation period, rural development projects added information and communication technology (ICT) to provide individual need-based information in broad development areas through Internet. In the post economic liberalization phase without abandoning the extension model "social marketing approach" to rural development has been adopted.

Government Initiatives

After independence, the government took upon itself the major responsibility of development. Hence, the central and state governments carried out development projects. Four such projects are briefly described. Radio for

Rural Development: Popularly known as "Radio Farm Forum" was one of the earliest efforts in the use of radio for rural development. The experiment was carried out from February to April 1956 in five districts of Maharashtra State by All India Radio (AIR). Rural listener groups were organized, who would listen to radio broadcasts twice a week at 6.30 p.m. for half an hour.

"The group then stayed together for discussion of what they had heard, the discussion lasted usually, about half an hour, seldom less, frequently more". The summative impact evaluation indicated positive outcome of radio rural forum. Impressive knowledge gains as a result of radio listening were reported across illiterates and literates, agriculturists and non-agriculturists, village leaders and others.

However, over a period of time the project withered away and could not be operationalised for large-scale implementation in one form or the other. Lack of political will and indifference of bureaucracy killed the rural development project even before it could help poor to take advantage of radio broadcast. Satellite Instructional Television Experiment (SITE) is considered to be one of the biggest techno-social communication experiments in education and rural development. The one-year experiment aimed to provide direct broadcasting of instructional and educational television in 2400 villages in the states of Andhra Pradesh, Bihar, Karnataka, Madhya Pradesh, Orissa and Rajasthan. Over 500 conventional television sets spread over 335 villages in Kheda district, Gujarat was also part of SITE.

Satellite technologists had called SITE as leapfrogging from bullock cart stage to satellite communication, which did not discriminate between rural poor and urban rich for information and communication. It had given 50 years communication lead to rural poor of the country.

SITE provided telecast for rural primary school children in the age group 5 - 12 years studying in grades 1-5. and teachers' training. Rural adults viewed television programmes on improved agricultural practices, health and family planning. They were also able to view news. Television was considered as window to the world.

The telecast reliability was above 99 per cent during the experiment period. More than 90 per cent direct reception television sets were in working order. Both quantitative and qualitative in-depth evaluation indicated modest gains in some areas, whereas no gain or negative gain in other areas. The one-year duration was thought to be too little for any positive results. Based on the experiences and positive gains, INSAT satellite was launched in 1981. Since than a series of INSAT satellites have been launched and used for nationwide television telecast for education and development. The sad part is that, in spite of best efforts, satellite television has been used for entertainment more than rural development. I am sad that my prediction came true that satellite television will be used for entertainment and not rural development.

Post Media Liberalisation Approach to Rural Development

The post media liberalisation phase, communication has been further re-emphasized and recognised as "missing link" in achieving development objectives. As early as 1995, Karnik, Nazareth and Dasgupta made an excellent proposal for creation of agricultural information and communication system for rural and agricultural sector. The report provides tentative outline of activities that should be carried out to create the information system and a rationale for setting up of such an information system that would meet the perceived needs and emerging needs of farmers to increase agricultural productivity in a sustainable manner.

The authors suggested the overall approach to be "demand driven". Almost all health care projects for rural poor, especially women and children have used demand driven social marketing approach for rural the development. United States of America, World Bank and other donor agencies have been advocating for such an approach for rural development.

At the same time, communication convergence, especially of media and Internet, opened up the possibility of individualised non-broadcast communication. Launch of "Kisan Call Centres" and an exclusive "Farmer Television Channel" are examples of social marketing approach for rural development. Let me give few example of social marketing approach of communication for rural development.

Community Radio Initiative: In post media liberalisation phase, Government of India, announced the policy for community radio broadcasting. "Community radio is expected to focus on issues relating to education, health, environment, agriculture, rural and community development".. Country's first community radio station became operational on February 1, 2004 at Anna University, Chennai. Sreedhar responsible for setting up of the radio station indicated that Anna University will serve the educational needs. How this community radio will serve the rural folks is yet to be ascertained.

However, given the low power of the radio station in heart of Chennai, it is clear that the major benefits will go to students rather than farmers, women and poor. Another "cable" community radio station, named as Namma Dhwani or Our Voices' was set up earlier in Boodikote, Karnataka. The villagers believe that "This radio station is ours because it speaks about us - in our language and in our accent". Community radio in Boodikote, according to Seema Nair, helps the villagers run the radio station "it is a new source of strength for poor people because it addresses their most basic development needs".

'Kunjal Panje Kutchji' is an interactive and participative development communication project. It is also the first time that a voluntary organisation, the Bhuj-based Kutch Mahila Vikas Sansthan (KMVS), has bought airtime on the radio as part of its communication strategy. The serial is broadcast on commercial time with the United Nations Development Programme (UNDP) support. The initiative is using existing commercial radio stations for community broadcasting. A feedback exercise was planned for continuous improvement and to ensure listener-ship not only decide what issues are taken up but also shape the script of the dramatized serial. 'Kunjal Panje Kutchji' has also focused on capacity building for elected women in panchayats on development issues.

No feedback is available to assess the effectiveness of the project. Community Television: Since the inception of INSAT satellite television system, Doordarshan achieved a kind of world record in setting up over 1000 low powered television transmission stations in the country. Each station in theory was supposed to telecast local television programme for rural development. A large number of television professional were trained for this purpose.

Doordarshan has been planning to introduce local television for rural poor and farmers to achieve the goals of rural development. Earlier similar attempts have been made to set up local television stations for rural development like in Nagpur.

Very little is known about the operations, achievements of local stations also their utility and effectiveness. Today, local stations have been largelly subsumed in the maize of urban national television. The advertisers have used the television time for selling consumer products that are not of any use to rural poor. Hopefully, small town neighbourhood restaurants, shopkeepers and television dealers will have a new venue for cheap advertisements.

Tamil Nadu Veterinary and Animal Sciences University (TANUVAS) Project

Currently TANUVAS tries to maintain contact with farmers and rural entrepreneurs through 14 University Training and Research Centres (UTRC), three Farmer Training Centres, and two Krishi Vigyan Kendras (KVK-Farm Science Centres) -all scattered in rural towns throughout Tamil Nadu. These outreach services are staffed with animal and agricultural specialists, most of whom hold post graduate degrees and professional level rank in TANUVAS. The primary means of contact with farmers at the centres is through face-to-face contact, either individually or during the training programmes and workshops.

This project has been experimenting as to how Internet can be used and combined with other technologies to benefit farmers and rural communities. Personal discussions with the project leader indicated that there are positive gains.

At present and no evaluation is available to base future decisions for expansion of the project. One inference that can be drawn from all these initiatives and experiments is that communication technology is not culture-neutral. It is no accident that not a single communication projects for rural development discussed here can be an unqualified success.

This calls for a serious reexamination and reflection of what we have learnt from the past and before getting fully committed to social marketing. The analysis presented so far indicates that "pro-poor" development issues have been pushed aside in favour of urban upcoming rich after media privatisation-leading to proliferation of private and public broadcasting and ICT in favour of consumerism and entertainment. The current communication policy of the country, which on the face of it is proactive for rural development, but remains urban "pro-rich" in effect. Besides, forces of market economy, focused towards profits, have begun to shape broadcasting and information technology programming philosophy, content and programme schedule.

CREDIT AVAILABILITY

The National Bank for Agriculture and Rural Development (NABARD) is a unique development financial institution, set up by an Act of Parliament in 1981 for bringing about integrated rural development. Owned jointly by the Reserve Bank of India and the Central Government, it is entrusted with agricultural credit responsibilities, and developmental activities besides supervisory role over rural financial institutions (RFIs). It seeks to promote sustainable agriculture and equitable rural prosperity through effective credit support, related services, institution development and microfinance innovations. It raises funds from the urban financial markets for deployment in rural India. Over the years, NABARD has established 16 Funds for enabling agricultural and non-agricultural development initiatives and innovations. In tune with national priorities and its own endeavours, NABARD has innovated, piloted and up-scaled credit products and services for rural development, aimed at building the capacities of RFI's/SHG clientele, building rural value chains, strengthening extension services, etc. for widening and deepening of rural credit absorption capacity in rural areas.

The major business loans are given for seasonal agricultural operations, for rural capital investments and for building rural infrastructure. Its major development initiatives are taken up through the Rural Innovation Fund and the Rural Infrastructure Development Fund, the SHG-Bank Linkage Programme, the Watershed Development Fund and the Tribal Development Fund besides the Financial Inclusion and Financial Inclusion Technology Funds and the Microfinance Development and Equity Funds.

The major challenges for rural India are as under:

i. Food Security especially in rural and tribal areas
ii. Financial Inclusion by 2015
iii. Poverty alleviation by ensuring Rural Livelihoods
iv. Credit Flow for the Rural Services Sector
v. Strengthening of Cooperatives and Regional Rural Banks
vi. Microfinance Institutions and addressing areas of concern

Food Security Issues

A major challenge facing NABARD is tackling the problem of hunger and malnutrition affecting one-third of the population. There is also the need to narrow the gap between producer costs and consumer prices so that farmers margins are enhanced through effective marketing support. To tackle global climate change, it is critical to have an institutional mechanism to help farming communities adapt to changing climatic conditions.

The food riots in some countries in early 2008 are not forgotten and with oil prices edging to US$100 per barrel, repeats of such food riots are not ruled out. The rising prices of inputs especially seeds, pesticides and fertilizers, diesel costs for pumpsets, spurious inputs, water shortages, controls on food prices, lack of rural infrastructure especially cold storages, godowns, etc. have culminated into lower agriculture production and productivity.

To arrest food prices, we need better management of water resources, better quality of seeds, scientific farming practices, rational use of fertilizers, integrated pest management and agricultural diversification. Capital assets creation in agriculture is essential for boosting productivity, such as cost-effective micro irrigation systems. The need to reduce cost of farm credit to 4 per cent (as per National Commission of Farmers, 2004) is another imperative while about 60 per cent of farmers have little or no access to institutional credit, are problems which brook no delay in finding appropriate solutions. The low seed germination rates and the seed replacement rates are also problems eluding solution.

In tribal areas, the need for community grain banks is felt and needs to be addressed. The needs of dryland farming are acute in view of 60 per cent of farms depending on monsoon rains. Tribal farmers who are mostly dependent on slash and burn farming techniques need to be weaned away from ecologically destructive farming practices.

Availability of agricultural credit in the right amount and in time, is being tested with the formation of Joint Liability Groups and the spread of appropriate or modern technology through Farmers Clubs and KVKs, is also being popularized.

The challenge of ensuring good crops for every drop of water, low cost credit, better margins for farmers rather than for traders and better rural infrastructure needs to be met urgently as ours is essentially an agrarian economy. The creation of Farmers Associations for aggregating, sorting, grading, packing and transporting produce, negotiating with traders, taking positions in commodity exchanges, are essential as also weather insurance/ crop insurance products that seek to mitigate some of the farmers' risks. The awesome challenge is to ensure that 85 per cent of the farmers who are small/ marginal farmers having un-irrigated land holdings less than 2 hectares, are able to eke out a living for their families.

Financial Inclusion

This is not brought about by opening a number of 'no-frills' accounts but must include safe bank deposits, affordable credit, safe funds transfers, micro insurance/ micro-pensioners and financial literacy/counseling. The formation of self-help Groups (SHGs) and SHG Federations as also microloans by microfinance institutions is also part of financial inclusion. There is a need to implement the Banking Correspondent/Facilitators Model by banks in unbanked areas so as to lower transaction costs for banks and clients as also set up a large number of micro ATMs so that cashless transactions within a common technology platform, is possible in rural areas. The Unique Identification numbers, proposed to be given to all citizens, will also enable quicker financial inclusion. The creation of a Rural Credit Bureau would help in quicker credit decisions than hitherto.

Poverty Alleviation

This is not possible without financial inclusion as a means of empowerment and pre-supposes some exposure to financial literacy and banking systems. Without a strong support system, poverty alleviation will remain a dream unless financial margins of farmers and rural artisans are improved. The quality of rural infrastructure especially for rural connectivity (roads, bridges, telecom, etc.) needs major improvement and upgrading. Also cluster development for farm and off farm activities would help in creating employment opportunities for rural growth.

The key to poverty alleviation is ensuring livelihoods in and around villages in rural areas. The need for infrastructure and amenities is a must if poverty alleviation is to happen. Today 48 per cent of our people are living below the poverty line and there is a need to address issues such as endemic starvation, hunger, child mortality and women's health issues. These social issues can be resolved only after urgent poverty alleviation. The need for rural employment (on-farm and non-farm sectors) is acute as is the need for environmental sustainability.

The Rural Services Sector

Credit for the rural transportation sector and for rural retail sector are available but for the other segments of the rural services sector such as cheap rural housing, drinking water, sanitation systems, rural eco-tourism and renewable rural energy, the credit flow is virtually non-existent. Unless lending to these sectors is stepped up, the quality of rural life will not improve and the unending migration of rural youngsters to urban areas in search of livelihoods and jobs, will continue. It is said that by 2050 half the population will be in cities! The question that begs an answer is "Will the 50 per cent people remaining in rural areas, be able to produce enough food to feed 100 per cent of the population"? Possibly biotechnology will provide an answer with improved production and productivity. NABARD has a critical role to play in reinvigorating the rural economy.

Strengthening Rural Financial Institutions

Cooperatives are the most farmer-friendly institutions in rural areas and most of them are non-viable or are non-functional. The Central and State Governments have pumped in millions of rupees so as to re-capitalize the Regional Rural Banks and the rural cooperative credit institutions, in view of the important roles played by them in rural capital formation and rural credit disbursal. These banks need to develop systems and processes to enable the smooth flow of rural credit and its timely recovery. The RRBs and Cooperatives also need to invest in BC/ BF agents and Computer/mobile technologies to enable a wider footprint area for their services without increasing operational costs sharply.

Microfinance Issues

The entry of foreign direct investment into microfinance institutions (MFIs) signals a trend of profiteering on poverty. The entry of investors who see easy pickings in MFIs and without any social commitment, are bound to create problems. In the SHG bank linkage programme, high interest rates as per group decisions reflect the risks and profits remain within the SHG. In MFIs the social bonding is lacking as is social collateral! Groups are formed for reducing transaction times and costs only and social motives in forming groups are absent.

Also, profits of MFIs are siphoned off for the investors. Prof. Mohd. Yunus, the Grameen Bank founder, terms these MFIs as institutional money lenders! There are other problems such as charging of high interest rates, non-transparency in imposing additional charges for institutional lenders, proliferation of MFIs in over-banked areas (whereas they would be welcome in grossly unbanked areas).

Relentless pumping of credit leading to over-lending and multiple membership of SHGs by rural women who often fail to juggle their loans from one SHG to another has led to religious 'fatwas' and non-cooperation in villages for loan repayments. There is also no exit policy of NGO's or MFIs and this results in stagnation if there is no move towards relevant upgraded products such as micro-insurance, health insurance, micro pensions, micro enterprises, etc. Also, there is no regulatory body to oversee the operations of these MFIs and self-regulation does not seem to have any telling impact. All this adds to problems brewing in the microfinance sector. Further, banks seem to have opted for lending funds to MFI's in bulk as these qualify for priority sector lending norms and are not perturbed by the problems being created by MFI's which are piling up, leading to an explosive situation later.

Perspectives

Institutional mechanisms for smooth flow of agricultural credit are needed along with new processes and IT systems, to enhance outreach and credit availability for farmers on favourable terms. Self-sustaining villages, rain-water harvesting structures to trap water, organic farming practices, SRI practices are all necessary.

However, for microcredit, the SHGs seem to be better placed than institutional lenders especially when social collateral norms are concerned. The need for constant upgrading of financial products and technologies adds to the costs of rural credit. The use of BC/BF models for expanding footprint area of banks without creating 'brick and mortar' branches is also a step in the right direction. The risk mitigation of agricultural operations for the farmer is a major challenge as also the challenge to provide adequate infrastructure for rural people.

The challenges of food security, environmental sustainability financial inclusion and poverty alleviation need to be addressed with urgency and sensitivity, so that tribal people and neglected parts of society are brought into the ambit of development. An inclusional model of rural development based on our credit plus approach has emerged to provide a base for equitable growth and prosperity in the rural areas. If this is not addressed, social strife and unrest under the guise of various revolutionary movements are inevitable, in the underdeveloped and tribal areas of the country.

RURAL MARKET SIZE

The Indian growth story is now spreading itself to India's hinterlands. The rural consumer market, which grew 25 per cent in 2008, is expected to reach US$ 425 billion in 2010-11 with 720-790 million customers, according to a white paper prepared by CII-Technopak, in November 2009. The figures are expected to double the 2004-05 market size of US$ 220 billion.

The Union Budget for 2010-11 has hiked the allocation under the National Rural Employment Guarantee Act (NREGA) to US$ 8.71 billoin in 2010-11, giving a boost to the rural economy.

FMCG

According to figures released by market researcher Nielsen, demand for personal care products grew faster in rural areas than urban areas during the period January-May 2010.

In shampoos, rural demand grew by 10.7 per cent in value terms, while in urban markets, it rose by 6.8 per cent. Similarly, toothpaste sales grew by 9.1 per cent in rural India and by 4.4 per cent in urban markets.

Several fast moving consumer goods (FMCG) companies such as Godrej Consumer Products, Dabur, Marico and Hindustan Unilever (HUL) have increased their hiring in rural India and small towns in order to establish a local connect and increase visibility.

Swiss FMCG giant, Nestle plans to make further inroads into the rural markets. The company has asked its sales team to deliver "6,000 new sales points every month in rural areas" to expand its presence in Indian villages, according to Antonio Helio Waszyk, Chairman and Managing Director, Nestle India.

RETAIL

The rural retail market is currently estimated at US$ 112 billion, or around 40 per cent of the US$ 280 billion Indian retail market, according to a study paper, 'The Rise of Rural India', by an industry body.

Hindustan Unilever (HUL) is planning to significantly increase its rural reach. According to Harish Manwani, Chairman, HUL, the quality and quantity of rural coverage will go up to the extent that "what we have done in the last 25 years we want to do it in the next two years." Currently HUL products reach approximately 250,000 rural retail outlets and the company intends to scale it up to nearly 750,000 outlets in two years time.

Direct selling firm Tupperware India, known for its storage containers plans to foray into the rural markets in the next two-three years. "We have solid plans for the rural market. We are working on bringing products for rural people as well," said Asha Gupta, Managing Director, Tupperware India.

Castrol India is pushing its rural sales by building up a distribution infrastructure to reach out to all villages. According to Ravi Kirpalani, Chief Operating Officer, Castrol India, "Our distribution now reaches 5,000-7,000 towns and villages, but we are planning to take our products to six lakh villages with a population of less of 5,000."

AUTOMOBILES

Car sales in rural India have been on the increase in the last three years since the government announced various schemes such as farm loan waiver etc, for the rural population.

Maruti Suzuki's share of rural sales has increased from 3.5 per cent to 17 per cent in the last three years. Mahindra and Mahindra (M&M) is now selling more Scorpios in rural and semi-urban markets. Scorpio sales have increased from 35 per cent to 50 per cent in the last two years.

Toyota Kirloskar Motor (TKM), in which Japan's Toyota Motor Corp holds an 89 per cent controlling stake, is planning at selling 40 per cent of its cars in rural markets in India. According to Hiroshi Nakagawa, Managing Director, TKM, "We are aggressively expanding our dealership footprint in India and quite a significant portion of this will be in country's heartland. By end of 2010, we plan to have 150 dealers across the country."

Yamaha is also planning a major initiative in rural India by launching more models in the affordable price range in 2010. "We are very strong in Tier 1 and Tier II cities. Now onwards, our focus will be rural India. As suggested, launch more models in the affordable price range to dominate the rural market," according to Pankaj Dubey, National Business Head, India Yamaha Motor. At present, around 15 per cent of its sales come from the rural market and Dubey sees this demand increasing substantially in 2010.

Tata Motors is also making efforts to sell its pick up truck Ace in rural markets. It has already opened 600 small outlets for the Ace in rural and semi-urban markets. It has also tied up with 117 public sector, gramin (rural) and co-operative banks to help small entrepreneurs buy the vehicle.

STRUCTURE OF INDIAN RURAL MARKET

The Indian rural market with its vast size and demand base offers great opportunities to marketers. Two-thirds of countries consumers live in rural areas and almost half of the national income is generated here. It is only natural that rural markets form an important part of the total market of India. Our nation is classified in around 450 districts, and approximately 630000 villages which can be sorted in different parameters such as literacy levels, accessibility, income levels, penetration, distances from nearest towns, etc.

The success of a brand in the Indian rural market is as unpredictable as rain. It has always been difficult to gauge the rural market. Many brands, which should have been successful, have failed miserably. More often than not, people attribute rural market success to luck. Therefore, marketers need to understand the social dynamics and attitude variations within each village though nationally it follows a consistent pattern.While the rural market certainly offers a big attraction to marketers, it would be naive to think that any company can easily enter the market and walk away with sizable share. Actually the market bristles with variety of problems.

The main problems in rural marketing are:

- Physical Distribution
- Channel Management
- Promotion and Marketing Communication

The problems of physical distribution and channel management adversely affect the service as well as the cost aspect. The existent market structure consists of primary rural market and retail sales outlet. The structure involves stock points in feeder towns to service these retail outlets at the village levels. But it becomes difficult maintaining the required service level in the delivery of the product at retail level.

One of the ways could be using company delivery vans which can serve two purposes- it can take the products to the customers in every nook and corner of the market and it also enables the firm to establish direct contact with them and thereby facilitate sales promotion. However, only the bigwigs can adopt this channel. The companies with relatively fewer resources can go in for syndicated distribution where a tie-up between non-competitive marketers can be established to facilitate distribution.

As a general rule, rural marketing involves more intensive personal selling efforts compared to urban marketing. Marketers need to understand the psyche of the rural consumers and then act accordingly. To effectively tap the rural market a brand must associate it with the same things the rural folks do. This can be done by utilizing the various rural folk media to reach them in their own language and in large numbers so that the brand can be associated with the myriad rituals, celebrations, festivals, melas and other activities where they assemble.

One very fine example can be quoted of Escorts where they focused on deeper penetration.In September-98 they established rural marketing sales. They did not rely on T.V or press advertisements rather concentrated on focused approach depending on geographical and market parameters like fares, melas etc. Looking at the 'kuchha' roads of village they positioned their mobike as tough vehicle. Their advertisements showed Dharmendra riding Escort with the punchline 'Jandar Sawari, Shandar Sawari'. Thus, they achieved whopping sales of 95000 vehicles annually.

One more example, which can be quoted in this regard, is of HLL. A year back HLL started 'Operation Bharat' to tap the rural markets. Under this operation it passed out low–priced sample packets of its toothpaste, fairness cream, Clinic plus shampoo, and Ponds cream to twenty million households. Thus looking at the challenges and the opportunities which rural markets offer to the marketers it can be said that the future is very promising for those who can understand the dynamics of rural markets and exploit them to their best advantage.

RURAL AND URBAN MARKET: A COMPARATIVE ANALYSIS

The market is a place where buyers and Sellers Exchange Things. In lay man terms "It is a place where buyers and sellers exchange goods/Service for some value in return such as Money". So the Market is same everywhere. But, The difference is in the consumer behaviour. There will be different buyers in each market.

This is because of different factors which Influence them. So the same way there is a difference between Rural and Urban Market. The factors are so many to define. There is a difference in all the marketing Variables. That is where most of the companies approach with different Marketing Mix and Strategies to Rural Market. The strategies differs from the urban to rural market. The companies which have understood the phenomena of rural market have succeeded in the market, For Ex: HUL, ITC, Colgate, Rajdoot Motorcycle.

These companies have done a perfect home work and Implemented in terms of effort and Operations. These companies approach shows that there is a difference between Rural and Urban Market.

The Differences can be Infrastructure, Economy, Lifestyle, Socio-Cultural Background, Availability or reach,Habits, Competition, Consumer Behaviour.

INFRASTRUCTURE

The facilities like Electricity, Internet, Roads and Buildings, Educational Institutions, Financial Institutions, Communication and Organised Market, Other Facilities differs in urban and Rural market. In urban everything gets implemented soon and Availability is also there. Where as in rural market everything takes a good amount of time.

ECONOMY

Here the Economy means, The earning Capacity in a rural Market. The cost of Living always depends upon their way of earning. So, the Income levels are unreliable, as Most of them are depended upon the seasons and Agriculture. So the Income levels cannot be a fixed one.

LIFESTYLE

The Lifestyle, that is living pattern of both the markets differ a lot. This can be important factor which influences the companies to think of when they approach rural market.

SOCIO- CULTURAL BACKGROUND

Due to the illiteracy level, and Culture adaptability from long time the rural market always gets differ than the urban market. The superstition and other belief as well as the way of thinking towards products and goods differ in these two markets.

AVAILABILITY OR REACH

Due to the areas which are diverted Geographically and Heterogeneous market the reach is very difficult. The logistics for rural market is a tough task than to reach the Urban Market.

HABITS

The daily routine of the people makes them to cultivate different habits. Apart from due to the awareness is low in Media terms there will be a difference in the habits.

COMPETITION

The competition in the market for brands and Companies always differ.

As in rural markets it is always the channel Partner and Retailer plays a vital role. But where as in Urban Market Brand Plays a great role.

CONSUMER BEHAVIOUR

Last but not least, The consumer behaviour is the task for the task for the companies. The mindset of the rural consumer is completely different from Urban Consumer. The Mindset of the consumer is different. For Ex: In urban market, to buy Electronic Item the customer thinks of Brand and Its updated feature. where as in rural market he thinks of in so many ways, such as money, Durability, Buying Capacity and so on. So these mindset makes a difference in both markets.

So these are the differences in the rural market and urban market. Those companies which have understood have done well.

UNIQUENESS AND NECESITY OF THE IMPLEMENTATION OF MARKETING IN RURAL TOURISM

SPECIFICS OF RURAL TOURISM RELEVANT FOR MARKETING IMPLEMENTATION

Rural tourism is a special part of the overall tourism industry. Application of marketing comes from the nature and specifics of it as a segment of tourism offer.

From above mentioned, it is still a logical conclusion that the application of marketing is based on three key components:

- Fundamentals of marketing philosophy (purpose, objectives and goals of the supply and demand holders),
- Application of marketing to the field of tourism and
- The specific application of marketing in the area of rural tourism, based on specific segments of demand and supply and adjusting to the specifics, especially of natural characteristics.

The fundamental thesis of this paper is that the *implementation of the marketing concept is one of the key factors of success in initiating activity and survival of rural tourism in the tourism market*. Specific characteristics of rural tourism "dictate" creating offers according to the modern requirements of demand.

Consideration of the needs of tourists in rural areas is only possible on the basis of marketing research, as a lever to create an adequate supply. In this area, particularly the application of marketing subtle due to the following constraints and challenges.

Large share of micro, small and medium enterprises and challenges of their (non) cooperation

As holders of rural tourism activities, there are primarily small and medium enterprises, and not a small number of micro enterprises. Among these tourism offer bidders, there's a strong competition rather than cooperation and it can be a significant problem. Clark concludes that the problems of small business at the same time the problems of rural tourism, bearing in mind the above mentioned. Problems of non-cooperation are common and appropriate stimulation by government bodies is necessary, as well as the legal framework that would discriminate the cooperation positively in order to encourage it.

Responsibility for development is scattered at different levels within the private sector, at all levels of the national to the local within the public sector, but also at the international level.

Integration and partnership between public and private sectors and the integration of rural tourism and other economic sectors are crucial, but often critical elements of rural tourism development strategy. Responsibility for the development of rural tourism is on several levels, from national to the local level, where you actually place the process of creating and consuming products of the rural tourism.

The above mentioned clearly requires coordination in planning, organizing and implementation at all levels. However it is considered as good when there is stimulation and leading the whole process from the national or even international level, because then it is possible to achieve the highest level of mutual coordination among the participants in the development process. Also, the normal development requires coordination among government departments to ensure compatibility in the legislation.

The issue of effectiveness and efficiency of marketing in rural tourism, which takes place on multiple levels and destination of the specific products. Is marketing really effective on so many levels of? Can the marketing be adapted to each destination and the product level in an effective manner? These questions can be added the fact that resources for the implementation of marketing decisions are very scarce in rural areas and that their ineffective and inefficient spending creates additional problems in the development of rural tourism destination.

Researching specific segments of rural tourism, which are significantly differentiated, segment selection and positioning of their own deals and destinations in relation to the chosen target segments of the customers

Development of rural tourism destination requires a very careful analysis and selection of those market segments which can be met and that match the previously defined strategic goals of development. Each segment has a different impact on the strategic goals of destinations such as, for example to increase spending or extend the tourist season. However, the creators and supporters of tourism development policies have a limited amount of information, which is caused by insufficient marketing research. Even traditional statistics and indicators (*e.g.* number of visitors, length of stay, consumption) are not recorded, and methodology through which data are obtained can often be of a very dubious character, while calculating market share and any comparisons are often not possible. Understanding consumers of rural tourism requires knowledge and motivation, needs and desires, image, perception, and behaviour before, during and after consuming the product.

Quantitative indicators are not enough, and unfortunately they are, usually, the only ones at disposal. The choice of market segments should be based on realistic estimates of destination competitive advantages. The goal is to meet expectations and offer value that the selected segment requests. Dividing segments may be based on a series of characteristics such as age, family status, income, behaviour and interests, place of residence and mobility. As an example of market segmentation of rural tourism the following segments of consumers of rural tourism can be mentioned: Daily visits, short (weekend) holidays, families with children, older generation, tourists with special interests, study groups, people with disabilities and others.

Expressed need for association of holders of supply due to scarcity of their own resources, and the use of cooperative marketing

Gorman (2005) identified cooperation as cooperation between two or more bidders, where each partner brings some but not all of their resources, thus contributing to the overall marketing competencies of cooperation, with a view to mutual benefit.

The same author stresses the importance of cooperation in the tourism sector, particularly for those bidders that are located in peripheral areas or centres, in case of rural tourism.

However, in order to lead to successful cooperation it is necessary to bear in mind the following challenges and constraints:

- The existence of interdependent stakeholders, and incentives that would induce cooperation and participation of partners,
- An effective way to share decision-making,
- The existence of constructive solutions that respect their differences,
- The existence of collective responsibility for future results,
- Awareness of the dynamic process of collaboration.

However, the benefits of cooperation have been identified in a number of rural tourism destinations, and some of them may be: economies of scale, preventing the outflow of income from the destination and the multiplication of the economic effects in the local community, managing visitors in terms of spatial and temporal dispersion, access to new knowledge and marketing skills, technology and distribution channels, support education and training and access to greater financial resources.

The use of modern information technology for communication and distribution of rural tourism product

The role and importance of marketing communications in practice is often misunderstood and simplifies the production of leaflets as accompanied with some form of direct mail. On the other hand, the possibilities opened up by the application of Internet and its services (e-mail, web, blog, etc.) are not fully recognized. It is necessary to take this opportunity for two-way communication (instead of former one-way), with leaflets and brochures as well as tangible support mechanisms. PR as a tool of promotion is often neglected, and only occasionally used as a supplement to the propaganda efforts. Rural tourism development requires the integration of all forms of communication and achieving synergetic effect in creating and sending promotional messages to the environment.

Nature conservation and respect for the principles of sustainable development

Sustainable development is an essential element of any strategy for developing rural tourism. Rural tourism development must contain three essential elements of sustainability including: environmental, social and economic sustainability. The key elements of each of the rural tourism offer are clean air, clean water and distance from urban agglomeration, even more than other types of tourism. The above mentioned points to the need of promoting the social aspects of marketing whose principles receive its full confirmation just in this kind of tourism.

Global context of rural tourism is particularly interesting

Namely, for international visitors, rural tourism products are interchangeable or there are significant substitutes on a global level but also within a country. The above mentioned is not well understood among individual bidders at the local level and the rural tourism offer in the immediate environment is often seen as the only competition. In addition, Clark states that the concept of rural tourism for the consumer does not have a consistent global interpretation. It is not about technical definitions but rather about the perception of consumers. The same author explains that what is seen as a "green", "clean", "rural" or "free" in one country may not be so in another. Visitors from various countries bring cultural expectations determined by "rural" and which does not and often does not match the rural tourism offer of the host country.

NECESSITY OF MARKETING IMPLEMENTATION IN RURAL TOURISM DEVELOPMENT

In order to achieve a higher level of business effectiveness, holders of rural tourism activities have to implement marketing as a business philosophy more thoroughly. The understanding of the existence of a link between market orientation and business success must increase in order to allow the application of a long-term marketing concept rather than a strategy of survival from one season to the next. Regarding the long-term planning, greater shift has to be done in the area of strengthening of the market research function, product diversification, pricing policy, promotion and distribution. The role of marketing philosophy is to answer these key challenges.

The holders of rural tourism activities usually do not have formal strategic and operational planning documents, or such cases are quite rare. Due to this fact, the use the marketing information in the regular management information system, and carrying out intensively the marketing activities is less possible. The basic component of marketing effectiveness is the existence of adequate planning and marketing plan as a result of this process. The role of an effective marketing plan, at micro- or macro-level, is to focus the scarce resources of an offer bidder (*e.g.* tourist farm), towards selected market segments with adequate combination of marketing instruments.

With regards to planning on macro-level, one of the main roles of marketing philosophy is to protect the rural character of an area as the main element of a rural tourism product. Rural tourism cannot enjoy the benefit of being too successful because success will change the nature of the product. When a village becomes successful, it will attract investment and the development of tourist services. Actually, success itself can seriously destroy the distinctive character of an environment.

The role of marketing philosophy is to define the guidelines for image creation and protection, via adequate strategic marketing plan, in order to protect the long-term interests of an area. The awareness of necessity of various innovations, especially regarding further product diversification, is also seen as quite problematic. The lack of awareness that the change is the only constant in the business could be solved via continuous education. For example, farmers as offer bidders are opened for external advice and consulting, especially if these activities are part of free of charge training or certain governmental development programme.

When the level of awareness reaches its critical point, the offer bidders need the strategy to improve their tourism product. Market research is the first step, and that means that market research is not an end in itself. The holders of tourism activities should find the ways for compiling accurate databases of personal life-stage, socio-economic, and behavioural characteristics for prospective customers, and other elements of market, as well.

Such a growing database may create a wealth of marketing opportunities. The data obtained through extensive research should have an immediate and practical impact on planning and organization of rural tourism offer. The focus of marketing philosophy has to be on providing the highest level of tourist satisfaction. The marketing of rural area is not about the marketing of a place, but of providing a range of experiences. To concentrate solely on 'place' leads to a product orientated perspective that loses sight of the delivery of experiences. Regarding rural tourism product development and diversification, it is highly recommended to develop the whole portfolio of products and services, well known as product mix of "see, buy and be" attractions. "Seeing" attractions encompass sightseeing attractions.

"Buying" attractions provide opportunities to buy physical goods (souvenirs, crafts, food, drink, etc.). "Being" attractions are related to the tourists who would like to spend their time in self-development and physical activities and recreation. Lack of "be" and "buy" activities and over-supply of "see" attractions represent the usual challenge facing great number of rural tourism destinations. The marketing concept could solve the problem in a way to develop adequate strategy which will generate better links between farmers, local tourism sector, travel agencies and other stakeholders, in order to provide necessary components of a rural tourism product. Promotion, as an element of a marketing mix concept, covers a range of activities including the main ones of advertising, public relations, personal selling and sales promotion.

The effectiveness of each promotion instrument depends on the available marketing skills and planned approach, rather than ad hoc approach with irregular communication activities. Due to the lack of financial support and marketing skills, the rural tourism enterprises need to achieve the coordinated promotion and pricing policy. But, the competition rather than cooperation among them is seen as serious obstacle for effective joint marketing activities and further rural tourism development. Special marketing opportunity offers the Information and communications technology (ICT) in sense that it reduces the reliance on intermediaries.

Also, Web site and other Internet services could be used for promotion and innovative direct communications with the market, especially with the independent tourists. Finally, marketing concept should be implemented in order to develop the distinctive image and enhance the brand awareness. In line with this process, the creation of an authentic tourism product based on the distinctive competitive advantages of a destination is seen as a key factor. Rural destination/product has to retain its unique identity, authentic sense of a place, and its traditional hospitality. Brand management based on these components, and emotion at its core, has the possibility to be effective in the long- term.

CONCLUSION

The need for a marketing implementation in the field of rural tourism is encouraged by increasing complexity of market and market relations on a very dynamic tourism market. The development of information technology, competition and growth in its global character, the new buyer and the need for sustainable development are just some of the factors that determine a new way of keeping the rural tourism business. Today, the marketing concept and philosophy of doing business are becoming essential to all policy makers and implementers of rural development.

Specifics of the implementation of the marketing concept in rural tourism development arise from the very specific characteristics of rural tourism supply and demand. In particular, the application of marketing philosophy required a subtle approach to the following limitations and challenges:

1. High share of micro, small and medium enterprises and challenges of their (non)cooperation,
2. Responsibility for the development is scattered at different levels within the private sector, at all levels of the national to the local within the public sector, but also at the international level
3. Questionable effectiveness and efficiency of marketing of rural tourism due to multiple destination levels and among specific products
4. Specific segmentation, targeting and positioning
5. The need for cooperative marketing
6. Modern information technology,
7. Nature conservation and respect for the principles of sustainable development, and
8. Global context of rural tourism.

There is no doubt that marketing in rural tourism should be seen as a means to achieve development of strategic goals of rural tourist destinations, such as long-term prosperity, guest satisfaction, profit maximization, extension of the tourist season, neutralizing the negative impact, stabilize employment, support and further diversification of existing economic activity, temporal and spatial redistribution of tourist demand and changing consumer behaviour in terms of increasing tourist spending. Therefore, marketing cannot be understood simply as propaganda or simply as printing leaflets, but as a platform for defining business objectives and strategies, and creation of tourist products which deliver unique experience to consumers and generate profit for rural tourism destination and others who appear as the bidders.

6

Exhibition of Rural Products and Tourism

EXHIBITIONS

The Exhibition with act as a platform to showcase varied rural artifacts and represents artisans from various states and promotes the same. Benefits for poor and needy artisans under corporate social responsibility and provides opportunity is expected to draw buyers/visitors and would be a potential market place for 20 days. Mall being a favourite destination for ethnic products bought from various parts of India, will indeed help women entrepreneurs derive some incremental income and increase their awareness level leading to self and enterprise development.

This consent to support the needy artisan/women will be a source of great inspiration and encouragement to the work of 'SOS CARE India' for the Artisans in need. This support will provide invaluable encouragement to the poor and up coming entrepreneurs/poor artisans in India and make them feel that they are not alone. This activity helps the artisan for through out a mediator who takes maximum profit on item of needy artisan.

OBJECTIVE OF THE EXHIBITION

- To get an exposure a new ideas to Women Entrepreneurs and Artisans.
- Exhibition encourages Women entrepreneur and Artisans to come up with their latent potentials, Which Would act as a role model for the new and young Entrepreneurs.
- The Product display on various types products to help Women entrepreneurs their business relationships directly with the actual buyers.
- Extensive publicity and contacts would be given to women entrepreneurs and Artisans through display their Products.
- Improve the exposer level of artisan.
- Display of Products is created a comprehensive marketing network for export purposes.

- Efforts for poor and needy artisans under corporate social responsibility and provides opportunity to organize this

FAIR

- Giving Indian women a positive direction and boosting their self-esteem through several programmes of SOS CARE.
- Provide invaluable encouragement to the poor and up coming entrepreneurs/poor artisans in India.
- An empowered and economically independent woman takes a whole generation of her family several steps

EXPECTED OUT COME OF THE EXHIBITION

The exhibition first of its kind in mall will showcase products of rural and urban entrepreneurs and will create a new window for them to sell their product to urban visitors of MALL.

Apart from this the exhibition have following benefits:

- The visitor will get an opportunity to see the artisan products of rural India.
- The participants will get bulk orders both national and regional level.
- The exhibition will attract more visitors to the mall.
- Artisan will assess their product demand in such big commercial places.
- Help artisan to derive incremental income.
- Enhance the exposer level of the artisans.
- Exhibition would provide greater access to latest technologies, know-how and services to one and all.

ADVANTAGE OF EXHIBITION TO THE MALL

SOS CARE exhibition not only provide platform to the needy artisan but also provides extensive direct or indirect benefit to the sponsors/ malls.

These benefits are as:

- The exhibition and side-by-side cultural events will attract more visitors to the mall.
- Buyers will get the opportunity to purchase their items from exhibition and spare the valuable moments in the mall.
- Exhibition will be covered in different media, news channels that will indirectly publicize the status of the mall.
- It will help the mall in income generating activity.
- Thousands number of new outsiders visitors will also gather in the evening which will increase the sell of the mall products.
- Providing opportunity to the needy artisan/entrepreneurs will fulfill the objective of Corporate Social Responsibility.

- The name and logo of mall will be emblazoned on the press releases, invitations, advertisements and banners of the exhibition as the sponsor of the exhibition.
- Mall can avail of every possible way to publicize itself and its services among the participants of the Exhibition.
- An opportunity for mall to reach out to 15,000 FIWE Members and the thousands of women artisans and Entrepreneurs from the 28 FIWE affiliated associations from all over India who could turn out to be its

POTENTIAL CUSTOMERS

- Continued SOS CARE partnering with mall on the local and regional projects and the big events and programmes organized by SOS in future.
- We mutually identify new strategy for the 1500 women entrepreneurs and also tie with the Thousands artisans in all over the India.
- SOS CARE India plan to be organized a combined press conference with mall and announced new facilities/ product. Also display the logo and banner of the SOS AND mall.
- SOS CARE India also take the initiative on the behalf of the Artisans/ E ntrepreneurs that in future SOS CARE India motivate poor artisans to start there small business with the help of mall policies, where Mall will take special care of that client.
- SOS CARE and mall instigate the small artisan to help in the social economic status in the community.
- Mall will support event for social cause and cash under corporate social responsibility
- SOS CARE India publish all combined initiatives to the publish materials, newsletters, brochure, magazine etc. If the tie-up is having great way than SOS CARE permitted mall for using of SOS NAME and LOGO for other product also for national level, through electronic media, Print media and TV

ADVERTISEMENT

- We are planning to open help lines in mall with the joint initiative of mall and this will assist rural and urban entrepreneurs to address their problems in quick time. This will also assist mall to reach Customers in quick time and promote their marketing initiatives.

SOS successfully organized the exhibition and event in the spice world mall with the prime support of Mr. Summit Ghosh and mall committee members. In continuation of its previous Events of the same level and magnitude SOS and Spice World organized Exhibition named-2006 from 29 sep. to 22nd oct.2006 in Spice world mall, Noida, Combined initiative of SOS & SPICE Exhibitions provides an avenue for the POOR AND NEEDY Artisans and *Indian Women Entrepreneurs* to explore the new vistas to Promote. In 25 days long exhibition we created mall as a Spice world village, which was looked like Delhi Haat. Selected and Talented Artisans from the above states with their products invited to participate in this Exhibition. 20 stalls covered the Exhibition in side and outside mall.

The organization in its endeavors to contemplate the objective of empowering the POOR AND NEEDY artisans, craftswomen's for provide strong foundation for independent and secure life and responsible citizen in the society. On this occasion Social Mass was admired the efforts being put by SOS towards the empowerment of Needy Artisans/women through development of entrepreneurship. Govt. of India offered his support to all the women entrepreneurs/artisans from rural and urban India who, breaking the shackles of rigid patriarchal society, have made strides towards economic independence by setting up their own enterprises, at micro, small or level.

An empowered and economically independent woman takes a whole generation of her family several steps forward. The Exhibition in spice mall acted as a platform to showcase varied rural artifacts and represented artisans from various states and promotes the same. During these exhibitions our endeavor was to spread the message of love, caring and friendship amongst Artisans of our country. Indian Artisans from Federation of Indian Women Entrepreneurs, Indian rural artist, craftswomen, member associations spread across the country participated in this endeavor. This endeavor drew attention of the general mass to support the cause of Artisans in need.

The exhibition first of its kind by SOS CARE,catering to the marketing needs of women entrepreneurs from various walks of life engaged in promotion and marketing of rural handicraft product will showcase handicraft products bought from All North - Eastern States, Madhya Pradesh, Gujarat, Andhra Pradesh, West Bengal, Bihar, Chattisgarh, Goa & Orissa and others states.

We will invite women entrepreneurs; Rural/Needy Artisans from the above states with their products will be invited to participate in this fair. The Products include jewelry items, bamboo products, metal items, medicinal plant extracts, paintings, furniture, pottery, and utility items etc. The sole purpose is to disseminate the technicality and other entrepreneurial measures, and the focus would be to assess selling effect of the product and market demand. The probability of producing particular products on a mass scale will be ascertained with thorough analysis.

Genesis of each product will be documented from artisan's own word of mouth and description of individual products and will be sent to leading technological institutions and government departments. With exhibitor/artisan SOS plans to provide opportunity to the bucolic renowned artist to show their potentiality during exhibition, which will attract thousand numbers of buyers in mall. In this cultural activity special attention will be on.

The stagnancy as well as the disguised unemployment that has crept into the Agricultural Sector in India has resulted in the rapid migration of people to urban areas in search of greener pastures. Correspondingly, the recent past has been characterized by greater emphasis on the manufacturing and service industry notwithstanding the fact that agriculture is still the main stay for the majority of the people especially those living in the rural areas. The focus is now back on agriculture with the realization that the economy cannot progress rapidly without the equitable development of this core sector.

This rapid migration of labour to the urban areas has also resulted in the slow but steady decline in the traditional and hereditary customs that have passed down generations and have since been a great source of pride. A group of enterprising villagers in and around Karamchedu, in association with the Federation of Farmers Association, Honey Bee, A.P. and National Innovation Foundation, Ahmedabad propose to hold a 'JAATHIYA GRAMEENA PRAGATHI PRADARSHANA', the first-of-its-kind in the country being organized at the village level.

This exhibition seeks to address a myriad of issues ranging from increasing agricultural yields through the usage of modern implements to the conservation of water, energy and the usage of organic manure. The farmers, rural artisans and occupational groups from different states in the country would participate in this exhibition not only with a view to improve their economic conditions but will also exhibit their talents in order to safeguard and restore the traditional heritage of rural villages. This event is scheduled for a period of 10 days from 01st of June to the 10th of June, 2007 at Karamchedu village, Prakasam District, Andhra Pradesh.

Participation is expected from all quarters and will not be restricted to farmers alone. The related State Government Departments as well as the people from across the country with an interest in either agriculture and its allied activities or rural development are enthusiastically expected to participate in this exhibition. Various stalls are proposed to be erected during the exhibition which will enable new products to be displayed besides providing a source of revenue to a large number of people.

The salient features and benefits expected to be reaped by rural villagers are as follows:

- Cohesiveness among rural villagers would be developed irrespective of their caste, creed and religion by mobilizing them on the basis of larger and more important issues such as agriculture and rural development. The exchange of ideas will also help people appreciate the traditions and customs prevailing in different states thereby promoting harmony among people from various walks of life.

- The Northern States *viz.* Punjab, Haryana etc. are in advanced stages of developing small scale agricultural processing industries and value added products for which remunerative prices have been obtained, which resulted in an improved standard of living. Such technologies and innovations would be showcased during this exhibition and would be adopted wherever they are feasible. This would not only facilitate an increase in the income of rural villagers but also contribute to the GDP of the nation.
- This exhibition will facilitate crop wise commodity groups to acquaint themselves with the innovative practices adopted at different places thereby improving their yield. For instance there are variations in the yields of a particular crop from mandal to mandal. Display of innovative and updated practices provide an opportunity to replicate the same with a fair degree of success.
- Resources like water and energy are scarce and there is a common tendency among people to misuse such precious resources either out of negligence or due to lack of proper knowledge. The importance of conserving such precious resources shall be highlighted which in turn shall benefit the society as a whole.
- This exhibition also intends to highlight the importance of the agricultural sector in promoting self employment in the rural areas. This can be facilitated through the development of agriculture which will correspondingly lead to an improvement in the standard of living thereby providing more employment opportunities to a larger number of people.
- The villagers are not aware of many Government schemes introduced for rural development. They are also not adequately informed of the different innovate implements and modern technologies that have been developed by the private organizations. This exhibition would, therefore, facilitate the transfer of such technologies besides enlightening them with regard to the various schemes available to them.
- This exhibition would not only facilitate transfer of technologies and exchange of customs of rural artisans but also help strengthening of net working of farmers' organizations throughout the country for articulating their problems and demand higher investments in the agricultural sectors, development of rural infrastructure and remunerative prices for the farmers' produce besides other services connected with agriculture and rural village development.
- Various important issues concerning the society relating to areas such as women and child development and their empowerment etc shall

also be dealt with through the organization of informative lectures and stalls.

- Glaring deficiencies exist in the health services in the rural areas with neither the Government nor the private sector taking interest in this important field. Modern health services as introduced in allopathy, homeopathy and ayurveda could be exhibited thereby benefiting rural villagers.
- Last, but in no way, the least rural sports and games play a significant role in developing social cohesiveness in rural areas. These sports initiate the concept of team work and also facilitate rural youth to exhibit their hidden talents. This exhibition would also enable youth to deploy their leisure time towards useful activities.

GRAMASHREE MELA

Swadeshi Science Movement is organising the Grama Sree Mela 2007 from 15 to 24 December 2007 at Thiruvananthapuram, the capital city of Kerala. The exhibition venue is "Manjalikulam Ground (SMV Higher Secondary School Ground), Near Thampanoor.

As it is the tourism season of Kerala, this event is designed as an Indian Village Fair to attract the consumers and potential clients and to maximize the marketing potential for the rural products.

Rural artisans voluntary organisation under the purview of CAPART and Self Help Groups from several states and various districts of Kerala will converge at Thiruvananthapuram for a 10-day Exhibitioin of their products.

Over 100 non-governmental organisations (NGOs) and groups receiving assistance from the Council for Advancement of People's Action and Rural Technology (CAPART) and others will participate in the exhibition-cum-sale, showcasing various products, including jute bags, soft luggage and carpets, garments, handloom cloth toys, herbal medicines, leather, cane, bamboo articles, handicrafts, furniture, ceramics, metal works, food products, hand made soaps, natural fibre products etc.

DIRECT MARKETING EFFORT

This event is a direct marketing effort by bringing together discerning consumers in cities and rural artisans and traditional craftsmen thereby making their ware available at a relatively less price to the public. Since freight charges were borne by Organisers and daily allowances paid to the participants and arrangements made for their stay, the cost would be less. CAPART will be helping them by providing designs, technical inputs and marketing support. The products are environment-friendly and help to reduce the use of products with plastics.

EVENTS

As a part of the Grama Shree Mela, the following events are also arranged:

- A beautiful exhibition of products made by rural artisans and SHGs
- Home Pavilion explaining the activities of CAPART
- Buyer-Seller Meets to help the rural products marketing
- Demonstrations of cut flower cultivation and mushroom cultivation
- Workshops on product development, marketing support
- Public talks with eminent scientist from the concerned areas
- Web marketing support for rural products
- Cultural evenings
- Seminar on Horticulture for rural development
- Home Pavilion showcasing traditional handicrafts from different parts of India
- Photo exhibitions of traditional village fairs

ORGANISERS

CAPART is an autonomous body involved in catalysing and co-ordinating the emerging partnership between Voluntary Organisations and the Government of India for sustainable development of Rural Areas. CAPART is a society under the Ministry of Rural Development, Government of India established to promote voluntary action towards implementation of projects for the enhancement or rural prosperity and to act as a catalyst for development of technologies appropriate for the rural areas. CAPART was formed in 1986 with the amalgamation of CART (Council for Advancement of Rural Technology) and PAD-I (People's Action for Development-India). Since its inception, CAPART has been providing financial assistance to voluntary organisations engaged in rural development.

ROLE OF MELAS IN MARKETING OF RURAL INDUSTRIES PRODUCTS

a. To study the Gram Shree Mela's role in marketing of rural industry products.

b. To analyse the customers' attitudes towards the rural products vis-a-vis the melas.

c. To understand the perception of participants/entrepreneurs on the role of melas in improving their living standards.

d. To suggest a few innovations for making the mela an effective instrument for bridging the gap between production and consumption.

The overall objective of this study is to see to what extent these melas are helpful to the producer and the consumer in bridging the gap between them.

METHODOLOGY

The study is based on empirical data collected on all aspects of Grama Shree Mela during 26th December 1998 to 4th January 1999 at Adarshnagar, Mumbai. The participants (entrepreneurs), the customers (buyers) and the organisers of this mela form the major source of information. Two, separate questionnaires are used for both the entrepreneurs and customers.

STUDY AREA

The study was conducted in Mumbai during December 1998 - January 1999. CAPART organised Grama Shree Mela in Mumbai during the same period. Melas in Mumbai are expected to attract not only a large number but also various categories of customers.

Mumbai also attracts a large number of participants/entrepreneurs from almost all the states in the country. Mumbai Mela was selected on the advice of CAPART officials.

FINDINGS

- The role -of these melas in marketing the rural goods in the cities is gaining recognition over a period of time.
- The melas organised under the banner of Grama Shree Mela have really created certain degree of awareness among the urban people about the rural products.
- These melas have also helped the rural entrepreneurs to acquire competitive strength in the urban- market.
- A large number of rural entrepreneurs had an opportunity to interact with the urban people and understand their tastes so as to improve their production process.
- The participants/entrepreneurs come to mela not only to sell their products but also to exhibit the innovations of the producer. The customers come to the mela only to have the best and rare products at reasonable price. The perceptions and the expectations of both the parties may be different but achieve the same goal.
- The customer represent different sections of the society and background. They have a number of reasons to visit the mela. A few come to mela to buy certain products and few others because of their liking for these products. Many customers have a special flavour for rural products. Many of them are regular visitors to such melas. There are also a few who are regular buyers of rural products because of their product's unique features.
- It is observed that majority of the customers are satisfied with the quality and price of the products.
- While identifying a few deficiencies in the present mela the customer

felt that organising these types of melas effectively by itself could be a very good strategy for market promotion of RIP.

- The participants/entrepreneurs represent all the states and UTs and a wide rage of product lines.
- The investment and production capacities of these entrepreneurs appear to be reasonably good. The employment potential of all these enterprises is significant. The share of women employment is more than 50 per cent.
- The major market channel for these products is the mela for the last few years. However, there are many that depend on various other channels such as government, direct sale, merchant middlemen and exports.
- The expectations of these entrepreneurs on the present mela are varied. A few think that the exposure to urban and open market would help them in improving their product. A few others wish to explore new products by attending these melas. There are a few who want to learn the techniques of good marketing from these melas. Some hope to observe the new design and packaging in these melas so as to improve their own presentation in the future marketing of their products.
- The turnover of these participants during the last mela appears to be reasonable.
- Their expectations on the present mela could not be realised due to the interior location as well as lack of proper publicity.
- The feel that there are a number of advantages that could be derived from these melas for the marketing of rural products. Of the entire advantages, interaction with their entrepreneurs and gaining knowledge about new products become important for the entrepreneurs. By participating in these melas many entrepreneurs appear to have made a number of improvements to their own products for better marketing.
- A few express that they are forced to sell their products at a throw away prices. Many other feel that the actual sale and the profit derived from the sales of these melas are much less than expected.
- They also admit that the products many not give satisfaction to all the varied interests of customers. However, they express that, by and large, the customers go away with a sense of satisfaction.
- While explaining the difficulties encountered in the melas, they suggested that the melas need to be organised monthly at all state capitals so as to expand the market network for the rural products.

POLICY IMPLICATIONS

Since melas are recognised as an effective strategy (channel) for marketing of rural industry products, they need to be strengthened not only by increasing the frequency but also by organising them in several locations. Further, they need to be extended to different sectors as is done by Government of AP with regard to DWCRA/Chief Ministers Empowerment of Youth (CMEY), TARUNI (Exhibition/stall of women entrepreneurs) and Farmers Market (Rythu Bazaar).

SARAS

The promotion of Swarozgaris under the banner of SARAS was one of the major steps taken by the Ministry of Rural Development during the year 1999-2000 for the improvement of rural business. The main aim of the Ministry of Rural Development in subscribing most of the rural products under the banner of SARAS was that, it wanted to give the rural products a globally recognized brand name which would be an added value to the trading of these products. This task taken up by the Ministry of Rural Development has opened up a galore of opportunities for the rural artisans or entrepreneurs or officials who are deeply involved in the programme of Swarnjayanti Gram Swarozgar Yojana (SGSY). The business people got a vast exposure in the international market with the help of this programme.

This can be claimed to be one of the beneficiary activities performed by the Rural Ministry for the welfare of the state's economy especially the rural sector. SARAS was recognized to be an umbrella brand under which a variety of products were marketed not only in the domestic market but in the international markets as well.

The chief concern of the Rural Ministry was to tap a big opportunity in the markets across the country and also to deploy its programmes all across the world. The SARAS also acts as an awareness programme to promote the rural products manufactured amongst the urban consumers in Delhi and the neighbouring places. This is a strategic step to expand the market for the consumption of rural products.

SARAS has been a regular annual event every since 1999 when it hit the market at one go with its innovative approach to the consumers. The SARAS exhibition is also a portrayal of the skills of people residing in different corners of the rural sector. The products are directly displayed in the exhibitions executed by SARAS for rural products, and the visitors enjoy the privilege to make their choices directly from the exhibition. The products are highly adored by every section of society and people from all across the country participate in the SARAS exhibition.

The sales graph of the rural products are growing higher and higher and every year there is a phenomenal rise in the selling of products. Some participants even order these products in a bulk apart from buying single pieces. The products range includes handicrafts, textiles, artwork, furniture, draperies, household artifacts, items of daily use, and many more.

The exhibition of rural products under the banner of SARAS has also been a participant in the India International Trade Fair (IITF). Such enhancements in the programme have fueled the confidence and enthusiasm within the craftsmen and they are giving their best of production every year for it. SARAS has not only recognized the in-built skills of the artisans that were subdued but also provided them with a plethora of opportunities to make the best use of it. The goods manufactured by these rural poor are made popular to adorn the domestic markets and has also paved its way through the urban, metropolitan, and global markets.

SARAS exhibitions have also won the confidence of the stakeholders in the development of rural products or craftsmen. Apart from opening up of new roads for these hidden talents, SARAS has been also playing a key role in connecting these talents with various markets. SARAS 2003 will be strictly focusing on improving the skills of the artisans and increasing the richness of products by developing more awareness programmes among the rural poor.

"Exhibitions provide best opportunity for marketing the produced goods, especially for the rural products and thereby support production," said Chikmagalur former MP D C Srikantappa. Inaugurating the 30th State-level exhibition arranged as a part of Lakshadeepotsava at Shree Kshethra Dharmasthala. He lauded the efforts of Dharmadhikari Dr D Veerendra Heggade in bringing about social reformation through Shree Kshethra Dharmasthala Rural Development Programme (SKDRDP). Dr D Veerendra Heggade who presided over the programme said that the idea behind the exhibition was to arrange a festival which is devoid of all unnecessary systems like gambling, drinking and so on. He said that 'Lakshadeepotsava' thus stresses on the disciplined way of entertainment and religious acts.

DISTRICT SUPPLY AND MARKETING SOCIETY

District Supply and Marketing Society (DSMS) is a registered Body under society Registration Act, 1860 registered Body under Society Registration Act, 1860 under the administrative control of Orissa Rural Marketing Society (ORMAS) Bhubaneswar. It was set up during 1993-94 by the D.R.D.A., Keonjhar as it sister concerned with an objective to provide all backward, forward linkage to the Government poverty alleviation Scheme.

PROGRAMME IMPLEMENTATION

a. To identify groups with sustainable feasible activities under the scheme of SGSY with an intent of facilitating higher scale of operation, technology up gradation, and marketing support would like to strengthen the groups in identifying their critical gaps with require inputs.
b. To act as a catalyst in enabling the rural flock to make their products

competitive in internal and external market through provision of comprehensive marketing support in:

- Market identification.
- Activity selection.
- Costing and type fixation.
- Standardisation and quality control.
- Product designing and packaging.
- Selling channel.
- Product launching.

c. Providing inputs of training in skill up gradation technical skills.
d. Awareness building and organization of beneficiaries.
e. Strengthen the capacity of group by forming and monitoring the self-help groups.
f. Act as a facilitator (not direct marketing) tying of the groups with market for selling of the Rural products.
g. Organising and participating in various exhibition both in state and National level for selling of the rural products produced in the District by the Group.
h. Conducting workshops/ seminars for the grass root level workers, NGOs and others.
i. Selling of rural products through DSMS sale counter named "GONASIKA" at the Collectorate premises.

ADVANCE LEAF-CUP-PLATE MAKING

Keonjhar district in Orissa is known for its predominate forest cover which has been depleting very first in the recent past. The economic of the areas is forest base. Collection of monor forest produce is the main occupation of the people. The rural mass in the district have been stitching the Sal and Siali leaves into plates and cups for so many years sale those to the local brokers who in turn sell those products through different channels. The bottom line is that the producers earn the lowest of all benefit about six hundred per month.

However to give maximum benefit and profit to the producers 'ORMAS" (DSMS) has identified advance leaf-cum-plate machine which not only improve the earnings of minimum ₹.2000/- per month but also we will enable them to form their groups for their Economic empowerment and sustainability. In this regard already some groups of Ghatgaon and Banspal block have taken training of advance leaf-cup-plate making where first the leafs are stitched by swing machine and then LDPE(Polythene) and card board is used for preparing Buffet plate 250 leaf plate per house can be prepared by single skill operation.

These Buffet plates are of hygienic quality and used for social purpose like Marriages, other functions which has a lot of demand and outside the State. 'ORMAS' has also made marketing tie-up with outside agencies for marketing these leaf cup-plates to give maximum profit to the producers. In this regard DSMS, Keonjhar has already supplied advance leaf cup-plate to the agencies (ACI), Hyderabad and to other district. DSMS has identified other groups for advance leaf cup-plate trade to be assisted under New Scheme of 'SGSY'.

PACKAGING DEVELOPMENT OF SPICES, PICKLES, BODI

There are many groups in the district who produce spices, (Chillipowder, turmeric Powder, Dhania, Jeera etc.), Pickles, Bodi of good quality. But due to poor packaging these products are not available. DSMS, Keonjhar has developed better packaging in the name of 'GONASIKA' brand and Bottling of pickles for better selling. Tie up has been by DSMS, Keonjhar with local and outside markets for selling of spices, Bodi and Pickles.

SLOGAN

DSMS, Keonjhar will act as a facilitator and wants to give maximum profit the rural producers.

Work side/ Project that can be visited by interested group/ Press/ media:

a. DSMS sale counter 'GONASIKA' where rural products are available at Collectorate premises, Keonjhar.
b. Advance leaf cup-plate making centre, Suakati, Keonjhar.
c. Spices and Pickles making Centre, Suakati, Keonjhar
d. Paper Terracotta, Barigaon, Anandapur, Keonjhar
e. Terracotta, Haldharpur, Ghatgaon, Keonjhar.

Periyar PURA (Providing Urban Amenities to Rural Areas) in coordination with NBARD (National Bank for Agriculture and Rural Development), RTC-IOB (Rural Training Centre-Indian Overseas Bank, Thanjavur), BEED-Thanjavur (Bamboo Extension and Enterprise and Development) organized a two day bamboo workshop and exhibition on May 12th and 13th 2007 at Periyar Maniammai College of Technology for Women, Vallam on Bamboo Cultivation and its applications for Cauvery delta farmers.

Scientists and Professors from various institutions such as Indian Institute of Technology, Mumbai, Kerala Forest Research Centre Kerala, and Tamil Nadu Agricultural University, Coimbatore were presented in bamboo seedlings production, nursery management, establishment of bamboo plantation, post harvest technology and product development. A demo session about propagation was arranged.

Over 350 farmers from various parts of South India participated in this programme enthusiastically. They realize Bamboo is a good alternative and it gives more income then any others. As an average all the farmers participated in this workshop agreed to cultivate the bamboo in 2 acres. As an outcome, Tamil Nadu Bamboo Farmer"s Association was formed, Mr. R. Pannirselvam, was elected as president.

Bamboo growing and product development workshop cum exhibition was organized at PMCTW, Vallam, Thanjavur on May 12-13, 2007. The goal of the workshop was to establish Bamboo as an alternate crop in the Cauvery delta for enhancing the income and employment generation as well to lend sustainability and eco-development in the region. There had been overwhelming response not only from the Cauvery delta farmers but from the entire length and breadth of Tamilnadu as well. Over 350 farmers enthusiastically participated through out the workshop sessions.

Various aspects of bamboo growing from nursery preparation, choice of cultivars, planting and management were explained and demonstrated by experts on the field. With the acceleration in the economic growth of the country, various new products of Bamboo are entering the domestic and international market. Experts from IIT, Bombay exposed these new products to the stakeholders who evinced keen interest in knowing and venturing as entrepreneurs. The tools and machineries for processing and value addition to bamboo were also exhibited and explained.

The farmers convinced of the profitability of Bamboo growing were however apprehensive about marketing. The commitment of farmers resulted in the formation of an association of Bamboo growers of Tamil Nadu. Establishment of small and medium industries with the present available stock of Bamboo in the delta region will enhance the confidence building and commitment of farmers in taking up new plantations on a larger scale. The central and state governments should come forward in a big way in establishing industries and assisting the institutions that desire such ventures.

7

Industrial Heritage and Agri/Rural Tourism

SPECIAL INTEREST TOURISM: AN INTRODUCTION

Agri-tourism, rural tourism and industrial heritage tourism are all niche market tourism areas, part of a global expansion of special interest tourism, defined and explained in Weiler and Hall's 1992 classic text on that subject. The three themes must be seen, and understood, as one of a series of fascinating developments in the post war evolution of tourism, summed up by the UN's World Tourism Organization in 1985:

- "New kinds of life-style and a new realization of the importance of relations between people and between people and nature are features of the 1980s. Gaining in importance are participation in outdoor activities, aesthetic judgement and improvement of self and society. The search for these new values in the exercise of tourism is reflected in organized recreation and the new products that have emerged, such as active holidays and special interest tourism".

Ten years later official recognition of the growth and value of special interest consumer expenditures in general, and in tourism in particular, came from the Organization of Economic Cooperation and Development in its work on the growth of niche markets and of niche market tourism, and the need for the private and public sector to understand and use their potential for socio-economic development. Earlier, the OECD had set guidelines for rural tourism.

Special interest tourism continues to grow, spurred by the rapid expansion of the mass media into niche markets, by the internet's ability to inform, by new transport facilities, and by the surge in individualism and intellectual curiosity that society has seen.

TOURISM'S POST WAR GROWTH

To understand the background to special interest tourism in general and to rural tourism and industrial heritage tourism in particular, it is necessary to briefly outline the story of tourism's post war expansion, and its underlying drivers.

The standard global statistics come from the annual surveys of the UN World Tourism Organization. They show international tourism arrivals on a global basis rising from 25 million in 1950 to 982 million in 2011, worth €740 billion. Over that period there has been average year on year growth rates of 6 per cent. UNWTO looks forward to 1.4 billion arrivals by 2020. Domestic tourism arrivals are, of course, very much greater, and much more difficult to quantify accurately.

They may be up to eight times greater. In financial terms, not only is tourism a huge financial force; it is also a re-distributor of income within countries, typically from large cities and industrial regions to resort areas and increasingly to rural areas. It also redistributes income within the developed world, and from the developed world to the developing world. With that redistribution comes jobs and additional investment capital flows.

Europe is the largest receiving continent for international tourists, with 504 million arrivals out of the world's 982 million, worth €333 billion. The Asia Pacific region is the second largest recipient of international visitors, with 28 per cent of the world total.

Within the overall growth picture, however, there are a number of important internal stories. Tourism grew in the nineteenth century as a largely resort based industry, with a property development base.

Existing resorts, which are typically sea and sand based resorts, along with some spa resorts, are now being challenged:

- By newer resorts - often in other countries and/or continents, especially in Asia, Oceania, and Australia.
- By cruise ship tourism - cruise passenger arrivals worldwide rose from 3.8 million in 1990 to 12.8 million in 2008; bed nights totalled 79.4 million worldwide in 2008. Numerous new cruise ships are under construction, and research results suggest that younger people are now beginning to cruise.
- By city tourism - until recently city tourism was restricted to the iconic heritage cities of the world: Paris, Rome, Sydney, and New York amongst many others. But increasingly city and regional planners are using tourism as a tool for the regeneration of dozens of medium size/ large industrial cities world-wide, seeking to diversify their economies, change their image, and create jobs. Beginning with the transformation of Baltimore's harbour district in the 1980s, urban tourism has flourished, with a powerful mix of speciality retail, new hotels, cultural attractions, heritage developments from industrial to post-modern, and the ever growing activity of partying, eating and drinking. Rotterdam, Dublin, Bradford, Glasgow, Turin, Poznan, Riga and many more are all examples of the rise of urban/city tourism in Europe. High speed rail services and low cost flights are key drivers

in this development. To emphasise the change, in 2010 the coal and steel based industrial cities of the German Ruhr region became Europe's Capital of Culture· Many once purely industrial cities are now becoming a new type of self-contained, professionally managed, "authentic" heritage/culture based full service resort. They offer very serious competition for existing resorts, especially in the winter season. Two points of special importance for readers of this study emerge from this development:

- Industrial Heritage Tourism is a part, and could be a greater part, of this rise in City Tourism – although the "fit" is not always achieved or possible.
- It is difficult to obtain reliable overall statistics for city tourism in Europe – and for industrial heritage tourism.

• By rural tourism -while existing in many parts of Alpine Europe for over a century, has grown rapidly, and in a unique way across most of Europe. It is unique because it is the first type of tourism that is not - as yet - resort based. EuroGites claims that there are now 400,000 rural accommodation units in Europe, with 3.6 million bed spaces (twice the total bed capacity of Spain, the second most important tourism destination country in Europe). Growth figures can also be found for most other developed nations: it has become a world-wide phenomenon. Rural tourism – as will be explained later – is extremely broad in content, encompassing nature tourism, ecotourism, agri-tourism, adventure tourism, food tourism, and many other emergent developments. It is also an area of activity for which it is hard to obtain reliable statistics.

WHAT ARE THE KEY FEATURES IN THE RISE, DIVERSIFICATION AND TRANSFORMATION OF TOURISM?

This is a complex question. Tourism is essentially a fashion industry: people travel to where they believe it is fashionable to be, and they are largely guided in their beliefs by a powerful media industry. It is no longer very fashionable to spend time at many traditional European sea side resorts. It is increasingly fashionable to take short breaks in cities and in the countryside, often as second or third holidays.

Holidays, once seen solely as time for relaxation, have diversified remarkably. The tourism analyst Stanley Plog noted the rapid growth of a new type of traveller, the allocentric, who focuses on activity and prefers unfamiliar, novel trips of many kinds. Education is also a growing motivation, in both formal and informal modes.

It must be added, however, that tourism remains a leisure pursuit that, despite its links to education, must be enjoyable and uplifting. The emergence of the term "infotainment" – linking learning and enjoyment – is noteworthy. Holidays remain dream times, fulfilling dreams, enabling experiences.

In addition to the above, there are many powerful technical, economic and social factors to be noted, including:

- Rising car ownership;
- The spread of the high speed divided highway across Europe – including autobahnen, autoroutes, and motorways;
- Low cost airlines;
- Speciality tour operators – the UK's Association of Independent Tour Operators, for example, has over 140 specialist small tour operators;
- Rising levels of education;
- The introduction of credit cards, internet banking and the European common currency, making travel easier and less demanding;
- The internet, better fixed line and mobile telephony, and the ability to book holidays, transport and accommodation on line on a 24/7 basis;
- PLUS – until recently – the essential enabling factor - rising levels of disposable income;
- The rise of the pensioned and active older traveller, creating new markets.

Further complicating the picture, there have been a range of new paradigms and understandings in tourism which complete the background picture.

TALC – THE TOURISM AREA LIFE CYCLE

This concept, originating from Richard Butler in the 1980s, is a strong and valid influence on tourism planning. It explains that tourism destinations, like all consumer products, have a period of discovery, growth, maturity and then decline (unless regeneration measures are taken). Each destination brand needs to be refreshed after circa 25/30 years, sometimes earlier, if it is to avoid decline. The TALC concept helps explain the decline of many 1960s Spanish resorts, some resorts in Southern Italy and some North Sea resorts. It also sends a strong warning of potential problems to all destinations – conventional, rural, or industrial – that are not professionally managed, that do not invest in market research, and do not update their products.

THE RECOGNITION OF THE EXPERIENCE ECONOMY

For many years, tourism was sold as a commodity, to be purchased like any other tangible commodity. As both society and marketing moved forward, it was realised that tourism was *a service* as well as a tangible commodity. The service element was a major determining factor in consumer choice. This was especially the case as tourism moved into supply surplus, and competition grew between different parts of the industry, and different destinations. From circa 1990 the marketing literature moved on to see many businesses, including tourism, as selling *experiences* as well as services. A number of pioneering publications explained the emergence of "the experience economy". These include those by Gerhard Schulze and his book *Erlebnisgesellschaft*, later published in English as *The Experience Society;* Rolf Jensen's book, *The Dream Society* and Pine and Gilmore's *The Experience Economy.* All of those writers noted that more and more people are able and willing to spend money on great/satisfying experiences, often emotional experiences, rather than conventional consumer goods.

The marketing techniques required to tap into the experience economy are both demanding and new. Tourism businesses have been slow to realise these important developments, which are especially important to the rural and the industrial heritage development sectors. Both are extremely experiential: they are not conventional passive leisure products. But uninformed marketing is a problem in both sectors.

To help understand the role of experience marketing in tourism, Visitor Experience Plans, were pioneered by the US National Park Service in the late 1990s. Although originally designed as a conservation tool, visitor experience planning and experiential marketing can help boost visitor numbers to destinations, especially when linked to market informed heritage interpretation plans.

PLACE ATTACHMENT

One of the growth areas in understanding tourist preferences has been the concept of "place attachment studies". Place attachment relates to the psychological "hold" that places have on people, through the enjoyment or admiration of landscapes and townscapes, of their ambience, and through the remembrance of experiences and relationships. Place attachment helps explain repeat visitation, and the way in which recommendation and word of mouth marketing works. Put briefly, both rural and urban destinations can develop strong place attachment; industrial heritage tourism, however, is weak on place attachment. A key reason for this appears to be poor site marketing in comparison to place/regional marketing, and the ability of regions with a full suite of visitor facilities (accommodation, hospitality and attractions) to develop much stronger place attachment than sites. It follows that industrial heritage tourism needs to address this problem.

SUSTAINABLE TOURISM

The relatively unregulated rise of mass tourism in the 1970s created widespread concern about its social, cultural and environmental impacts, especially in fragile natural environments. From that concern emerged the concept of creating more sustainable forms of tourism. Early criticism focussed on mass tourism. We now know that in many ways mass tourism is more easily managed than the spread of less intense forms of tourism – including rural tourism – but the stigma attached to mass tourism still exists. Sustainable tourism systems are related to the rise of the more general interest in sustainable development and the pioneering work of the Brundtland Commission.

There are many definitions of sustainable tourism. The following is one of the many normally cited:

- "Sustainable tourism is a positive approach intended to reduce the tensions and frictions created by the complex interactions between the tourism industry, visitors, the environment and the communities which are host to holidaymakers. It involves working for the long-term viability and quality of both natural and human resources. It is not anti-growth, but acknowledges that there are limits to growth"

The increasing interest in Corporate Social Responsibility in the travel and tourism industry is linked to the sustainable tourism concept. And, directly related to this study's findings, sustainable tourism researchers and practitioners normally link sustainable tourism to the use of rural tourism as a tool for the conservation of rural society, landscape and ecosystems. Equally there is a direct link from sustainable tourism thinking to the conservation of industrial heritage.

THE TRIPLE BOTTOM LINE

Sustainable tourism employs the concept of triple bottom line accounting. This is the idea that as an indicator of sustainable tourism, enterprises, communities, regions and nations should record not just economic results – plus or minus – but also environmental, social and cultural results – plus or minus. Triple Bottom Line accounting is now a required feature of tourism strategy making and plans.

ECOTOURISM

The term Ecotourism is much used in the USA as an alternative for sustainable tourism, and also for rural tourism. Many commentators in the USA fear the political overtones of the word "sustainable".

Strictly, and across the rest of the world, Ecotourism is defined by Ceballos-Lascurain as:

- "Environmentally responsible travel and visitation to relatively undisturbed natural areas, in order to enjoy and appreciate nature (and any accompanying cultural features– both past and present), that promotes conservation, has low visitor impact, and provides for beneficially active socio-economic involvement of local populations."

That definition is used by the International Ecotourism Society, who recognise it as a specialist sub-set of the wider concept of Sustainable Tourism, and applicable to rural areas. The word ecotourism is of value, but rarely used, within Europe.

TOURISM AS A REGENERATION TOOL

Many writers on sustainable tourism recognise that tourism should not be an end in itself, but should also be a conservation and regeneration tool for urban and rural areas. This study illustrates a range of cases where tourism has been used as a regeneration tool.

It is important to note, however, that tourism cannot always succeed in that task if:

- The site and its situation is not good for tourism purposes
- The stakeholders involved in the project are unwilling to work together, or have weak entrepreneurial and related tourism skills and
- If the funding is insufficient or the time scale is too short.

SLOW TOURISM

The concept of slow food emerged in Italy in 1986 as a protest against the industrialisation of food, against "big business" in the food industry and in favour of traditional foods and cooking, traditional agriculture and small scale, local production. It has grown, and it has been joined by a range of other "Slow" movements, including Slow Tourism. Both slow food and slow tourism have links to rural and agri-tourism; food related tourism is also a fast growing sector.

Slow tourism can be defined as:

- "An emerging conceptual framework which offers an alternative to air and car travel, where people travel to destinations more slowly overland, stay longer and travel less."

Slow tourism stresses the importance of the travel experience, the enjoyment and understanding of destinations, cultures and landscapes, slow food and drink, and it has a very strong link to the issues of climate change outlined below. It is an important element in future thinking on rural tourism, and links to a number of transport elements in industrial heritage tourism, especially to canal and heritage rail modes. Tangible examples are, as yet, hard to find, but the tour operator Inntravel has a fast growing business based on Slow Travel; there are discussions in Austria about developing the 107 km Stainach Irdning to Attnang-Pucheim rail route as a slow tourism corridor.

CLIMATE CHANGE

Climate Change issues are an increasing problem for the tourism industries of the world. Although tourism is regularly cited as contributing just 5 per cent of the world's total Green House Gas emissions, that figure is a minimal one: many researchers find the full contribution of tourism to GHG is between 5.2 per cent and 12.5 per cent.

The real fear is, however, about the future. Because of tourism's high growth rates, the rising use of air travel, and the rise in long-haul travel, tourism related GHG emissions could rise by 130 per cent by 2035 from 2005 figures. Given rising sea levels and changes in climate that effect food production, tourism could face strong pressures to change its approaches, and tourists could face equally strong pressure – financial and social – to change their travel and tourism behaviours and habits. While there is evidence that travel is addictive, many addictions can be broken.

Climate change presents both threats and opportunities for rural tourism and, to a lesser extent, for industrial heritage tourism. Some aspects of rural tourism may be threatened by climate change: landscapes may change and become less attractive in parts of southern Europe and wildlife resources may be lost.

The latter is already an issue for whale watching in northern Europe. A specialised branch of rural tourism, winter sports tourism, is also concerned about climate change. Key areas include winter tourism areas in relatively low lying parts of Germany and Sweden. Rising sea levels could be a problem for some industrial heritage sites, and for many coastal cities.

A further negative influence on rural tourism could come from rising fuel prices, (caused by taxation and/or world scarcity) impacting on both car and air travel to rural destinations. The car is currently a vital element in the rural tourism market strategy. But there are also positive aspects to climate change and its influences. Slow tourism appears to have some romantic appeal, and already rural walking and cycling are strong "slow" markets. Increasing prices for long haul tourism may encourage more domestic, intra Europe, holidays. Industrial heritage tourism could benefit from "staycations". Heritage rail travel could become more attractive. Behavioural change is a key way to tackle climate change: short-haul rural holidays with little car use while in the rural area could be a valuable anti-climate change approach. Austria's rural resort of Werfenwang has long experience of such approaches·

For an up-to-date detailed but accessible report on Climate Change see World Bank; for a review of tourism adaptation to climate change see Scott and Becken.

INDUSTRIAL HERITAGE TOURISM AND RURAL TOURISM: AN OVERVIEW

In summary, rural tourism is essentially a tourism activity which relies on landscape and related heritage, the conservation of which is usually paid for by the public sector. Industrial heritage is primarily a conservation activity which relies in large part on tourism, along with public sector and volunteer funding. Both have the capacity to expand, be much better organized and to spread good practice more widely and deeply. Both have a small number of world beating enterprises, and very large numbers of much less effective enterprises. Both have many organizational and technical problems which could benefit from strong pan-European networking organizations to carry out basic research and advisory/lobbying roles. They have some common origins and some issues in common – but in other respects they can be very different from each other.

WHAT IS INDUSTRIAL HERITAGE TOURISM?

It is tourism that visits industrial heritage sites, or museums with a special interest in industrial heritage. It is important to note that industrial tourism, or factory visits, are not seen as being industrial heritage tourism: normally heritage sites are not in production, except for demonstration or small scale production purposes.

There is little discussion of definitions of industrial heritage tourism in the academic literature, nor is there very much refereed tourism research on the subject. This is an area which falls between study areas – it does not fit easily with tourism research, or with heritage researchers, or with regional studies.

In 2001, Michael Falser, an Austrian architect and art historian working at UNESCO, produced a global analysis of industrial heritage sites entitled *Is Industrial Heritage under represented on the World Heritage List·*

His definition is lengthy and a little vague, but he suggests a 10 point classification of industrial heritage:

- Extractive Industries
- Bulk Products Industries
- Manufacturing Industries (*e.g.* machine textile manufacture)
- Utilities
- Power Sources and Prime Movers (*e.g.* water wheels, steam turbines)
- Transportation (*e.g.* railroads, canals, harbours)
- Communication
- Bridges, Trestles, Aqueducts
- Building Technology
- Specialized Structures/Objects (*e.g.* dams, tunnels, hydraulic works)

Of those ten, categories 1, 2, 3, 5, 6, 8 and 10 are the categories most developed as industrial heritage tourism sites. Of those seven, categories 1, 2, 3, and 6 – (mines, metal working sites, factories and transportation systems) appear to be the most visited.

There are three additional categories not listed above which are also very important. There are a number of industrial heritage complexes comprising factory or factories complete with workers housing and related buildings and infrastructure. Examples include Saltaire in England, New Lanark in Scotland, and La Chaux de Fonds/Le Locle in Switzerland: all are World Heritage Sites. The second additional category comprises the many industrial museums, such as the Catalonian Museum of Science and Industry in Spain, the Chemnitz Industrial Museum in Germany and the Museum of Technology at Hengelo, the Netherlands. And finally there is the very special category of industrial museums that attempt to replicate industrial heritage complexes, rather than be conventional museums. The largest example of this type in the world is the UK's Beamish – The Living Museum of the North· Beamish is an open air museum in the North-East of England which in its 120 hectares presents a working re-creation of everyday life at the early twentieth century climax of the industrial revolution, complete with working tramways, an accessible coal drift mine, costumed interpreters, period retail shops, etc. It raises very special issues of management and design, and is the subject of a case study in this study.

It should be noted that the categories discussed above fit reasonably well with those adopted by the European Routes of Industrial Heritage group – see section 5 of this study.

In 2003, the TICCIH, (The International Committee for the Conservation of the Industrial Heritage) set out the Nizhny Tagil Charter for the Industrial Heritage· It is the industrial heritage equivalent of the well-known ICOMOS 'Venice Charter for the Conservation and Restoration of Monuments and Sites', dating from 1964. The Nizhny Tagil Charter defines industrial heritage, sets out guidelines for its conservation and use, but has no reference to tourism except to say that "public authorities should promote tourism to industrial areas". There is no definition of industrial heritage tourism.

Typically, industrial heritage tourism is largely site, building, machine and technology based. It is rarely regional, although there are some very important exceptions to that rule, notably in Germany's Ruhr region. And industrial heritage tourism tends to be relatively weak on the social and cultural heritage of the industrial revolution. Jones and Munday call for industrial heritage tourism to not only cover physical remains from the industrial past, but also sociofacts – "aspects of social and institutional organization", along with mentefacts – "attitudinal characteristics and value systems including religion and language". This issue will be covered later.

The majority of industrial heritage sites inevitably date from the eighteenth and nineteenth centuries, the era of the industrial revolution, and, using the UNESCO list of 962 industrial heritage sites as a guide, Europe has a near monopoly of this activity. Of the 33 listed industrial heritage related sites, 28 are in Europe.

Most sites are, not surprisingly, in northern Europe, the heartland of the early industrial revolution. Large parts of Eastern Europe industrialised only in the twentieth century; many parts of southern Europe did not industrialise. Within northern Europe, Germany and the UK, the leaders in nineteenth century industrialization, each have far more industrial heritage than any other country, and have led the way in many aspects of industrial heritage conservation and tourism development.

Four other key issues in industrial heritage tourism need to be highlighted.

It is typically a site only phenomenon. It rarely includes accommodation elements, unlike rural tourism. That is important: up to 50 per cent of the gross income from tourism into an area comes from overnight accommodation. The ability to offer overnight accommodation also increases the likelihood of local food and beverage sales, which can account for up to 30 per cent of tourism income.

Many former industrial areas do not have existing accommodation facilities, nor do they often have many domestic properties large enough to offer bed and breakfast facilities: both omissions are linked to their industrial pasts. Again, unlike rural tourism, few industrial regions have as yet evolved into even proto-resorts, capable of offering a range of attractions and accommodation, and offering a brand image. Because of the failure of many industrial heritage sites/ museums to link with tourism interests and agencies, it is hard to progress the evolution of industrial heritage into full destination status. Industrial sites find it hard – but not impossible – to develop place attachment. Ways forward on these key questions will be given later, especially in the discussion of the Beamish Museum in the UK and the Ruhr area of Germany in Sections 5.1.4 and 5.1.5.

Secondly, the drivers behind the conservation of industrial heritage are usually quite different to those driving rural tourism. Most industrial heritage site management is undertaken by non-profit, local government or state agencies, and often by volunteers rather than paid labour. Funds come largely from the public sector. The aim is normally to conserve, not to make money. Chhabra provides an interesting commentary on this, albeit from a USA perspective. Tourism is sometimes seen by those managing heritage sites as somehow outside their remit. There is often a lack of partnership between tourism agencies and heritage sites.

Thirdly, industrial heritage tourism labours under serious psychological and aesthetic burdens. The link between industry, hard work and the often tough living conditions of the past is deeply engrained in the psyche of much of the population. Both Cole and Jansen Verbeke note the desire of many to tear down monuments and relics of the industrial past, let alone visit them. An appreciation of the industrial landscape is a taste that can be hard to acquire for some.

While most will enjoy the sight and sound of a steam train climbing a steep hill, with sparks, black smoke and steam shooting skywards, not so many appreciate derelict industrial sites and the remains of industrial waste. It is not surprising that railway heritage tourism is popular: it is an easily absorbed visitor experience.

Finally, it is a popular belief that health and safety issues, and trends in society towards litigation, are becoming problematic, especially for industrial heritage. As part of the research for this study, the authors wrote to all the national rural tourism organizations linked to EuroGites, and to all the national heritage railway organizations linked to Fedecrail to ask about legal and other constraints on their activities and those of their members. They reported very few problems with health and safety rules, or with tourists taking legal action. Most did not feel this to be a problem because most health and safety legislation applies to all businesses, not just tourism. Most had insurance against legal disputes. The impact of safety standards were largely seen as acceptable in the twenty-first century and lobbying against unacceptable demands appears to have been successful. The problems of obtaining market share, finding public and private funding, appointing quality staff and trading profitability were seen as much more pressing.

WHAT IS RURAL TOURISM, AND WHAT IS AGRI-TOURISM?

Rural tourism is tourism which takes place in the countryside. Agri-tourism is rural tourism that takes place on farms. However, such a simple definition of rural tourism is inadequate for many purposes.

Problems include:

- Urban or resort based tourism is not confined to urban areas, but spills out, through excursions, employment and purchases, into rural areas.
- Rural areas are themselves difficult to define, and the criteria used by different nations vary considerably.
- Not all tourism which takes place in rural areas is strictly "rural" - it can be "urban" in form, and merely be located in a rural area. Many so called holiday villages are of this type: in recent years numerous large holiday complexes have been completed in the countryside. Their degree of "real" rurality can be both an emotive and a technical question. They may be urban in layout and architectural style and scale. They may be urban in ownership and management. They may be urban in purchasing policies for food and drink. And they can be completely self-contained in terms of function - visitors may never, or only rarely, leave the complex and enter the "real" rural world.

Getz and Page in their review of *The Business of Rural Tourism* conclude that a definition of rural tourism is valuable for public sector policy makers and planners. They need to define the subject to determine eligibility for grants and other incentives, and equally, to have definitions which ensure that permission for development goes to rural initiatives which can help conserve the countryside, rather than urbanise it. But Getz and Page are less sure of the value of defining rural tourism for others: "the question of what is rural is irrelevant to rural tourism business operators... not really of importance to visitors either".

This is an uninformed view. Businesses need to consider very carefully how they pitch their enterprises, to take maximum advantage of the marketing opportunities afforded by rural images. They also need to understand how to understand "perceived rurality" so that their activities do not damage the reality or image of the countryside. And rurality is an essential requirement for many visitors: tourism is ultimately a form of escapism from everyday urban and suburban life: understanding how the market defines rural is, therefore, vital. There is also a broad environmental and ethical goal in seeking a definition. The search for a definition of rural tourism brings with it a search for the value judgements which should underlie the rural tourism development and management process.

The OECD's Rural Development Programme tackled the definitional issue in the early 1990s.

They concluded that rural tourism, in its 'purest' form, should be:

- Located in rural areas
- Functionally rural - built upon the rural world's special features of small-scale enterprise, open space, contact with nature and the natural world, heritage, 'traditional' societies and 'traditional' practices.
- Rural in scale - both in terms of buildings and settlements - and, therefore, usually – but not always - small-scale.
- Traditional in character, growing slowly and organically, and connected with local families. It will often be controlled locally and developed for the long-term good of the area.
- Of many different kinds, representing the complex pattern of rural environment, economy, history and location.

The OECD's Rural Development Programme applied to that definition above their threefold geographical criteria, noting differences between tourism according to location:

- Peripheral or remote regions, characterised by sparse populations, small-scale often traditional enterprises, high servicing costs and economic poverty.
- Intermediate' regions, which make up the majority of the rural land mass, and lie midway between the extremes of peripheral regions and economically integrated rural regions.
- Economically integrated regions, often close to large urban complexes, tend to have large farm units, a diversified economy, good services and relative affluence.

As pointed out earlier, in contrast to Industrial Heritage Tourism, Rural Tourism is normally a "complete", albeit unplanned, package of tourism facilities, comprising a range of accommodation facilities, a range of hospitality facilities, attractions both natural and man-made, retailing, and often co-ordinated information facilities provided by a local partnership, a local council or community. Almost all accommodation facilities will be privately owned, along with many of the attractions. Because of this, rural tourism can be, and often must be, more attentive to market demands. Equally, however, rural tourism benefits enormously from the work of the romantic poets, painters and composers of the past who have endowed us with an appreciation of nature, rural landscapes and open air recreation. Rural tourism owes much to Beethoven's 6 Symphony, William Wordsworth's nature poems, and the paintings of Germany's Caspar David Friedrich and Spain's Carlos de Haes.

THE DECLINE OF THE TERM AGRI-TOURISM?

Traditionally, agriculture was central to rural life. It was the main employer of labour, the main source of income within most rural economies, and indirectly the farming process and community had a powerful influence on traditions, power structures and life styles. Decisions made by farmers determined land use and landscapes.

Early forms of rural tourism were, not surprisingly, strongly linked to accommodation on farms. That linkage grew as farm diversification began to be officially encouraged in the 1960s and 70s. The use of the term agri-tourism became common, and some of the agricultural ministries of Europe supported agri-tourism development. But gradually, the term rural tourism has taken over, with agri-tourism becoming just one sub-sector of a more holistic rural tourism.

There are a number of reasons for this. As tourism developed in rural areas, it became clear that visitors might stay overnight in farms, but much of their time was spent away from farms, exploring the countryside in general, and villages and country towns in particular. And the central role of farming in the countryside continues to diminish.

By the early 1990s only five OECD countries employed more than 15 per cent of their labour force in farming, forestry and fishing: in eight OECD countries that figure was less than 5 per cent. Even the role of agriculturists as guardians of the traditional landscape has declined: farmers must now often ask planners and conservation agencies for advice and finance to carry out their landscape and nature conservation work. And many smaller farms are opting out of agriculture, and becoming full time tourism enterprises. The large farms that remain tend not to need tourism income. Meanwhile, there has been a surge in accommodation and attraction development in villages and small country towns.

WHAT WERE THE ORIGINS OF INDUSTRIAL HERITAGE TOURISM AND RURAL TOURISM?

The growth of both activities can be traced back to the late 1960s and early

70s and are products of economic and technical changes, which threatened the status quo of society, life styles and long existing economies.

Agricultural change threatened traditional farming patterns and techniques in much of the developed world. In 1968, Sicco Mansholt, then European Commissioner for Agriculture, suggested that small farms had no agricultural future.

The Mansholt Plan envisaged five million farmers giving up farming. Mansholt also noted that heavy industries – coal, iron and steel, textiles, and shipbuilding - were shedding enterprises and labour rapidly. These development trends helped create both industrial heritage tourism and rural tourism. Farms diversified to maintain their income: tourism was a way out of dependence on agriculture. It also helped to valorise and conserve rural areas themselves, their lifestyles and cultures. Industrial areas saw the creation of industrial heritage based on redundant heavy industrial plants and infrastructure. Tourism helped valorise and conserve aspects of vanishing heritage, lifestyles and cultures.

Conservation emerged as a key word. It is timely to recall Robert Shannon Peckham's words from 2003: "The prospect of loss haunts heritage"· That prospect became a powerful driver for the heritage industries and for heritage based tourism.

Nostalgia – for lost industrial and agricultural worlds - became a powerful force for conservationists and heritage tourism. That fear of loss is still important in tourism terms. It is partly behind the rise in food tourism. It manifests itself in political ways too. José Bové and François Dufour's book "Le monde n'est pas une merchandise" is simultaneously a manifesto for sustainable farming on traditional lines, a political document, and a romantic marketing presentation for rural tourism.

Both industrial heritage tourism and rural tourism have a purpose beyond simple economics. Both can act as a guardian of the physical record of the past, and as a justification for the conservation of that past. In 1990, Peter Keller, reporting to the Tourism Committee of the OECD, on *'Tourism Policy and Rural Development'*· wrote 'The countryside as a creative counterbalance to the hyper-civilised urban centre is no illusion... hill farmers must be kept on the land... highly developed economies should be able to afford the luxury of safeguarding typically rural areas'· Peter Keller was not a rural sociologist or a representative of the farming community: for over 30 years he was responsible for tourism policy at Switzerland's Federal administration.

In more detail, the growth of both industrial heritage tourism market and the rural tourism market reflects increased levels of public education and the interest and endorsement of both activities by the mass media. Both have also benefited from changes in the school curricula in many countries which now require knowledge of the recent past, of geography and environmental issues, and for many, some knowledge of the countryside.

The rural tourism market has two additional features. Most surveys reveal that both "peace and quiet" and access to nature are key attractions. Secondly, exercise – largely walking, but increasingly leisure cycling, and to some extent more extreme activity sports such as climbing, orienteering and similar pastimes, have become very popular. Much depends, however, on the legality of countryside access in specific nations. Britain, Germany, Austria, Switzerland and France for example have dense networks of footpaths and other routes, typically well mapped and signed, with relatively clear legal rights of access.

THE BENEFITS OF INDUSTRIAL HERITAGE AND RURAL TOURISM: AN ECONOMIC, ENVIRONMENTAL AND SOCIO-CULTURAL ANALYSIS

Both Industrial heritage tourism and rural tourism claim to offer benefits to the economy, to heritage protection, to local communities where they operate and to the wider society. While there is little evidence that this is not true, except in very specific circumstances, there is equally not a lot of evidence about exactly how effective their activities are in creating overall benefits.

The lack of evidence stems from:

- Poor, conflicting and numerous definitions of industrial heritage, of rural areas, of tourism, of tourism in general, of heritage tourism, and of rural tourism.
- Lack of statistical data and serious problems in collecting such data.
- Lack of funding for detailed single site, and especially for regional, research.
- The nature of tourism and visitation. A very large number of tourists take part in more than one form of tourism on any given trip, and often on any given day. A family might visit a cathedral in the morning, enjoy culinary tourism in a small city at lunchtime, ride a heritage tourism railway in the afternoon, include a visit to a nineteenth century woollen mill as part of that ride, and then spend the night in a farm. Even within that family, there will be very different interests and demands – as shown in the classic study of rural tourism by Palacio and McCool.

Despite the above, this section describes, assesses and discusses the existing and potential benefits of industrial heritage and rural tourism, according to their economic, environmental and socio-cultural impacts.

THE ECONOMIC IMPACT OF EUROPEAN INDUSTRIAL HERITAGE

Like many other tourism attraction sites of all kinds, industrial heritage sites generate income from visitors. Their primary income comes from entrance fees. But there are also numerous secondary incomes. The majority of site visitors are usually making day visits from their home: secondary, indirect income comes from food, beverage and retail spending, plus travel expenditure in the regions they visit. But, in many cases, by attracting day visits they add to the tourism 'offer' of an area and attract overnight visitors. These overnight visitors generate further secondary income for local areas in the accommodation and food and drink sectors; this is normally several times greater than their spending at the site alone and much greater than spending by a day visitor.

In addition, the direct spending by tourists at industrial heritage sites stimulates further spending by these organisations and their employees in the local economies. This *indirect* and *induced* spending can increase the total economic impact of tourism significantly. For example, a study of the West Somerset Railway, a heritage steam railway in south west England, estimated the value of the *multiplier* at 1.9. For every one Euro spent with the railway a further 0.9 Euros is generated in the local economy, almost doubling the value of the initial spending.

These conclusions were verified by a study of the impacts of the Ffestiniog and Welsh Highland Railways, in North Wales. Both railways are purely heritage tourism lines, with a combined length of 60 kilometres: the Welsh Highland railway has been recently rebuilt and reopened, 70 years after its closure as a conventional line. The primary income from the 128,000 passengers, 95 per cent of whom are tourists, is circa €6 million; secondary indirect and induced income injects an estimated €5 million more into the local economy. An estimated 12,000 of its passengers visit the area primarily because of the heritage railway. The peak gross income of the railway is forecast to be €14 million as the brand image and marketing work of the lines grows. The average firm in the rural area surrounding the railway employs 6.6 people: the railway employs the full-time equivalent of 60 people.

There is currently no single or comprehensive source of data on the impacts of the industrial heritage sector. The sector is highly diverse, in terms of size, governance and the industry involved. Some sites are small, preserving just one piece of heritage and rely wholly on unpaid volunteer support; others are much larger with a greater business ethos often combining a professional management and workforce with voluntary labour. Whilst some have grouped together to form national or international umbrella organisations others remain 'undiscovered', and membership of the national or international organisations is by no means comprehensive.

Given the diverse nature of industrial heritage and that many sites are small and unrecorded, there is no or limited data on the demand for and spending within the sector. There is also an overlap with other similar activities such as cultural heritage, archaeology, science and technology, built heritage, and museums. However, there are some studies that give an indication of the potential economic impact of industrial heritage sites and the associated tourism impact. A report by the Heritage Lottery Fund and VisitBritain *Heritage and the UK tourism economy* estimated that the total heritage sector is worth over €24 billion to the UK economy, supporting over 250,000 full-time-equivalent jobs. Although industrial heritage tourism is a small part of the overall heritage industry, it is likely to result in direct and indirect income of around €2.5 billion using the formula discussed later.

In 2010 a detailed study of the potential of industrial heritage tourism in the Brandenburg Region in Germany estimated its value to the region at €50 million annually. They also note the difficulty in estimating the level of employment created, partly due to the use of volunteers to undertake many tasks, but estimate the number to be below 500.

The world's largest railway museum, the UK National Railway Museum in York, attracts over 770,000 visitors annually. A recent study by the Yorkshire Tourist Board estimated that the museum brought almost €29 million expenditure within the county. Over half of this was from domestic and international overnight stays.

There are a number of approaches to estimating the demand for and the economic impact of industrial heritage tourism across the European Union. In general these fall into two categories, bottom-up or top-down. A bottom-up approach requires extensive data collection, normally on a site-by-site basis. Even if such data were available these normally include site admission charges and spending at sites but are less likely to include spending on accommodation, retail, transport, and food and drink away from the site.

A top-down approach relies on general tourism data which includes 'off-site' spending, but assumes that the characteristics are similar to the average tourist, which may or may not be the case. There is a lack of consistent European data in this area; therefore, a 'topdown' methodology has been adopted. This involves taking general data on tourism in Europe and refining this based on a series of assumptions. Through a progression of steps this enables an estimate of demand and economic impact to be estimated.

As discussed above one of the benefits of using a top-down approach is that the wider impacts of the tourism activity can be captured rather than just the direct spending at the site. For this study average spending figures from Demunter and Dimitrakopoulou have been used; €v349 for international tourists, €220 for domestic tourists and €28 for day visits. It is estimated that demand motivated by industrial heritage generates €4.8bn from overnight tourism and €4.1bn from day visits for local economies.

There is no definitive value for industrial heritage tourism to the European Union economy. This study has estimated its economic impact based on fractions of existing tourism flows. The total number of tourism trips and day visits motivated by industrial heritage in the EU is estimated to be approximately 157 million, with a direct spend of almost €9 billion annually.

Total impact is likely to be significantly larger when the indirect and induced impacts are taken into account. This is particularly the case for many industrial heritage sites which tend to be locally based with strong links to local communities, increasing the local economic impact·

THE ECONOMIC IMPACT OF RURAL TOURISM

The problems of data collection noted above are equally great for rural and agri-tourism. As a result, it is often not fully realised how strong the rural tourism sector can now be. In part that is because of the integration of many parts of the sector within other sectors.

Many farm accommodation enterprises are financially integrated into the agricultural activities of the farm: profits from accommodation are set off against losses on the farm. Visitor purchases in village and small town shops are not differentiated from local people's purchases. Visitor numbers are rarely recorded separately by public transport undertakings, yet they are often essential in maintaining viability; that is a very real problem when assessing the viability of rural railways, where a majority of tickets may be issued outside the rural railway at stations in large urban areas. In terms of jobs, the prevalence of pluriactivity in the rural tourism sector – (one person working in more than one job, and often in jobs in more than one sector) – makes accurate assessment of job numbers difficult.

The importance of rural tourism in the UK was only fully realised in 2001, when Foot and Mouth disease spread across the countryside and rural tourism was largely stopped by movement restrictions of various kinds. In calculating compensation measures, the government found that national rural tourism revenues in 2000 were estimated to be around €14 billion, compared to €18 billion from the agricultural sector. Rural and farm tourism in the UK employs over 380,000 people in 25,000 businesses. In many of the UK's rural regions, tourism is more important financially and in employment terms than farming.

EuroGites, the European rural tourism umbrella group, collected financial data from its member associations in 2008, and extrapolated that information to include known bed numbers from associations outside its membership. These calculations suggest that rural tourism supports 900,000 direct and indirect jobs in Europe, and generates €150 billion in gross income each year. These figures are estimates but there is currently no way of getting more definite statistics. It seems that they are unlikely to be wildly inaccurate – indeed they may be underestimates - when set against the few national statistics that we have for rural tourism. The UK government found that national rural tourism revenues in 2000 were estimated to be €14 billion. Government figures for 2009/ 2010 for England alone now show that rural tourism is worth over €34 billion, and accounts for over 12 per cent of rural employment: 10 per cent of rural businesses are tourism related.

The potential demand for rural tourism can be seen in the impacts of visitor numbers and tourism spending in Europe's protected areas, many of which are national parks. UK statistics show that the percentage of tourism related business and employment in National Parks is double that of rural England as a whole: in National Parks 27.5 per cent of businesses and 21.2 per cent of rural employment are tourism related· Similar figures have been reported for other parts of Europe. National Parks have strong brand image and obtain marketing benefit from that brand image: similar brand images could be created by skilled marketing for other – though not all – rural areas.

Rural tourism is, therefore, worth approximately 10 times in income terms that of industrial heritage tourism on the basis of the available statistics.

OTHER BENEFITS OF INDUSTRIAL HERITAGE TOURISM AND RURAL TOURISM

There are a range of other benefits to be found for both the above special interest tourism areas over and above income and job numbers. Some of these are discussed below:

New skills and training

Both types of tourism encourage people to train to gain new skills, especially in customer care, hospitality, IT skills and marketing. In the past, these areas were relatively unknown in declining industrial and rural regions. There are many anecdotal instances of tourism trained people then using their new skills to take other jobs, often in service industries or in manufacturing which has relocated to an area. In former coal and steel areas, this can be an important part of the de-industrialisation process, tourism helping to train a new type of service skill amongst workers. It begins the slow process of changing mindsets. Jones and Munday commenting about the Welsh industrial heritage town of Blaenavon note that it is on-going process for the Blaenavon Partnership even after 15years. It helps former coal and steel towns to become attractive for new industries.

Within some branches of industrial heritage tourism, special skills training linked to metal and wood working have evolved. Discussions with FEDECRAIL, and with heritage rail and heritage waterways operations, reveal a range of specialist skills training schemes operated in Austria, Belgium, Germany, the Netherlands and the UK. Some have prospered. Many have found problems in obtaining recognition from educational authorities, in working in partnership with educational organizations, and in finding national and European contacts with which to confer and learn. Comprehensive heritage conservation training schemes to allow qualified people to work in wood and metal for both historic buildings, machinery and equipment have been considered, although as yet none of these holistic schemes appear to have been successful. In the UK a privately financed and well publicised foundation, the Waterman Railway Heritage Trust, currently employs 30 apprentices through a government Jobs Fund Scheme aimed at 18–24 year olds who have been unemployed 6 months or more.

In Germany, the Meiningen Steam Locomotive Works in Thuringia is a major example of skills training and transfer linked closely to industrial heritage tourism. Originally opened in 1863, it is now the major centre for parts production for the over 3,000 heritage steam locomotives in Europe, along with heritage electric and diesel locomotives and rolling stock. From time to time it builds new or replica steam locomotives. It has become a major tourist attraction in its own right. It employs over 100 engineering specialists plus support staff.

Addressing depopulation

Depopulation has been a problem in rural Europe since the nineteenth century, linked largely to the decline in the agricultural workforce, and the tendency for manufacturing and services to concentrate in cities. Although, in principle, depopulation is not "wrong" as a rebalancing of population distribution, it increases congestion in urban areas, brings a depressed outlook in rural areas, and creates problems in maintaining rural services. Declining industrial areas now have similar issues. Rural tourism, and to some extent industrial heritage tourism, has begun to reverse that trend, directly through increasing local incomes, and employment, but also in other ways:

Service retention

As noted above, one of the problems in declining rural and urban areas is that of maintaining essential health, retail, educational, transport and other services for ever smaller populations. Tourism increases the local market for services and begins to create a virtuous rather than a vicious circle for service retention in these areas.

Attracting in-migration

While out migration and depopulation still goes on, a reverse and often equivalent flow of in-migration has been noted in many parts of rural Europe, and in some formerly declining industrial areas. Tourism has been responsible for part of that process, especially in rural areas. This process, known as counter-urbanization, owes much to the movement of life style entrepreneurs from cities to countryside, bringing with them capital, market knowledge, entrepreneurial skills and contact networks. This process, while owing much to tourism, is also linked to the spread of e-mail and internet communications, allowing distance working in many sectors.

Housing

The building sector has grown as a result of industrial heritage tourism growth, and especially because of rural tourism. Both have encouraged property improvements, extensions and some new build. In turn this is linked to rising property values. Tourism has created demand for re-using redundant farm and industrial properties for either overnight accommodation or for tourism linked retailing/workshop and food/beverage service purposes. In some cases, arts performance or heritage centres/museums have recycled redundant buildings. Rising property values help restore confidence in an area, although as noted later may become a problem in some cases.

Opportunities for women

In both rural and industrial areas, tourism development has brought employment opportunities for women in areas once dominated by male employment. This has increased participation rates, cut female outmigration, raised incomes and introduced new initiatives into communities – classic examples include the several women's co-operatives in Santorini, Crete, the Clatt community tea rooms in north – east Scotland, and many others.

Image building and synergies

Synergies between farm production and tourism has had beneficial effects on marketing and image building for both sectors, a development commented on by the OECD's pioneering studies in niche market development and picked up notably by the emergence of wine tourism.

Creating a focus for regional planning and regeneration initiatives

Tourism developments have begun to be chosen as key players within regional planning and regeneration initiatives, chosen for their ability to change the image of a region, attract potential life style entrepreneurs, make better use of heritage assets, increase employment, increase income and attract new capital. The best known use of industrial heritage tourism is that of Germany's Ruhr Industrial region but smaller scale initiatives include Blaenavon in Wales and Haslach in Austria which brings rural tourism and industrial tourism together.

Environmental benefits

Both industrial heritage and rural tourism can have environmental benefits, largely because they valorise environmental conservation and enhancement. Industrial Heritage tourism development has encouraged public sector and in some cases EU investment in the urban environment and in clearing contaminated and unsightly land in former industrial areas. Without the input and justification provided by rural tourism, the conservation of Europe's rural landscapes, ecosystems, built environments, communities and cultures would be hard to justify. Many more farmers now realise the value of landscape and wildlife conservation, and that rural environments can produce wealth through visitation rather than solely through food production.

Conservation is valorised by rural tourism. The wider community, urban and rural, requires traditional countryside for sport, physical and mental wellbeing and for educational purposes. There are now over 10,000 rural landscape and biodiversity protected areas in Europe, each requiring public sector financial and political inputs for conservation purposes. These inputs can be justified by the economic benefits flowing from tourism. The need for a strong linkage between the finances of protected area management and sustainable tourism was recognised and discussed by Shipp and more widely by Eagles. Ways to make those linkages work have been researched and outlined by Merkl, Emerton and Drumm.

Socio-cultural benefits

In socio-cultural terms special interest tourism has maintained social life and traditional ways of life in many areas.

Perhaps the most typical socio-cultural benefit in both rural and declining industrial areas is the recognition and celebration of past ways of life, giving relevance to the lives and memories of older inhabitants, and linking those lives to the present day and to the future. Local pride increases place attachment and place identity for both local people and visitors.

Secondly, many communities have gained considerable benefit from taking part in the development and management of local tourism, gaining community strength from that involvement·

A third benefit comes from "traditional" skills retention, be they agricultural, architectural or industrial. Loss of skills loses inter-generational links and begins a process of loss of authenticity and can mark the eventual end of the road for the conservation process. The founder of the traditional small craft heritage centre at Mystic Seaport, USA, a key early industrial tourism centre, the late John Gardner summed up the need for hands on socio-cultural conservation linked to tourism:

- "Museums for the most part are very short sighted ... interest in old boats and ships is bound to die out as the generations that were close to them pass away ... (and as for heritage in general ...) You can't preserve skills unless you acquire them, and the only way you can acquire and retain them is by practice, by use."

Three practical European examples of the John Gardner philosophy can be quoted. The Roskilde Viking Ship Museum's Boatyard in Denmark – has regenerated lost skills in traditional boat building through enlightened commercial use, building new "Viking" longboats. In Wales, the Big Pit at Blaenavon now trains heritage miners to a professionally certified level. In Italy the European Centre for Training Craftsmen in the Conservation of the

Architectural Heritage, Isola San Servolo, Venice, trains people in working on a range of heritage materials. But there is little coordination and rational expansion of this area of activity, and a European level approach could provide important economies of scale and networking opportunities. Heritage techniques training facilities can also become tourism attractions in their own right.

Finally there is a wider community benefit that needs to be stressed. Without tourism, much of our man made heritage would have been lost. Tourism has, when well-managed, become a great conserver. At the same time as it has created jobs, brought capital and income to declining areas, and acted as a conservation agent, it has enriched the lives of enormous numbers of people by giving them added insights into the past, and how people have managed their lives and their communities in the past. Industrial heritage and rural tourism have moved tourism on from rest, relaxation and sometimes hedonism to provide a thinking person's tourism, encouraging enquiry and understanding. In doing so, it has helped create new art forms – applied art of a special kind. That art form needs tourism to unlock its worth – national parks, eighteenth century canals, and heritage buildings are not transportable, cannot be auctioned like great paintings or sculptures.

DIS-BENEFITS

There can be some dis-benefits, especially in sensitive areas, arising from both industrial heritage tourism and to a much greater extent, from rural tourism development. Most can be reduced by informed management.

They include:

- Physical damage to fragile ecosystems can be created by too much unmanaged visitation. Krippendorf listed the main issues nearly 20 years ago. Loss of tree cover on mountain sides because of ski-run, road and car park construction leading to landslide and related erosion; trampling of vegetation by large numbers of hikers; the growing urbanisation of scenic areas; noise and litter disturbance to wildlife. Shipp extends the list of issues in Europe's protected natural areas - including pollution of water courses, air pollution and new types of damage created by mountain biking, rock climbing and orienteering and other technological developments.
- The arrival of incomers purchasing properties for second home use can be a problem, especially in conservation areas where new building is restricted. Competition for limited numbers of houses can increase house prices beyond the reach of local people. While planning and management measures can address that problem, they can be politically controversial.
- Loss of rurality: tourism can be an urbanising influence on the

countryside, encouraging cultural and economic change, and new construction.

- The economic stability of the rural world can be threatened by new, perhaps large scale, tourism businesses seeking short-term gains, upsetting labour markets and land values, and becoming powerful in the governance of the region.
- The cultural heritage of the countryside may be at risk from outsiders and powerful outside cultures.
- Visitors can now penetrate any and all rural regions, no matter how remote. The long-haul flight, the hire car, the 4-wheel drive vehicle, GPS, coupled with the power of television's travel programmes which seek new "undiscovered" areas – all present a challenge to the survival of traditional rurality – and to wilderness, a very rare and precious commodity in Europe.
- An over-reliance on tourism can create economic risks, given volatile exchange rates, growing competition from other tourism areas, and economic downturns.

While most of these dis-benefits can be addressed by management techniques there needs to be political will to devise and use them. That will is not always easy to bring to bear in some circumstances.

Finally it is important to comment on the popular belief that a more professional approach to these niche forms of tourism will result in loss of local character and regional diversity. There is no evidence to support that belief. In part that is because rural tourism is very much a micro-business activity that owes much of its character to the many thousands of individual entrepreneurs. The role of multi-national branded and standardised hotel chains is very small in this sector. In part, the huge variations in geography, climate and history across Europe act as a brake on trends towards uniformity. Many emergent niche products are built upon diversity and locality – food tourism is a classic example. And tourism management scholars are very much engaged in the search for, and retention of, local authenticity – Xie and Lane provide an entrée to this issue. It could be that professional management will seek to prevent rather than encourage regional uniformity.

CASE STUDIES

This section provides case studies designed to show the rich complexity of the issues surrounding industrial heritage and rural tourism. This is important: any European policy and/or initiative need to understand that complex background.

The studies do not follow an identical pattern in all cases. In part that is because they cover many very different organizations and subjects. In part it is because they are drawn from very many sources, and from a range of countries:

"official" sources rarely report to a common format, even within the same country. Those based on peer reviewed research have similar problems. Tourism is researched by agricultural researchers, business specialists, economists, ecologists, geographers, land use and regional planners, marketing specialists and sociologists as well as in over 140 specialist tourism research journals. Each specialises in different activities, and has different cultural and technical requirements.

INDUSTRIAL HERITAGE CASE STUDIES

Industrial Heritage tourism seeks, where possible, to:

- Conserve heritage *in situ,* and often in a relevant landscape or townscape, not taken away to a museum.
- Display *working heritage* – of great interest to visitors because it is working and very apt since industrial heritage is about work.
- Provide a link to a fast disappearing social and cultural heritage – it conserves "the arenas in which that... historic drama is salvaged and retold" –.

There is a complex and fascinating story to tell, peopled by remarkable characters.

Industrial heritage tourism was begun not by enthusiasts seeking to develop tourism but by enthusiasts seeking to conserve industrial heritage. Tourism was a way of financing conservation through entrance or user fees and an advantage when seeking public money to conserve heritage. Tourism has increasingly funded, and could further fund, industrial heritage conservation. The case studies illustrate the problems that industrial heritage tourism faces, and some of its great successes.

The selection of case studies was difficult. Key thematic areas were selected, and within those areas studies were taken to illustrate both common problems and good practice. *Coal Mining* based tourism was chosen because of the central role of the coal industry in Europe's industrial revolution, and the large scale, and financially demanding nature, of coal heritage tourism sites. *Textile industry* based tourism illustrates another major European heritage industry, very different to coal mining tourism, linking to art and design as well as to specialist machinery. Despite the importance of textiles to our daily lives, textile tourism requires very skilled marketing, product development and hands on interpreting facilities. An additional textile based case study can also be found at 5.3, a study of Haslach in Austria, an area that brings industrial heritage and rural tourism together.

Railway based tourism was chosen for its ubiquity, and its strongly visual and frequently hands-on attractiveness for many tourists. It is an activity that attracts many volunteers. Railway based tourism can also have a life after railway closure; railways can live on as walking, cycling and riding routes. The operation of an *outdoor industrial heritage museum* is described. A case study of Europe's premier industrial heritage tourism area, *Germany's Ruhr region* illustrates the use of industrial heritage as a powerful regional planning and regeneration tool. That study is followed by an analysis of a much lower key, but more typical, industrial heritage region in Germany, the *Brandenburg area*, setting out issues and possible solutions.

Some important study areas, including canal and maritime heritage tourism, have been omitted because of pressures of space.

Coal Mining-related Heritage Tourism

Mining is central to industrial heritage. Coal mining helped launch the industrial revolution. Europe's greatest industrial complexes were based on coal. Iron mining came second to coal as a major extractive activity.

Industrial heritage tourism linked to mining is, however, rare. The most interesting tourism mines are open to the public, underground and deep. They are all potentially dangerous. They require stringent and expensive safety precautions, expensive pumping systems to prevent flooding, forced air ventilation systems to remove gas and improve air quality, plus highly qualified staff. Public ownership in various forms seems the norm. The case study below illustrates these points.

In addition to many small surface museums, there are a few small-scale coal, iron and other heritage underground mines that are open to the visitation.

Examples include:

- The German Mining Museum - Das Deutsche Bergbau-Museum – in Bochum, North-Rhine Westphalia, one of the best visited museums in Germany, with approximately 400,000 annual visitors, is in public ownership and has an underground demonstration mine, especially constructed for visitation.
- Austria's Iron Ore Mine at Eisenerz, in Styria, offers summer only access to the now inactive underground mine – surface mining continues. Opened in 1986, it is in the ownership of a Foundation owned by the province of Steirmark, and operated by a local company. Visitor numbers are high at 80,000 per year during its operation from May to October. It offers underground tours, trips in adapted mega-transporters and observation of ore blasting.
- Italy's Talc and Graphite mine at Scopriminiera, 70 km from Turin, offers a museum and 3.5km of guided underground tunnel access

The Big Pit, Blaenavon, South Wales

The Big Pit at Blaenavon in South Wales is about 50 km, or an hour's drive, north–east from Cardiff. It is part of the Blaenavon World Heritage Site industrial heritage complex. It is a rare example of a deep coal mine open to the public with underground guided tours throughout the year. It is a major national attraction, and most visited part of the WHS.

The mine opened in 1860, producing coal for the local iron works and for distribution by rail around the UK and beyond. By 1910 it employed 1300 men. Employment slowly declined to 400 when it closed as a working mine in 1980. By 1983 it had reopened as a visitor attraction operated by a local Charitable Trust. It quickly became popular but had financial problems because of the need for capital investment in visitor facilities, and because of competition from other regional attractions. In 2001, it became part of the public sector National Museum of Wales, joining a slate mine and a small textile museum plus 5 other more conventional museums across Wales.

This study shows that high visitor numbers that can be achieved by a relatively remote site that is well financed, well marketed and well interpreted. It has access to skilled staff at the National Museum, who can afford to carry out and act upon the visitor research shown above. And visitors do not pay to enter the Big Pit. There is a large and interested audience for an authentic deep coal mine visitor experience. But such attractions appear to need constant public sector support. Despite many years of WHS management, Blaenavon has not become a full service resort, has no accommodation sector nor has it developed place attachment.

Becoming part of the National Museum gave the Big Pit access to capital investment, professional marketing and interpretation and to the national policy of free access to all visitors. A new shop, restaurant, a multi-media virtual gallery, a blacksmith's shop and state of the art interpretation centre complimented underground tours led by trained and experienced ex-miners. The Big Pit became a must-see part of the curriculum for most schoolchildren in Wales – and in adjoining parts of England. Visitor numbers peaked at 158,000, and are currently around 150,000 per year. Total turnover of sales and grants is now €2.4 million per year and 65 people are employed. A survey in 2008 suggests that the contribution of the Big Pit to the national economy is approximately €4.8 million per year. The Big Pit is an Anchor Point on the European Route of Industrial Heritage, and an enthusiastic member of ERIH.

A visitor survey taken in 2007 found that:

- All visitors travelled by car: 85 per cent came from within one hour's drive
- 32 per cent were on holiday; 68 per cent were day visitors from the local area
- Average length of stay was 2 hours 30 minutes
- 39 per cent were repeat visitors – a remarkably high figure

Main motives for visiting were:

- Recommended by friends etc., good reputation—28 per cent
- Wanted to experience history, etc.—20 per cent

- Wanted to show a visitor Wales and its heritage —18 per cent
- Free entry —20 per cent
- The children —9 per cent
- A day out —14 per cent
- Want to go underground —8 per cent
- Had a mining background/family —8 per cent
- Been before and liked it —10 per cent

Best liked features were:

- The guides —65 per cent
- It was free and offered so much —32 per cent
- Going underground —28 per cent
- The whole thing —25 per cent
- The galleries —24 per cent
- The darkness without lights —14 per cent
- The baths/interpretation —8 per cent

In both the above, interviewees could name more than one motive – hence these numbers add up to more than 100 per cent. Interestingly, the majority of visitors -over 80 per cent - were not influenced at all by the sites World Heritage Site status

Textile Industry Heritage Tourism

Textile heritage tourism is widespread in Europe. It is supported by an active group of artisan textile producers and enthusiasts. It finds the public hard to convince about its value as a tourism attraction, but there are many pointers which suggest that the situation could be improved by better market knowledge and marketing, better management and better interpretation.

The Audax Textile Museum Tilburg, The Netherlands

Textile production was a traditional industry in the eastern Netherlands; by the seventeenth century hand-loom weaving was well established in Tilburg. By 1881 there were 145 mills in the city.

Mills and mill buildings deeply influenced the life and townscapes of the region and especially in Tilburg. It employed many thousands of often highly skilled people. And then, in the 1960s, like other textile regions in Europe, the industry declined rapidly, with both domestic and export markets suffering price competition from low cost producers outside Europe. The majority of mills closed; many were demolished.

The Audax Textile Museum Tilburg honours that almost totally lost history. It has created a very special place, and potentially, an ideal industrial heritage tourism resource. More than any other textile industry heritage site, it has bridged the tantalising gaps between the textile production of the past, the present and future. It is revered by textile experts across the world.

It holds exhibitions and master classes; it has exciting educational links and courses in partnership with European institutions across Europe, and an exchange programme with the renowned American Textile Museum in Washington DC. It is a working museum: it produces avant garde textiles in full view of visitors. It is an aesthetic feast of colour and texture. And yet it is visited by relatively few tourists. This case study examines why this vibrant and valuable resource comes so close to being a model site – but yet does not quite achieve the holy grail of linking past and future for non-specialist tourists, of stimulating the minds of tens of thousands of potential visitors.

More prosaically, it is far from self-sufficient in financial terms. It is, however, important to say at the outset of this case study that the management of the museum is fully aware of these problems and is working on them. There are three key questions highlighted by this case study. First, financial resources are not a major problem, but lack of knowledge of the markets for industrial heritage tourism is major problem. Secondly, there is insufficient knowledge about how to supply the markets with the products that are wanted by those markets. But the third and key problem for the Museum lies beyond their immediate control. Tilburg does not try to attract visitors, despite the rise in city tourism noted earlier. The city's web site is unattractive, dull and unhelpful. There is no tourism development campaign. Without an active city/regional tourism marketing campaign it is difficult for industrial heritage sites to attract visitors from beyond the local area. Linkages between tourism and heritage interests are essential.

The Museum's past

The museum was founded in 1958, moving to larger premises, Mommers former textile mill, in 1982. It expanded further, and in 2008 a stunning ultra-modern glass based entrance building was added, housing a reception, cafe/restaurant, expanded shop, and a range of conference and exhibition rooms.

The museum has always prided itself on being a working museum. While it has an important archive collection of textiles, machines and documents, it is also a place where the visitor can watch artists and technicians producing exciting new works. It buzzes, if quietly, with activity.

The museum was originally founded by the Tilburg City Council. In 2002, it became a non-profit foundation that brought together three other Tilburg museums – the Tilburg City Museum, the De Pont museum of contemporary art, and the Scryption museum for written communication. The City Council continues to fund 70 per cent of the textile museum's expenditures. Annual turnover is around €5 million.

Visitation and the Future

The museum had 50,000 visitors in 2011, a number below its peak. It is far less than a visitor attraction of its size and location would expect: at least 100,000 should be a possibility. There are 40 paid staff (some working in textile production), and about 50 volunteers.

Why does the Museum attract so few visitors?

This museum is a case study of a living museum, connecting the past with the future, and doing many things well. But it is also a case study of the problems which hold industrial heritage tourism back from attaining its full potential. It is a wonderful place for those who know about textiles. Its staff know about textiles: they do not seem to know about tourism.

The main issues are presented below:

- Not all industrial activities are suited to tourism. Textiles are not an easy subject to attract visitors. There are few members of the public who know about how textiles are made. The last mills in the Netherlands closed over 40 years ago – the local nostalgia market is not strong. Special efforts must, therefore, be made to attract people and to get place attachment and repeat visits.
- The museum is a must-see for textile specialists. The museum assumes that it is relevant to the average person: it does not, however, offer a "layered" programme of interpretation, attractive to different types of people.
- There appear to be few exhibits/activities for families with children, normally a strong market for museums of all types.
- While textile production can be seen, it is not explained in a way that is accessible to non-textile specialists. The technicians are, rightly, too busy to speak to visitors. There could be, however, many alternative ways of making useful contact.
- Welcome is weak. This is a common problem and could be easily solved by well trained volunteers.
- The number of volunteers is not very large: it could be much larger. For an example of a very successful technical museum with a very successful volunteer programme, go to the Sydney Power House Museum web site·
- It is widely known in museum and gallery circles that the cafe and shop are of great importance in attracting visitors and raising revenue, even from people who do not visit the museum. The layout of the entrance area does not allow this to happen, and the atmosphere of both cafe and shop are not stimulating.
- The museum is largely explained for Dutch speakers only. Yet Tilburg is situated close to large numbers of German and French speakers, and many other nationalities can speak English.
- The Museum is hard to find. It is signed off the main ring-road, but

with a few small signs, using thin blue script on a white background, scarcely legible for drivers concentrating on traffic. Brown Signs are used for tourism purposes in many European countries, and are much more legible.

- Once close to the museum, it is again hard to find, being set back from the road. Surprisingly, there are no large hanging textile banners which are now readily available, and are used, for example, very successfully by the Canadian Textile Museum in Toronto.
- There are no obvious links between the four museums within the foundation – even though one of them is close to the textile museum. They could share marketing, practice synergy marketing, become the Tilburg Museum Quartet.
- The museum is less than 130 km from the German border. German museums have been revolutionised in recent years, not least by the "Long night of the Museums" concept. There is little sign of German ideas here·
- There appears to be no Visitor Experience Plan, no Interpretation Plan, and no Marketing Strategy. This is not uncommon in museums, and often reflects the training of Museum Directors which centres on Curatorship.

Railway Heritage Tourism

Railway heritage tourism is widespread and often seen as the jewel in the crown of industrial heritage tourism. This section includes examines a successful heritage railway, a rail route that is now a cycle and walking trail but retains its heritage infrastructure, and a brief discussion about using conventional railways as heritage routes.

The West Somerset Railway, UK

The 33km West Somerset Railway, in south west England was completed in 1874, linking the seaside town of Minehead via rural communities to the county town of Taunton and connections for London. It closed in 1971, but was re-opened by a group of local people and enthusiasts as a heritage line in 1976. They were supported by the Somerset County Council who purchased the track and land of the railway as a strategic investment and now leases the line back to the West Somerset Railway.

This study shows that railway heritage that responds to market niches in a professional way and that works closely with tourism agencies and other providers, can be very successful. It also indicated the value of local community links and the enormous value of a highly developed and sophisticated volunteer programme. The railway is a public limited company; this status enables the company to gain a licence for railway operations and it remains connected to the national rail network. Although trains stop short of the national network for technical reasons, the physical connection remains, allowing summer season charter trains to the line.

The railway operates from February to November, with additional trains in December and between Christmas and the New Year bringing extra income. There are 4 daily trains each way in low season and 7 in high season. Many, but not all, trains are hauled by heritage steam locomotives. There are in the region of 200,000 passengers per year, with August the peak month with approximately 42,000 passengers. The line is ranked in the top 10 of the UK's heritage railways, and recognised as an example of best practice management.

In synthesis, the West Somerset Railway's location, near to both resident and holiday populations is critical to its success. As a 'stand-alone' attraction it would be unlikely to draw many visitors, other than enthusiasts and those arriving on charter services, from further afield. It works very closely with other tourism providers and agencies.

The use of volunteers – in common with many forms of industrial heritage - is very important. The railway would not be financially viable without the volunteer workforce, which is used for both highly skilled and less demanding jobs.

The railway uses a complex fund raising and ownership system which has been very successful. It is a viable company, requiring no direct public support for its operations. It has a large reserve fund and added €190,000 to that fund in 2011.

Marketing

The railway produces an annual marketing plan for the year's special events and the scheduled services. Both traditional paper and Internet based marketing is used, with information/timetable leaflets distributed to all local accommodation providers.

The railway's web site has full details of scheduled services and special events; they also have a Facebook and Twitter presence. The railway attends trade shows, where they represent West Somerset tourism as well as themselves. They have a director's seat on the Somerset County Tourism Association and chair the marketing sub-group of the Exmoor Tourism Partnership; they also work with tourist information centres and tourism officers in the wider region. They participate in Visit England campaigns and research.

The railway's location is central to its success. The region is one of the UK's most popular holiday areas, with in excess of 20 million overnight visitors and 141 million day visits annually. It is within less than two hours travelling time of the Bristol region with its population of around 900,000 and Exeter, with around 140,000 people. The railway is a working heritage experience for the important day visit market. It works closely with other tourism providers, offering tickets packaging the railway with entrance fees for specific local attractions, thus broadening its market and assisting other local tourism attractions.

Employment and volunteers

The railway has 45 full and part-time staff and is supported over 1,000 volunteers. Without volunteers the railway would not be financially viable. Volunteers are used throughout the organisation; the railway employs no engine drivers, all are trained volunteers.

Social benefits

The railway has good relationships with local communities. Some village stations have been adopted by local communities; as well as developing community pride in those facilities, small station shops/cafés run by local people raise funds towards station maintenance.

Although the railway spent approximately €18,000 last year on external training it undertakes most training 'in-house'. As well as developing 'softer' skills (*e.g.* customer service through *welcome host* courses), many volunteers learn heavy engineering skills in the railway's workshops, including welding and machine tool operation. This builds local social and skills capital, a factor often overlooked when assessing the value of heritage tourism.

Income, funding and economic impact

The railway's turnover exceeds €3 million annually. Although a public limited company there is no profit distribution; all surpluses are retained for future investment. The total economic impact of the railway on the local economy, including direct, indirect and multiplier effect is €5.7 million.

The railway also raises funds through its membership of approximately 4,700 supporters and through share issues. Membership levels has been falling, whilst support for share issues, and legacies have increased. The latter two are used solely for capital projects; membership fees are treated as revenue. Both forms of support are encouraged by a sophisticated system of offering free or low price tickets.

In common with many other heritage railways in the UK a number of locomotives are privately owned by enthusiasts either personally or through enthusiast groups, reducing the railway's capital costs and maintenance risks.

Where possible the railway supports local suppliers, for example local beers are highlighted on buffet menus. This increases the indirect economic impact of the railway in the local economy. In a reciprocal arrangement, the railway promotes local accommodation providers on their web site who earn a small commission as ticket agents for them.

External issues

New regulations, from the Office of Rail Regulation and Rail Accident Investigations Branch, have increased the administrative burden on the railway. Not only has this increased the importance of maintaining more detailed records and audit trails, it has also limited the type of work some volunteers are able to undertake unless they have the necessary safety critical training and can demonstrate appropriate competency.

Vias Verdes: Spanish Greenways

A remarkable feature of railway heritage is that it can be valuable for tourism even when the train service has ceased. The post 1960s reduction of the European railway network made redundant much rail-related industrial heritage, but left a huge legacy of unused traffic free rights of way. There began a random process of either losing the heritage and selling off rights of way and land for development, or using the disused routes for cycle/pedestrian/equestrian leisure and tourism as "greenways" with great tourism potential.

In the USA this problem and opportunity was tackled from 1986 onwards by the creation of a non-profit organization, the Rails to Trails Conservancy, aided by federal tax breaks and land banking legislation, backed by a membership of over 150,000 supporters. It has created 20,000 miles of traffic free routes at 1,400 sites. This idea has taken place only piecemeal and on a very small scale in Europe. This case study looks at a Spanish state initiative that seized this major opportunity before heritage and routes were lost.

The Vias Verdes programme in Spain was launched in 1993 to assess and plan the use of closed railway routes for non-motorised transport. The Minister for Public Works, Transport and Environment, together with the two state railway companies RENFE and FEVE, commissioned the Spanish Railway Foundation to audit disused railway lines. This identified 98 lines totalling 5,700 km and over 900 stations. An additional 89 privately owned former mining and industrial lines were also identified. This took the total to around 7,600 km of abandoned railway lines across Spain. The case study illustrates the ways in which much can be learned from a knowledge of non-European approaches to industrial heritage, and that heritage assets can be "recycled" to great effect, with tourism acting as a catalyst to valorise that recycling process. The advantages of effective co-operation with national backing are also clearly demonstrated.

The FFE was given on-going responsibility for creating the Vias Verdes from these disused lines. Working in partnership with local and/or regional authorities a detailed viability plan is produced including current ownership, design requirements for visitor use, and future management and maintenance arrangements. The latter can take a number of forms; local, provincial or regional authorities, communities, or through consortia, companies or foundations established specifically for this role. Over 90 greenways have now been created covering 1,900 km.

They offer good surfaces and gentle gradients suitable for cycling, walking and disabled users. There has been no consistent monitoring across the Vias Verdes, but the Girona Greenways Consortium estimated that the Carrilet Via Verde which runs from the foothills of the Pyrenees to the Costa Brava attracts around 1 million visitors a year including around 23,000 tourists from outside the region. This may seem a small number but given *"the area through which the greenway passes is relatively undeveloped in terms of tourism and 23,000 tourism-related trips is an important figure considering the size of the local tourism industry"*.

Heritage Preservation

In addition to working with Vias Verdes the FFE has a wider responsibility to identify, restore and conserve Spanish railway heritage, including cultural elements. It supports the work of the Museo del Ferrocarril de Madrid – Delicias and the Museo del Ferrocarril de Cataluña-Vilanova i la Geltrú in conserving the documentary heritage of the railways.

The development of the Vias Verdes has secured the future of a large amount of railway infrastructure, including over 500 tunnels and 1100 viaducts. About 60 former railway station buildings have been renovated and converted to hotels, information centres, museums, restaurants and bike hire centres.

Marketing

Most of the marketing for individual routes is undertaken by the regional authorities, in common with most tourism marketing in Spain.

In 2000 the FFE launched the Vias Verdes web site· This provides online maps, background information, contact details and route guides. Three detailed route guides have been published, covering over 2,000 km of routes. These are currently only available in Spanish: most of the current demand is domestic. In 1999 an annual *National Vias Verdes Day* was launched, typically on each second Sunday in May. Events are organised by the different consortia for each route encouraging local people to walk and cycle on the routes; these are often supported by local dignitaries or professional cyclists. All routes use standardised signing; Lumsdon *et al* identified this as important for tourism users of cycle routes. Route markers show the Vias Verdes logo, display route information and often use old railway furniture such as sleepers, thus reinforcing the heritage connections.

Social benefits

In addition to encouraging the active involvement of local communities in their development and providing a valuable resource for healthy recreation for residents, the restoration of redundant industrial assets improves the local environment which is valued by users and non-users alike. In a study comparing the costs of traditional recreational facilities, such as sports centres and swimming pools, Palau *et al* concluded *"that investment in the improvement, development and maintenance of the greenways offer far superior returns per use for the public authorities administering sports facilities."* A survey undertaken on routes near Girona in Catalonia found that on average 50 per cent of users were women walking and cycling for up to an hour, who are traditionally less likely to engage in active recreation than men.

Tourism Issues

Vias Verdes is a good model for the preservation of railway heritage and provides a valuable resource for local communities that has been lost in many other countries. However the FFE's remit limits its ability to extend its work beyond the preservation of railway infrastructure and this prevents it from linking up with other long-distance or local networks of walking/cycling routes.

The Danube Cycle Path in Germany and Austria, part of EuroVelo-Route EV6' is the most popular cycle route in Europe, reputedly with a million users per year, with many tourists from all over Europe and beyond. Guide material is available in many languages. Because the web site can only partly function in languages other than Spanish, and because the guides are only in Spanish, the Vias Verdes are not yet fully used as a tourism resource. Its potential could be considerable in spring and autumn because of Spain's climate advantage in those periods.

Operational railways as Heritage Tourism

Most discussion about industrial heritage railway tourism refers to railway lines outside conventional passenger operations, typically railways operated by heritage preservation groups. Heritage tourism can also take place on "standard" operational lines with imagination and initiatives, boosting both rail use and heritage tourism. The value of taking a broad view of industrial heritage tourism development - going beyond the museum concept - emerges here, coupled with knowledge of international ideas, and the key role of market knowledge to guide product development.

The world leaders in using operational railway are to be found in the USA. *Trails and Rails* is an innovative partnership programme between the National Park Service and Amtrak, providing rail passengers with educational opportunities that foster an appreciation of a selected region's natural and cultural heritage. The programme links cities and National Parks and provides audio heritage interpretation on selected trains, with texts designed by staff from Texas A&M University. In 2011, 371,865 Amtrack passengers participated in *Trails and Rails* on 1,580 trains.

Attempts at similar programmes have been made on UK railways but have failed because of train operating company disinterest, opposition from trade unions and lack of funding. The Association of Community Rail Partnerships – a federation of over 50 community rail partnerships and rail promotion groups in the UK - has worked on a number of ideas to overcome related problems, and been successful in promoting increased use of railways for rural tourism, and encouraged local groups to "adopt" and look after a number of heritage stations. They have also developed rail linked walking and cycling routes, brought station buildings back to life, and encouraged art and education projects. A German equivalent of ACORP is currently in discussion.

Research on rural tourism use of rural rail lines in UK by Dallen found that up to 60 per cent of rural rail users were tourists, and that 37 per cent of users had a special heritage related attachment to using trains.

Finally, it is worth noting that heritage rail operation, using volunteer staff, mixes successfully with modern scheduled operation in at least one case in Europe. In Stockholm a modern company operated tram system using 30 metre long cars, line S7, from the City Centre to Djurgården, the city's museum area, shares operations with a volunteer operated heritage tramway using trams up to 100 years old. Over 2 million passengers have used the heritage trams since 1991 without problems.

The Industrial Heritage Museum

Beamish - The Living Museum of the North

Although industrial heritage tourism is typically found on former industrial sites, there are some cases of successful museum development. This case study looks at a very special type of Industrial Heritage Museum which is recognised as a world leader: the re-created replica open air museum. It examines Beamish in north-east England, situated between the cities of Newcastle and Durham. The purpose of this case study is not to describe the museum in detail, nor to look at the ethics and many issues involved in recreating a "living" past, but to look at the managerial and financial issues of this form of industrial heritage, and as a source of ideas for the development of industrial heritage conservation and tourism. Beamish's experience shows that industrial heritage sites – if well designed and well managed – can be sustainable economically, and can contribute positively to regional incomes. Beamish has strong market knowledge and works very closely with regional tourism stakeholders. Beamish is a special case because of its size and expertise. However, groups of smaller sites working in partnership could achieve similar results. (Beamish is considering setting up a consultancy company to advise others.)

The north-east of England was a major and proud industrial region specialising in coal, steel, shipbuilding and associated engineering. As early as

1958, the idea of a museum to commemorate the region's industrial past was discussed: it was set up in 1970 by the four major local government units in the region. The 120 hectare site was opened in 1972. It has over 300,000 objects in its collection. It focuses on the region's industrial heritage, largely from the period 1800 – 1940. It includes a small number of buildings originally on the site: the majority of the buildings are, however, either relocated buildings from the region or newly built replicas. It has a range of streets, costumed interpreters, working exhibits, shops, and uses period buses and trams to carry visitors around the site. Purists were and are shocked by it. In his polemic against the heritage industry, Hewison described it as "more real than the reality it seeks to recall... a lovingly reconstructed fake". It has, however, been a market success.

While still controlled by local government, the museum operates as a charitable foundation with its income coming from a separate trading company in order to be tax efficient.

After its opening in 1972, visitor levels grew to around 500,000 per year by 1989, and then declined slowly to 300,000. The Tourism Area Life Cycle – see earlier at 2.1 - was in operation. By 2008 the cost of running the museum was close to €5.4 million per year. It was close to an operating deficit. The museum employs 240 paid staff and has approximately 150 volunteers, and it faced a common problem for most forms of industrial heritage that repairs to major items of working heritage machinery and to heritage buildings can be very expensive. At the same time, public sector spending cuts made it imperative that it covered its full operating costs, plus a surplus for future repairs and improvements. A special programme was put in place to solve its problems, based on principles that many other heritage sites might consider.

They included:

- Reviewing their weaknesses and treating them as opportunities.
- Creating a detailed recovery plan which positioned the visitor at the heart of the business, carried out market research, sought to increase visitor numbers, offer better value and address seasonality – especially the low level of winter visitation. The detail is important -no single action could have recovered the museum from its serious situation.

In detail, Beamish:

- Created many more events and special exhibitions to attract repeat visits.
- Concentrated those events in the winter "low" season.
- Changed ticketing policies to offer tickets at a slightly higher price that would allow unlimited visits for a year. That gave a strong incentive for repeat visits. Surveys show that repeat visits result in additional expenditure on food and retail sales.
- Offered low priced "one visit" winter tickets to tempt new visitors.

- Worked with local/regional hotels to encourage low season short breaks linked to Beamish, to attract tourists from beyond the region.
- Developed heritage eating, including a coal fired traditional fish and chip shop.
- Developed its retailing activities.
- Developed new programmes for the school market and other groups, an important source of low season visitation.
- Improved staff training.
- Attracted and trained more volunteers.
- Sought and received capital funds from the Heritage Lottery Fund and the Arts Council to develop new exhibits.
- Began to open at night for special events.
- Developed outreach events in a range of regional centres.
- Introduced better public transport links and shuttle buses: this is especially important in the UK because people over 65 years old can travel free on local buses – opening up a potentially large pensioner market.
- Considered developing its own accommodation.
- Raised its profile and its marketing work.

Visitor numbers recovered to 498,000 by 2012, despite the recession. Earned income recovered to €7.2 million in 2011, allowing €720,000 to be added to the reserves.

The important figures to note are those for catering, the new fish and chip shop, and retail sales. It is no longer enough to have industrial heritage. The whole site has to be operated as a visitor experience – and a holistic experience includes eating and shopping.

Tourism

Beamish was planned as a regional museum, with its catchment area limited to the northeast. It is now a long distance tourism attraction, with 68 per cent of Beamish's visitors arriving from outside the north-east region in 2010/11. Of those 55 per cent came specifically to visit Beamish; 87 per cent of those– 215,000 people – stayed in serviced accommodation or campsites and 60 per cent stayed in hotels. The income from the over 120,000 people staying in hotels would alone have been enough to cover all Beamish's operating costs, an indicator of industrial heritage's potential to boost local economies.

Regenerating Communities and Regions Through Industrial Heritage Tourism

The Ruhr Tourism Region

The Ruhr region of Germany is probably the biggest collection of industrial heritage in Europe. It was Europe's largest industrial region, with 300 coal mines operational by 1850. That coal was exported to other parts of Europe and worldwide, used locally to develop a very major iron and steel industry, and to provide power for numerous manufacturing plants. The population of the Ruhr metropolitan area is now over 5 million, in 53 towns and cities: only four working mines remain. It is one of Europe's top 6 urban regions. It has witnessed a considerable outflow of population to parts of Germany deemed more attractive, and an outflow of industrial production. But it has also become Europe's largest urban regeneration area, a process on-going for over 20 years, beginning with the International Building Exhibition at Emscher Park in 1989. Industrial Heritage Tourism has become a vital part of that regeneration process, changing attitudes, changing the image of the Ruhr, and providing jobs and financial inflows.

Within the concept of the Ruhr as a region capable of attracting tourists, there are a number of key ideas:

- That changing the image of a region can help retain and attract people, enterprises and visitors.
- That the industrial past should be understood and celebrated as living history and as a series of art forms.
- Retaining and re-using industrial buildings for tourism and other purposes can be both a "green" solution to recycling and retaining local character and can build brand and place attachment.
- That the industry-linked culture of the region should be recognised and used.
- That investment in the arts and cultural industries can pay dividends in terms of image changing, regeneration and tourism, and that former industrial buildings can provide a unique stage for art and culture.
- That regeneration and tourism should be approached on an active regional partnership basis, not just on a site by site basis.

The dream is expressed in an amended extract about the Ruhr's Emscher Park project "The region's massive and muscular industrial structures are now filled with art, culture, housing, commerce and offices. Concerts are staged in the ageing steel frames of former factories. Grassy recreational areas complete with hiking trails and climbing walls, have been sculpted from the old hills of coal pilings. Cycle and walking paths through glades of trees linking the many different components of the park follow the former industrial roads and rail lines".

The Ruhr has a long history of regional planning dating from the SVR (Siedlungsverband Ruhrkohlenbezirk) of 1920, which planned housing and open space across the region, through to the Regionalverband Ruhr of 2004, which extended the regional remit to include developing the regional image as well as regional planning of the built and natural environment. These grand partnerships all aimed to pool the low purchasing power of the many small municipalities within the Ruhr, improve derelict landscapes and overcome the legacies of the region's structural transition. Tourism development based on its industrial legacy is seen as selling an authentic and attractive Ruhr regional image, creating something special, reducing travel away from the region and thus boosting the local economy while bringing visitor income from Germany and beyond.

The resultant policies of cultural, recreational and tourism development resulted in €2.5 billion being invested – 80 per cent of it from the public sector – between 1982 and 1999, and the eventual creation of Ruhr Tourismus, a process that began in 1998 with Ruhrgebiet Tourismus Gmbh, leading to Ruhr Tourismus Gmbh in 2009, owned by the RVR, bringing together in partnership the tourism marketing, product development and event planning for the whole region – acting as an umbrella organization rather than supplanting the work of tourism organizations across the 53 local authorities in the region. It also acts as a tour operator, ticketing agency and event organiser. It has a staff of 36.

Ruhr Tourismus uses the concept of the *Die Metropole Ruhr*, the Ruhr Metropolis, as a brand name to emphasise the region's importance, its new and fashionable approach to the past and the future. Its web site opens with the following words:

"During your trip to the Ruhr metropolis, you may choose from 3,500 industrial monuments, 200 museums, 120 theatres, 100 cultural centres, 100 concert halls and 2 famous musical theatres – an exciting composition of culture and entertainment "

Note that industrial monuments come first. But they are not alone, industrial heritage alone does not make a destination – see the earlier study of Tilburg's Textile Museum.

Ruhr Tourismus has been successful. Much of that success come from intensive and ongoing market research, market linked branding policies, excellent web sites, and a strong "can-do" mentality. The work of the organization can be judged from its valuable detailed review and strategy document for 2012-2016. It has seen 10 per cent year on year tourism growth in bed nights in recent years, and 49 per cent growth over the decade 2000-2010, well above the all-Germany growth rate of 29 per cent for that period. A total of 6.8 million bed nights were achieved in 2011. Industrial heritage experiences scored well in several visitor surveys – but so did shopping possibilities, events, sport, parks and theatre, reinforcing the point that industrial heritage tourism does best when accompanied by other activities. This is not a peculiarity of industrial heritage tourism – it also applies to nature tourism and to a range of other situations.

One of the Ruhr's major achievements was to have Metropole Ruhr chosen as Europe's Cultural Capital 2010 alongside Istanbul and Pecs in Hungary. More prosaically, but of enormous practical significance, was the introduction in 2011 of the Ruhr TopCard, a prepaid chip card giving free entry to over 90 attractions and half price admission to many more. This helps ensure longer stays and can reduce carbon emissions by helping retain the local population in the region.

Could the Ruhr Tourismus concept be introduced elsewhere and on a smaller scale? There seems no reason why not. A similar small scale company was created recently by the several local governments working along the Hadrian's Wall Roman site in the UK some years ago. Hadrian's Wall Heritage Ltd, a company limited by guarantee, aims to make the most of the Wall for its community and region, while ensuring the conservation of Hadrian's Wall·

Specific Examples

Two specific examples of the remarkable re-use of industrial heritage should be mentioned amongst many.

The Oberhausen Gasholder/Gasometer Oberhausen

The largest disc type gasholder in Europe, a huge cylinder 118 metres high and 68 metres in diameter, was completed in 1929 as part of the gas control and storage system for the local iron works. It became redundant in 1988. It had become not just industrial heritage but a local and regional landmark. By 1994 it had been converted into two huge exhibition and performing spaces, hosting up to 500,000 visitors each year·

The Zollverein Coalmine and industrial Complex

The Zollverein coal mine complex, opened first in 1847 and completed in 1932, with an ultimate working depth of 1200 metres, was closed for production in 1983. The enormous site, with its famous Bauhaus style pit head gear dating from 1932, was in danger of clearance but was purchased by the regional government in 1986 as an historic monument, and is now controlled by a foundation. It became a World Heritage Site in 2001. It now acts as a heritage site, museum, gallery, shop and restaurant – with an all time visitor total of 2.2 million in 2010 – when part of Europe's capital of culture. 2011 was a more "normal" year with 1.5 million visitors·

Industrial Heritage Tourism in Brandenburg, Germany

This review, based largely on a consultancy study is included as a contrast to the case study of the Ruhr area. The Brandenburg region, though close to Berlin, still suffers deprivation from its time in the German Democratic Republic.

A consultancy study explored what could be done to use its industrial heritage to improve its position. The situation revealed is typical of very many regions. Equally, the answers to the problems are typical of an effective informed partnership development approach likely to work in most parts of Europe, and reflects the need to add tourism skills to conservation skills at most sites. The existence of a small number of well-run sites found in Brandenburg, against a background of many less professional sites is quite usual, as is the need to restrict the number of sites to avoid oversupply and market failure. Themed, layered and relevant interpretation was found to be essential – which in turn requires a basic knowledge of the market segments involved, and linkages to marketing strategies.

Brandenburg is one of Federal Germany's 15 semi self-governing regions; it surrounds, but does not include, the capital city, Berlin. It has a population of 2.5 million, on a land area of 25,000 square kilometres. Never heavily industrialised, it nevertheless has 3 major industrial heritage sites and at least 88 other recognised sites. The survey results discussed here were based on a postal questionnaire to 79 sites followed by 10 semi-structured interviews with key players in the region.

Key survey findings included:

- Industrial heritage is widespread and varied: it concentrates on open cast brown coal production, textile production and brick production.
- 60 per cent of the replies came from museums.
- Half of all the sites have only opened to visitors in the last 10 years.
- Most sites are not open every day.
- 75 per cent of sites charge an entrance fee; most are €5 or less.
- Most sites had exhibitions and/or events.
- Together the 58 sites have 900,000 visitors per year, 8 sites accounted for over half of the 900,000; 61 per cent of sites had less than 10,000 visitors each year.
- Modern interpretation methods (audio guides, print materials in a range of languages etc.) were rare, but most sites did offer guided tours.
- Transport between sites is not easy. Marketing linkages between sites are few.
- Signing was not good.
- The main audiences were school groups, families with children and the over 50s.
- Most sites relied on web sites and print materials for marketing. Marketing was very limited with 75 per cent of sites having an annual budget of under €5,000.
- The average number of paid employees was 6, plus volunteers.

The key points made in the interviews were:

- Many sites were aimed at educating and informing local people about their local history rather than tourists.
- It was felt that the region has greater potential for tourism growth if marketing was improved.

- One part of the region, the Lausitz, was the only area with high potential, with its concentration of sites and good transport links to Berlin.
- The tourism agencies and authorities knew little about industrial heritage and gave it low priority. Heritage sites had weak links to tourism agencies.
- There was no organization or network responsible for improving or developing industrial heritage tourism.
- Tourism infrastructure was poor, with insufficient hospitality and accommodation, information and interpretation.
- Shortage of trained staff and shortage of younger guides.

Possible solutions to these problems included:

- The creation of a forum to take forward the idea of a development network and to lead in introducing innovations.
- Better marketing and linked marketing between sites.
- Staff training about tourism and working with tourists.
- Better links between sites and the tourism industry and vice versa.
- Concentration on improving existing sites rather than creating more sites.
- The development of themes and story lines.
- Concentration on specific markets especially the schools market.
- More use of sites for events.

Staff training is especially interesting because it is part of the task of re-skilling industrial society and changing mindsets, commented on in section 4.3, and backed by a number of researchers. Staff training although required for tourism can contain key transferrable skills for many other sectors.

RURAL TOURISM CASE STUDIES

Rural tourism differs from industrial heritage tourism in that it covers not just sites used as tourist attractions, but the entire span of the tourism phenomenon – from accommodation through food and drink to sites and the wider culture of a heritage region. And yet rural tourism can have very low capital investment demands compared to industrial heritage tourism. Occasionally rural tourism forms a hybrid with industrial heritage tourism – a theme discussed in the railway studies earlier in this report and covered in the Haslach, Austria study at the end of this section.

Rural tourism has pioneered a range of innovative ideas. It has seen the notion of establishing a rural area's Carrying Capacity for tourism overtaken by Limits of Acceptable Change. It has worked on the ideas of local tourism development groups, local and regional sustainable tourism strategies, trails, rural festivals, nature and ecotourism and many other discussions and techniques. And it has moved on to the concept of second generation rural tourism as a possible way forward to beat off competition from other types of destination. It is an ideas-rich subject. But it suffers from fragmentation, from being a grouping of thousands of micro businesses. Within rural tourism, agri-tourism plays a strong role in farm diversification and heritage landscape conservation. Farm tourism is closely involved in a new, fast growing, tourism area - food tourism.

Rural tourism has also developed a range of local development groups, and series of national agri/rural tourism marketing organizations. One of these organizations, Austrian Farm Holidays, is featured here.

Accommodation is a central theme of all rural tourism – offering strong opportunities for economic gain, for conserving historic buildings as well as "green" new building. Accommodation has more enterprises than any other part of rural tourism: accommodation is part of the rural tourism product because rural accommodation is so different to resort accommodation. It also attracts a special type of rural tourism business – the life style entrepreneur.

Rural tourism is very much an area rather than a single site activity, a theme taken up in the Portuguese study, which brings together village, small town and community tourism development issues. Protected Areas will be discussed because they illustrate intensive rural tourism activities, potential governance and management regimes, special opportunities *and* dilemmas, with a series of contested issues to understand. Finally, a short study shows how in some cases, rural and industrial heritage tourism can come together to mutual benefit.

Rural Accommodation

Accommodation is perhaps the most essential ingredient in the rural tourism equation. Overnight visitors are valuable. Surveys show that overnight visitors have higher spending levels than day visitors, typically up to 300 per cent more than day visitors. Investigations also show that more of the expenditure on accommodation in rural areas is retained in the local economy than other tourism spending.

Up to 70 per cent of accommodation expenditure remains in the community compared to 20 per cent of retail expenditure. In addition, tourist expenditure on accommodation is a greater generator of jobs for a given capital expenditure than retailing, restaurants or attraction developments. Rural accommodation is almost always locally owned. Externally owned chains of hotels are relatively rare.

Accommodation helps create a recognised destination. It can open the way to the formation of local tourism associations, training, better marketing etc. A number of researchers have shown that small and very individual accommodation opportunities are a Unique Selling Point for many visitors, differentiating the rural tourism product. Personal contact is regularly reported to be a key reason why many guests choose rural holidays. The importance of accommodation provision explains why rural tourism has a much greater economic impact than industrial heritage tourism.

Accommodation statistics show the full extent of seasonality in rural tourism, and the large amount of spare capacity in the sector. Many less sophisticated enterprises, and many remote enterprises, have bed occupancy levels as low as 30 per cent. But others surpass the typical national urban and rural average hotel occupancy levels of around 65 per cent. Some unserviced accommodation providers can exceed 80 per cent occupancy. There are many reasons for these variations. Seasonality is one of them, but although a complex problem, it often be improved by market knowledge, pricing policies, product development and skilled marketing.

Unserviced accommodation provision:

- Campsites – including glamping and other upmarket provision
- Caravan/recreational vehicle sites
- Camping barns/stone tents
- Hay/straw barns/"Sleep in the Hay"
- Self-catering accommodation – new build
- Self-catering accommodation – conversions
- Speciality self-catering: typically using high quality heritage buildings
- Timeshare

Serviced accommodation provision:

- Bed and breakfast
- Farmhouse bed and breakfast
- Hostels/group accommodation
- Guest houses
- Hotels

Sustainability should be part of all rural tourism's activities: accommodation is no exception. Increased use of re-cycling and environmentally friendly building and business techniques should be incorporated into all rural accommodation types. The major hotel chains are already far ahead in this area· The classic example of environmentally friendly rural accommodation provision is the Hotel Ucliva in Waltensburg, Graubunden, Switzerland. This 70 bed hotel dating from 1983 is built of energy efficient, environmentally friendly materials, specialises in locally purchased, organic/semi-organic home cooked food, offers a range of low impact activities for guests and has exemplary employment and local involvement policies·

A Rural Region Approach

The Schist Village Network in Portugal

The advantages for rural tourism of working in partnerships of various kinds are now widely recognised but rarely fully implemented. Rural tourism offers a complete tourism experience, including accommodation, attractions and activities and food and beverages. Partnerships can bring all those enterprises together, and use economies of scale to promote, market and help develop a rural region approach. They are not, however, easy to create, to energise, to maintain or to use. This study of two networks in Portugal is a long one. That length is justified because the need to work with local people in rural areas is very great, but the complexities in making such arrangements work are considerable and need to be explained.

The study shows the strengths and weaknesses of partnership approaches to sustainable rural tourism development.

The material for this section comes largely from the work of a three year rural tourism research project led by the University of Aveiro in collaboration with UTAD (University of Tras-os-Montes and Alto Douro). The ORTE Project, entitled "The Overall Rural Tourism Experience and sustainable local community development", began in 2010 and will end in 2013. This innovative and comprehensive research project is financed by the Portuguese *Fundação para a Ciência e Tecnologia,* and co-financed by COMPETE, NSRF and ERDF. Further information is available on: http://cms.ua.pt/orte/?q=node/20.

The Schist Villages Network Programme was created in 2000 in Portugal's Centro region, in the context of the EU's Community Support Framework 2000-2006· It takes its name from the local geology: schist is a metamorphic rock, with minerals such as mica, quartzite and hornblende. It is widely used in traditional building in the Schist villages, giving distinctive streetscapes. SVN is a sustainable regional development project, developed from an initial partnership of 16 municipalities. It now comprises 27 villages, 19 municipalities and over 100 operators with tourism related businesses in this territory. In 2011 the 19 municipalities had a population of 281,448 people, across 6,555 square km.

The programme was created initially through the elaboration of "Village Plans", assisted by a specialised and multi-disciplinary team working with each community. The Village Plan is a working document based on an in-depth study of each village, its surroundings and its population. From this study, essential actions were defined to promote the development of their territory. While this case study concentrates on rural tourism, the overall purpose of the programme was, and is, to assist the region's overall social and economic development.

Within the plans, the development of village inventories of both relevant tangible and intangible heritage were the keys to developing ideas about possible tourism experiences, and how to turn that heritage into tourism products. The Programme launched ADXTUR -*Agência para o Desenvolvimento Turístico das Aldeias do Xisto* (Agency for Tourism Development in the Schist Villages), as an entity that could then promote and market the actions developed in the context of the Programme. ADXTUR is a non-profit private association that brings together both public and private forces for the promotional purposes, the creation of wealth through tourism and the preservation of the heritage of the rural communities and their environment· ADXTUR has a staff of 5 employees and 7 contractors for consulting and other services. The overall programme aims, while developing tourism, to reduce the many common development problems of the inland villages of rural Portugal, including ageing populations, depopulation, isolation, fragmented/small scale productive capacity, lack of information and poor accessibility.

To gain the trust of local people through meeting with them and creating a community network building process. Each village set up community meetings, ADXTUR staff explained the project, worked closely with municipal staff and specialists from the regional coordination commission CCDR-C, the Coordination Commission for the Development of the Centre Region, who regularly met with the owners of historic buildings to explain how they could be restored and what could happen in the entire village. ADXTUR not only promoted visits by professionals to the villages, but also visits by people from some villages to other villages to gain awareness of the network and understand their similarities, differences, common problems and possible solutions. A special magazine was developed, dedicated to those involved in the project, passing on the message and illustrating the strengths and achievements of the Schist Villages.

The programme is holistic, not just involved with tourism marketing and development programmes: it emphasises the conservation of local architectural styles and techniques, job creation, local pride, heritage conservation and retaining authenticity. To assist this, an international project was set up linking the SVN with the Røros Museum and the UNESCO World Heritage Site at Røros, in Norway. This – grant aided by European Economic Area Norway funds – has assisted the painstaking conservation and re-use of 80 traditional houses in several villages, and trained new craftspeople in heritage repair using authentic methods and materials.

A key outcome has been the creation of the Schist Village's stores, selling local products, and offering tourist information, to reduce one of the biggest problems in this region – the producer's micro scale and lack of access to major distribution channels. The villages have a rich handicraft tradition, know-how associated with those crafts that reflect the culture and tradition of the region, but had previously no expression or economic dimension for that tradition. ADXTUR helped overcome this problem by creating their own network of stores, permitting the sales of local craft production, an economic return for the artisans that helps maintain tradition and provide a case for active people to stay in the villages. The Schist Village Network's 12 stores sell food, publications and handicraft products, sometimes associating traditional arts with modern design; they are located in the villages and also in Lisbon, Barcelona and Coimbra, with the last three creating a tangible form of synergy marketing between tourism and urban craft sales.

ADXTUR has also promoted the development of several other initiatives, for example: a magazine sold to tourists and the general public; a book with traditional cooking recipes, beautifully illustrated and linked to specific local people; a calendar of events; the promotion of products/ services associated with the territory's heritage, for example, routes – Schist Walking and Mountain Bike Trails - and a set of Theme Houses, related to traditional skills (The Weavers' House, The Mushroom House, The "Drum's" House and The Honey House), that now are fostered by another local development association – Pinus Verde (an association focused on forest management, working with the concept of multiple uses and integrated development of the forest). Additionally, all the marketing of the SVN (for example, the marketing strategy, the internet site, brochures, a magazine, participation in national and international trade fairs) is designed and promoted by ADXTUR.

The Schist Villages' three Mountain Bike Centres are permanent structures, each with a network of signed trails for mountain bikes, creating fully equipped hubs with information, car parking, showers and a bike self service station, with washing, air and small bike repair station. Each Centre offers Cross Country, Down Hill and Free Ride trails, with four levels of difficulty, thus being suitable for all grades of riders, from beginners to experienced bikers.

Marketing is done via the Internet and via close contact with inbound tour operators and attendance at tourism trade fairs including Berlin's ITB. The Web site brings together 70 accommodation providers and 6 camp sites. Market research is currently in an initial phase: partners (shops, accommodation, restaurants) may be asked in the future to use surveys to identify customer socio-economic profiles and tourist motivations. A new scheme of quality grading has been developed for the area.

ADXTUR's budget comes in part from an annual membership fee from local businesses and organisations, ranging from 10€ to 500€, depending on the type of activity). ADXTUR has also received €11,956,561 from the European Community Support Framework III to investments in public spaces and infrastructures (public infrastructures and facades of private houses). Currently, the National Strategic Reference Framework (in the context of PROVERE, ERDF, & PRODER) strongly supports activities, with more than €9,884,027 of EU financial aid allocated within the territory, since 2009. Funding is a problem because of the short term and volatile nature of some financial sources, making implementation of action programmes difficult. ADXTUR is, however, regarded as a permanent organization, rather than a short term project.

ADXTUR is governed by democratic decision-making and a bottom-up approach, with the participation and full involvement of all active partnership members, who articulate their interests, assume obligations and negotiate their differences, based on participation, transparency and accountability. To achieve this goal, the management of the Association is integrated with the Villages' Council – a body with representatives from all the villages, its own administration, independent of the Association and of other institutions that are involved in the Schist Villages. The Council, with leaders of each village meet on a regular basis, independently of ADXTUR's agenda.

ADXTUR's strategy, while focusing on tourism, is very much an instrument of regional and local development, improving the local economy and social development through the following elements:

- A strong social component, genuinely reflecting the living conditions in the area;
- The natural heritage, its management, qualification and protection, recognising natural heritage as a comparative advantages of this area;
- The built heritage, specifically the architecture of the schist buildings, characteristic of this area, which forms the essence of the Schist Villages brand;
- Local products, handicraft or agri-food products, which are seen as authentic, originally related with everyday life, containing traditional knowledge that is seen as a valuable and unique cultural dimension in the face of the demands of modern life.

ADXTUR puts special value on integrating the creative industries and innovation, both for commercial reasons, but also in terms of research and rural development, with the ambition of making the territory an experimental laboratory for rural development anchored in tourism.

Has ADXTUR solved the problems of the region? A number of problems have been reported to Project ORTE's researchers:

- Not all villages have an effectively integrated and appealing tourism product.
- Village de-population remains a problem.
- It can be difficult to create a critical mass of players in each village.
- Above all, a number of businesses report excessive bureaucracy and difficulty in gathering clear and simple information about the requirements for tourism investments, and great problems in obtaining the many licenses necessary to set up and conduct tourism businesses, with delays from government offices of, in some cases, years, not weeks.

The "Historic Villages of Portugal" Network was initiated in 1991 in the context of the EU II Community Support Framework and extended under the III Community Support Framework. It was a publically funded programme to reclassify 12 villages of Portugal's Centro region. Several organizations participated, including the IPPAR (Portuguese Institute of Architectural Heritage), the Coordination Commission for the Development of the Centre Region, local authorities and some private entities. This programme aimed to mitigate the problems associated with remoteness/ marginality, such as population aging, desertification, weak productive capacity and lack of entrepreneurship in the region, all of which compromise the development of the local and regional economy.

It also aimed to valorise and restore the historic built heritage of the villages. Interventions, supported by the European Regional Development Fund, between 1994-1999 and 2000-2008, amounted to €44.6 million. It appears that, compared with SVN, and based on local discussions, that this Programme was not fully successful. The branding does attract tourists, but the villages have not developed enough things for tourists to do and tourism related incomes remain low. The practical effects of the HVPN were mainly related to restoration of facades and buildings and the creation of the brand "Historic Villages of Portugal". The group is featured on an English and Portuguese web site·

Even though there are municipalities that integrate both HVPN and SVN,, there is no formal cooperation between these two networks. This duplication seems strange, and might be a lost opportunity. SVN appears to be the more successful organization, probably because of its holistic activities, and stronger links with tourism, job creation and marketing.

Rural Tourism and Protected Areas/ National Parks

This section has been included because of the strong role of protected areas in general, and National Parks in particular, in the distribution and growth of rural tourism, and in its potential future governance.

About 21 per cent of the area of the 32 member states of the European Environment Agency is in rural protected areas. Much of the land involved is in National Parks. There are six basic categories of protected areas classified worldwide by the International Union for the Conservation of Nature· Of those categories, Category IA and IB are very strictly managed and effectively not accessible to tourists. Category II protected areas, National Parks, are the major protected areas that are of interest to, and accessible to, tourism.

"Category II protected areas are large natural or near natural areas set aside to protect large-scale ecological processes, along with the complement of species and ecosystems characteristic of the area, which also provide a foundation for environmentally and culturally compatible, spiritual, scientific, educational, recreational, and visitor opportunities."

National Parks, because of their scenery, and their brand name, are areas of intense tourism demand, and intense rural tourism activity. UK statistics show that the percentage of tourism related business and employment in

National Parks is double that of rural England as a whole: in National Parks 27.5 per cent of businesses and 21.2 per cent of rural employment are tourism related· Similar figures have been reported for other parts of Europe, although there are variations between parks, and in how the statistics are presented in each study. Mayer et al, comparing visitor expenditure across six German National Parks, found that overnight visitor expenditures varied between the parks from €37 to €57 per person, while the national average overnight visitor expenditure in German as a whole was €120.

Secondly, National Parks have much more sophisticated governance and planning systems than other rural areas. As governance systems are important for encouraging improved performance from rural tourism, national park tourism governance systems may hold important keys to future progress.

Thirdly, there have been on-going and radical changes in the relationship between National Parks and rural tourism over the last 20 years. Tourism was seen as a danger to the protected area status of National Parks, encouraging questionable social and cultural change, and bringing environmental damage. New sustainable tourism management and marketing techniques have reduced the environmental threat.

Well managed tourism is now seen as a valuable aid to conserving rural societies, which might otherwise lose economic viability. Many national park environments rely on a viable tourism industry to help support and maintain agricultural systems that in turn help maintain ecosystems and landscapes. And even National Park administrations increasingly find financial contributions from tourism, plus its political support, essential for the maintenance of their planning systems. National Parks are also widely studied, providing large potential amounts of research based data on which to base development and management decisions.

This section, therefore, examines two western European National Parks and their governance systems and two central/eastern European National Parks to better understand the interplay between national parks and rural tourism. This process begins with an EU and Norwegian Research Council jointly financed comparison of Jostdalsbreen National Park in Norway, and the Hohe Tauern National Park in Austria.

It discusses a new concept National Park currently in formation in Transylvania, Romania, and closes with a review of the Polish part of the Bia³owie¿a National Park which straddles the border between Poland and Bielorussia. Low pressure, high pressure, experimental and transitional management approaches are illustrated.

Jostdalsbreen National Park, Norway

Jostedalsbreen National Park, established in 1991, covers an area of 1,310 km^2, much of which consists of the Jostedalsbreen glacier, the largest in continental Europe. The main management objective is nature conservation, although the park is one of several in Norway adapted for tourism purposes. Tourist numbers are rising slowly and are currently around 500,000 per year. There are currently few other serious management issues. In 2009, 11 small enterprises offered tourism activities, such as walks, climbs, and ski tours, to around 20,000 tourists. Most tourists were day visitors from outside the area, a large number from international cruise ships on the Sogne Fjord.

The management of Jostedalsbreen national park is a 'traditional' Norwegian model. National authorities hold management responsibility, while the regional County Governor's office is the executive body. The county government is a decentralized office of the national authorities; a National Park Manager is employed at the county's environmental department. He/she is executive officer for several protected areas, and on average 30 per cent of his/her time is dedicated to Jostedalsbreen National Park. In addition, there is a nature inspector connected to the park employed by the national Directorate for Nature Management: the inspector is based locally and is also responsible for several smaller PAs.

Approximately 90 per cent of the inspector's time is used on Jostedalsbreen NP. Three national park information centres are partly funded by the national authorities. Compared to international standards, the management model for Jostedalsbreen national park may be characterized as a low-cost, low input, low-output approach, with only 1.2 permanent positions dedicated to the direct management of the area. Another central characteristic of the Norwegian management model is its decentralization with several separate bodies responsible for particular management tasks. Total staff including visitor centres and national authorities' administration amount to eight all-year positions and 2530 seasonal workers.

The national park management is responsible for conservation and information. Tasks such as destination marketing and regional tourism management are outside the national park's remit. Participation and stakeholder involvement is carried out informally, based on personal contacts, and local discussion with elected representatives, staff and interested parties. The system functions because there are few conflicts, and relatively little pressure for change. The precautionary principle is maintained: there is little involvement in developing regional economic viability.

Hohe Tauern National Park, Austria

Hohe Tauern National Park, established in 1983, covers 1,834 km^2 of Alpine forests, grasslands, glaciers and rock formations. It is the largest national park in the Alps and has been a destination since the 19 century. Visitor numbers are estimated at 2 million per year. The park is established by federal legislation in three different federal states (Carinthia, Salzburg, and Tirol; political representatives from each federal state and the Austrian Minister of the Environment form the "national park council", an overall steering committee for the park, with local politicians, NGOs and landowners on several park boards. The park has 80 permanent staff members and about 20-40 seasonal employees and volunteers. They have responsibilities for conservation, environmental education, park interpretation, research and communication and, to some extent, regional management. In the Carinthian part of the park, park management is also the organizing body of tourism and destination management, including marketing. The new Tauernwelt visitor centre – one of 30 centres of various sizes - attracts over 100,000 guests each year.

Participation and stakeholder involvement is carried out through a range of formally constituted stakeholder boards, mostly with a range of associated committees. The park has close links with several councils at parish and regional levels, their elected representatives, and makes extensive use of the media including its own newsletters and web site.

The system is complex, and intensive, because there are strong development pressures. The Park is very actively involved in tourism and takes the view that positive but conservation based involvement is essential to maintain the triple bottom line of sustainable development. There are numerous partnerships between businesses, communities and the Park. Its management model may be characterized as a high-cost, high–input, high output approach. The precautionary principle is maintained but in a strongly evolutionary and innovative way: the Park is a key player in maintaining regional economic viability.

Transylvania, Romania

Romania has 13 National Parks, largely controlled by the National Forest Authority. Many date back to the 1930s. They have serious problems because of development pressures, underfunding, and the relatively slow development of conservation based, sustainable development attitudes at many – but not all – levels of Romanian society. The question of land restitution and the dismantling of the state's nationalization of land under communism add to the problems.

Given this background, a radical new idea in National Park creation, conservation and rural tourism was launched in 2007 by a group of Romanian and international biologists, conservationists and philanthropists to create a private National Park with an ultimate size of 50,000 hectares. Foundation Conservation Carpathia draws on the experience of similar projects in North and South America, and in Africa. It currently owns 12,000 hectares of forest and grassland, with 10,000 more in negotiation. The eventual cost of land purchases could be €130 million. The park aims to restore the natural ecosystems of the Carpathians, for the benefit of biodiversity conservation and local communities, and be large enough to maintain Europe's last remaining major group of Large Carnivores – a process begun by the World Wildlife Fund's Large Carnivore Project in 1992. The landholdings which form the nucleus of this embryo park are adjacent to the Piatra Craiului National Park, in the Brasov region.

The driving force behind this project is the conservation of wilderness and its wildlife; it believes that ownership is the only safe way towards that goal. This ownership, however, intends to be that of an enlightened despot: the promoters plan to involve nearby communities in employment opportunities, and develop a new style of wilderness tourism – one that will learn from the research of Higham into wilderness experiences, and probe new ideas, for example, using GPS rather than signposts and created trails to take visitors into the Park. It will extend local links between tourists and communities, drawing on the experiences of the Large Carnivore Project 1992-2002. This system places a premium on the precautionary principle, but also aims to create a sustainable rural economy, drawing on best practice worldwide.

The concept of a privately owned and managed park is a new one for Europe. It has historic links with the great estates of much of pre-twentieth century Europe. It also has possible links to the privatization movements across many European economies.

The Bia³owieza National Park, Poland

This case study illustrates the way in which, in the newer EU member countries, protected area administrations are changing their approaches to tourism, and taking account of new political, social and economic demands and opportunities· Bia³owieża National Park is an example of a slowly evolving and modernizing park, with few environmental pressures, and some links to regional economic development. Its management model is a medium-cost, medium input, medium output approach.

The Bia³owieza Forest is located approximately 230 km east of Warsaw, a 3 hour road journey. It covers an area of 150,000 hectares and straddles the border between Poland and Belarus. Its western part comprises 62,500 hectares, of which 10,500 constitute the Polish Bia³owieza National Park. Another 8,000 hectares enjoys other forms of protection, and there are 21 special reserves. Trees over 100 years old are not cut. The Polish part of the Bia³owieza Forest is administered by the Podlaskie voivodship, and Hajnówka County. The population density of the Polish part of the Bia³owieza Forest is around 7 people per square km, one of the lowest in Poland.

Bialowieza is the oldest Polish national park. In 1932 an existing forest reserve became the "National Park in Bia³owieza". In 1977 the Bia³owieza National Park became a UNESCO Biosphere Reserve, and in 1979 a UNESCO World Heritage site. The site, shared with Belarus, protects part of the largest surviving area of European primeval lowland mixed forest: pine, beech, oak, alder and spruce. Its rich fauna includes 50 species of mammals, 120 species of breeding birds and about 10,000 species of invertebrates. Iconic species include the tarpan, elk, stag, roe deer, wild boar, lynx, wolf, fox, marten, badger, otter, ermine and beaver. The European bison was reintroduced into the park in 1929.

In 1997 the park received the Diploma of Europe. Its most fragile area is a strict nature reserve, visitable only with a licensed guide. Other parts of the forest have marked trails and nature paths, and may be visited without a guide. The Bison Display and Breeding Centre presents the Bison, Tarpan type horses and hybrids of bison and domestic cattle called Zhubron. There is an Environmental Education Centre, a modern Forest and Nature Museum, and a small number of Tourist Information Points·

The Local Economy

Before 1989 the economy was based on the timber industry, forestry, agriculture and food production. Since 1989, the machinery sector has grown, along with services and rural tourism. There are now 72 registered tourism businesses, plus a number of accommodation providers with fewer than 6 rooms.

Tourism to Bialowieza Forest before 1989 was mainly educational tourism for organized school groups and for adults who travelled by coach. The only tour operator was the state owned PTTK. After 1989, the private sector grew, a number of local small tour operators and some external tour operators started work. Special interest tourism such as bird-watching and nature tourism has become important.

The role of the National Park in tourism

The National Park authority is responsible for tourism infrastructure in its area; the Forest authority is responsible for its own territory. The Hajnowka County authority is responsible for the rest of the territory and coordinates forest wide projects including working with NGOs. In 2011 Hajnowka County announced a tender for a common tourism infrastructure improvement project for the whole area. It includes modernization of trails, building a new information system, viewing towers and an animal garden with bison; 99 per cent of the area's bison roam freely. The National Park established a tourism administration department in 2011. It licenses around 100 local guides, the only people permitted to conduct tourists in the National Park. It maintains tourist trails for walkers and cyclists through the Forest including educational paths and 5 viewing towers. Visits to the main visitor centre have risen from 67,220 in 2002 to 84,277 in 2011. The park liaises with a number of key stakeholders including the Bialowieza Rural Tourism Association "Zubr", the Rural Tourism Association "Bialowieza Forest" in Narew, an Association of Local Products Providers, and the Local Action Group Leader+.

Tourism policies

The county of Hajnowka produced a Strategy for Tourism Development in 1999, followed by a Strategy for Sustainable Development with a special chapter on tourism. There are some Local Operational Plans. There is a Local Strategy for Local Action Group for 2009-2015. The first steps towards establishing a Destination Management Organization were taken in 2001; it is hoped to move towards that idea in 2013. The informal policy sector has seen the most interesting changes: the national park has increasingly seen the value of tourism, and begun to learn to manage rather than simply restricting it. National park staff, the industry and county staff are beginning to work more closely together. The national park has sought to expand its boundaries but this has met with local opposition.

Accommodation

There is a growing supply of tourist accommodation in the Forest, especially just outside the Park boundary in Bialowieza Village, the main centre of tourism. In 2002 there were 28 registered rural tourism units with 270 beds: by 2011 there were 1,200 beds in 71 units. Including hotels, 3,000 beds are now available in the whole county of Hajnowka ranging from camp sites, hostels, and rooms/apartments for rent to guest houses and hotels including a 250-bed 4-star hotel with conference facilities.

External public sector funding has been very important is financing accommodation development. The 1999-2003 Danish DANCEE small grants programme gave around €1 million to the area, of which 20 per cent was for tourism, increasing rural tourism accommodation units from 29 to 71, and bed numbers from 280 to 536. In terms of overall rural development, EU funds have included: LEADER+ €500,000; INTERREG - €407,000; Cross-border – €76,000; Open Forest – €14,000.

What does the area need to develop rural tourism further?

- Better collaboration and coordination between stakeholders and key players: the case for an integrated Destination Management Organization was made in 2001, but is still not implemented.
- Better awareness amongst tourism providers about nature and culture resources and the tools of product development and interpretation, despite there having been some training courses and study tours.
- Recognition of the cultural heritage significance of its wooden architecture, which currently does not receive enough protection, interpretation or marketing.
- Funds for developing tourism infrastructure and promotion (Hajnowka County is the most popular destination in the Podlasie region but is not recognized at regional level).

- Market research and a marketing strategy based on that research.
- A modern system of tourist information.
- Measures to reduce migration of young people; the average villager is 55 years old.
- Measures to retain the traditional architecture and special rural ambience of Bialowieza.
- Creating a number of integrated tourism products with professional promotion and distribution. Brand development linked to tourism products.
- Better dispersal of tourists by creating a second gateway to the National Park, reducing stress on Bialowieza village.
- Stronger involvement of local authorities in tourism.
- An independent structure for tourism management based more on the industry than the public sector, linking tourism and local products.

National Agri-Tourism and Rural Tourism Groups

This section discusses national Agri and Rural Tourism groups. Such groups formed in most European countries over the last 20 years to provide marketing, development and lobby networks, and are important to, and characteristic of, the sector. They have a range of common features. Where agricultural ministries are financial participants, their finances tend to be stronger, but membership is limited to working farms. They all seek to overcome the marketing problems faced by small enterprises. They all have web sites – though some are much better than others. All still have printed publicity, although that is a declining activity.

The majority offer some training and advice, and see their work as part of a wider endeavour to conserve and sustain a traditional countryside. All face rapidly growing competition from low cost international accommodation marketing web sites, which do not offer advice, training or development, but are cheap. All have a turnover of members each year, as some retire, give up taking guests, or seek to save money by resigning their membership: most get some new members every year as new enterprises start up. Because of competition from local Internet sites and from international sites, the future of weaker groups is now very unsure.

Austrian Farm Holidays/ Urlaub am Bauernhof

Austrian Farm Holidays is, without doubt, the most effective, the most innovative, and the best funded, farm holiday/agri-tourism marketing and development group in Europe, perhaps worldwide. It was founded in 1991 to consolidate a number of regional groups, one dating back to 1971. The consolidation created a more professional and powerful national organization. It was, and still is, supported in part by the Ministry of Agriculture and the

Ministry of Economy, Family and Youth: the latter Ministry is responsible for Tourism Policy in Austria. It aims to support farm based tourism enterprises, support agricultural areas and to create attractive vacations. It is important to note the high rate of enterprise contraction in Austrian agriculture, with 13 farms closing every day.

Austrian Farm Holidays is a highly professional, well-funded, and very effective marketing and development organization. Most other national rural tourism organizations are less effective, in part because of financial problems. While the Austrian model cannot be replicated exactly elsewhere, many aspects of its approach and systems could be used in other countries, but require financial inputs and highly skilled staff.

Austrian Farm Holidays is a private association, effectively a non-profit. It employs 22 full time equivalents. Governance is by a President and four board members, who are elected by representatives of the regional groups and key stakeholders.

The organization is funded in part by the two ministries and in part by its 2,750 members, who pay a basic fee with additional charges for specific marketing services chosen. Basic fees are currently €35 per bed per year, plus extra fees according to the brochures that members choose to be featured in. Total income is €1.25 million; €842,000 of that sum is spent on marketing and related projects. Austrian Farm Holidays' members have around 36,000 beds, approximately 1 in 7 of all guest beds in Austria. There are 2 million users of farm holidays each year, with a total gross spend of €1-1.2 billion. Approximately 50 per cent of bookings are repeat business.

Austrian Farm Holidays provide a very full range of services including:

- Two web sites' plus a range of social media and Web 2 activities;
- A regional advice and discussion system, as well as a national organization;
- Quarterly newsletters and statistics about individual members' performance;
- Representation at trade and tourism fairs in Austria, Czech Republic, Hungary, the Netherlands and Germany;
- Market Research;
- Media work, including press and TV, including editorial and paid spots on prime-time TV, and for 2012, two named express trains running between Vienna and Bregenz, and between Salzburg and Klagenfurt;
- Joint marketing with other organizations, and event sponsorship;
- Training courses held in conjunction with Chambers of Agriculture;
- Lobbying government;
- A range of specialist holidays and brochures including farm holidays for babies and children, for horse riders, on organic farms, and for those with special access needs.

Austrian Farm Holidays is unique amongst organizations of its type because it publishes performance figures which show how members' bed occupancy rates are changing – on average up 20 per cent over the last 20 years, and the price they obtain per bed – which is up 120 per cent, twice the rates of inflation over the same period. And while concentrating on marketing, it is important to stress its work on product development, staff/owner training, quality improvement, and its background role of maintaining rural community life and business.

In 2011, Austrian Farm Holidays published its *Strategy for 2011-2020*, the product of intensive market research and consultation processes with its members. The Strategy revealed to members a range of ways that they themselves could improve their own businesses, introduced them to a range of issues and trends in the holiday market and explained how their association would change to remain highly effective·

Organic farming and its links to rural tourism

In a number of European countries, efforts have been made to link organic farming to a special type of environmentally friendly rural tourism. At a European level, ECEAT – the European Centre for Ecological and Agricultural Tourism' holds records of, and publicizes, a number of organic farms that offer organic accommodation and food. At a national level, Austrian Farm Holidays have for a long time produced special marketing materials for organic farm members. One key linkage is missing in Europe – there appears to be no organization marketing organic farm holidays to the buyers of organic food. That potentially two-way marketing synergy could pay dividends, and is used especially successfully in Korea and to some extent in Japan.

Second Generation Rural Tourism: A concept case study

In western Europe, rural tourism was a growth phenomena in the 1980s and 90s; eastern and central Europe followed a similar path through the 1990s to the present day. Development in both cases was market driven, by consumer demand, and by supply side changes resulting from agricultural diversification. Some development has been driven by short term rural development projects. The only effective coordination and guidance of this complex process has come from farm and rural tourism accommodation groups, with some input from some protected area administrations. None take a holistic approach, although some seek that ideal. Most of the accommodation groups now suffer from income problems for a variety of reasons.

The market driven approach has problems. Because of the small scale and fragmented nature of development, few stakeholders have the training to understand the long-term requirements of tourism. They are unable or unwilling to develop tourism infrastructure, and they have little access to market knowledge. Product development ideas exist, but are implemented by only a few areas/enterprises. Links to conservation, to rural regeneration, and to synergy with agriculture are all possible, but poorly developed. Networking, partnership and governance tend to be missed opportunities.

More urgently, the agri-rural tourism sector now finds itself in a position of growing competition – in part from new rural tourism providers in low cost countries, in part from city based tourism and low cost chain hotels, and in part from cruise ship tourism. And – many of the first generation of rural tourism providers are now retiring from the field. Responses are needed if the economic and social benefits of tourism are not to be lost to rural areas, and if its environmental potential is to be maximised.

The concept of second generation rural tourism seeks to provide a series of blueprints to improve the situation described above, by developing branded rural tourism regions, created as partnerships between providers and stakeholders, increasing stakeholders' knowledge, using more effective marketing, and putting to use the ideas of slow tourism, food tourism, synergy with high margin agricultural production, and the use of tourism as a tool for rural regeneration, rather than just as an end in itself. A group of academic researchers is considering the creation of a "virtual" international rural tourism research group, in a bid to enable the professionalization of the sector. It would use the experience of the ALTER-Net model, a network of 26 partner institutes working on biodiversity policy issues from 18 European countries" see Section 7.2.

A MIXED RURAL AND INDUSTRIAL HERITAGE TOURISM CASE STUDY: HASLACH, AUSTRIA

The small town of Haslach in Austria, 60 km north of the city of Linz, lies in a quiet rural region of Austria, near the Czech border, far from the busy tourist centres of the Alps. Once a thriving linen textile region, based on fast flowing rivers, quality water and local flax production, its many small scale rural and small town producers thrived into the post-war period, secure behind protectionist tariff policies. Competition from Czech producers across the border ceased when the Czech industry lost its way under Communist rule, but in the 1960s serious problems were encountered. The market for linen products declined as alternative low cost easy care textiles flooded the market. Many producers went out of business. The rural region around Haslach began to lose population, as farm jobs declined and young people moved to the cities. The opening of the border to the Czech Republic in 1990 allowed a rise in cheaper cloth imports.

This case study shows how industrial heritage and rural tourism can, in some cases, come together to offer two positive trends. Two local mills have transformed themselves into high class niche producers of quality textiles using a mix of contemporary and heritage designs. An additional small producer has specialised in heritage products. Secondly, in the 1990s a group of local people decided to maintain their textile heritage, and a textile future, by setting up a self-help group. A textile museum was created and, of greatest importance, an annual textile festival was set up which became internationally successful, in part because of help from the European Textile Network. Up to 20,000 visitors are attracted to the region each year by the festivals, many of whom stay overnight, thus boosting the income of a number of rural tourism accommodation providers. Important practical links were made with textile experts at the University of Linz. And some of the rural tourism attractions of the region were developed.

Haslach and its rural area have a chance for the future:

- The venture was backed financially by both the local council, regional council, and by EU funding. All see the group's work as finding a new role for a town and its hinterland that had lost its way. That backing was financial, but also political, creating more confidence and an active cultural and tourism policy.
- The venture marks out the region as one to visit for its tangible cultural identity. It differentiates Haslach from the many other historic small towns in Austria. It has high media value: the annual conference events get air time regionally and nationally. The festival brings in income and is held in the "shoulder" tourism season. Other activities – notably courses – are also successful. The tourism potential of the venture is backed by its excellent graphics and quality marketing. The textiles concept has been extended to include a sub-regional tourism area brand: Weberland. The Weberland Trail takes walkers and bikers through the sites of the region. The town council's tourism officer is a leading member of the Self Help Group.
- The Group has recently moved into a former mill building in Haslach which has been restored and fitted out with help from Regional Government and EU Regional Funds. It is used for a range of activities including educational groups, the headquarters of a company arranging training and work placements for people with learning difficulties, and a successful bar/restaurant. It is adjacent to the working mill which now concentrates on heritage products. The capital costs of the Textile Centre are carried by a partnership of the Town and Regional Council. They retain ownership, and on behalf of the community, benefit from the area's physical, economic and social regeneration.
- The Heritage Products mill concentrates on felt products (felt slippers are a regional and Austrian speciality), and on traditional clothing and blankets. It has retail and mail-order facilities and is open to the

public. It offers training to people with learning disabilities: this type of traditional manual work seems well suited to this group.

- The Mill has developed an EU funded programme to help maintain specific regional sheep breeds in the area by purchasing the wool that regional breeds produce, sorting, cleaning and spinning it in house on a farm by farm basis, and then either returning it to its original farm for further processing, or selling on to craft workers or using it in-house in heritage products. Demand for this service and its products, has been strong. However:
  - The Haslach experiment remains very dependent on public funding.
  - Like so many industrial heritage centres, the town lacks accommodation facilities, hindering tourism growth, and textile heritage activities.
  - The local tourism office is excellent, but has limited capacity to innovate.

Haslach is still served by a single track rail line, which provides a slow but scenic link to the city of Linz, though connecting to main line services requires the use of a tram link. There could be a case for bringing together rural tourism and industrial heritage tourism to create a Slow Tourism Destination, combining more pro-actively new developments in community rail, heritage interpretation, food tourism, cycle and walking tourism, with the industrial heritage interests of the area. This would be beyond the capacity of the local tourism office, but could be managed by an experimental Slow Tourism project, perhaps involving academic and other interests known to be working in this area in Austria, and there could be cross-border links with very similar geographies and communities in the neighbouring Czech Republic·

Pan-European Organizations

This section reviews a number of the pan-European bodies specifically connected to industrial heritage and rural/agri tourism. Each has one major organisation which is pan-European; in addition, industrial heritage has a series of industry specific groups, two of which are outlined below, the European Textile Network and the Federation of European Museum and Tourist Railways. The highly fragmented nature of both industrial heritage and rural tourism makes both national and European partnership bodies potentially very valuable. As the market for both types of tourism product becomes increasingly transnational, European co-operation becomes especially important, both in marketing and in product development terms.

All the pan-European organizations are very short of money, and cannot get money from their membership because they cannot offer members many services – because they are short of money. There is perhaps a circle of eventual failure here. Both the major organizations, ERIH and EuroGites, survive only because so of the dedication and interest of their CEOs. Yet all the pan-European organizations have potential; some have special potential. A series of key questions have to be asked and answered about their roles, and their best ways forward. To be effective, additional skilled staff, additional resources and effective networking would definitely be needed. The dividends in terms of economic, environmental and socio-cultural benefits could be great - but only if investment and change takes place.

The European Route of Industrial Heritage

This organization is the only group working to promote the conservation of Industrial Heritage, and its presentation to the public, across Europe. It brings together 77 key industrial heritage sites, "anchor points", across northern Europe, linked by a series of 12 international industry theme route and 16 regional routes. It has records of 3,000 specific industrial heritage sites. Its title comes from the Route of Industrial Heritage created by Germany's Ruhrgebiet, in 1999. The so-called 'Tour de Ruhr' of around 400 kilometres, covers key industrial heritage sites in "the world's largest open-air museum". The story began, however, 10 years earlier. In 1989 the State Government of North Rhine-Westphalia created a pioneering regional redevelopment plan entitled the "International Building Exhibition at Emscher Park". It encouraged, by example, the ecological, economic, and urban revitalization of the industrial Ruhr Valley via a range of collaborative partnerships: see the earlier case study. In 1999, the successor plan to IBA – Project Ruhr – took over, and on a European level, ERIH was created.

ERIH was initially funded by an EU Interreg IIIB project. It is now funded by over 150 members, in 17 countries.

Annual membership fees vary from €100 for individual through site and corporate fees to €500 for Anchor Points, producing €60-80,000 income per year:

- ERIH is credited with helping change attitudes to industrial heritage conservation and tourism across Europe, by bringing key people – academics, planners, architects and politicians - together to discuss, learn and implement new ideas. It has a regular newsletter, offers conferences, lobbies on behalf of industrial heritage tourism, organises expert exchanges, and carries out projects if and when it obtains funding.
- Its web site - has between 60-100,000 hits per month.
- Special attention is given to the new EU members, and especially on building links between Germany and Poland. On June 30th 2012, for example, a Night of Industrial Culture was held simultaneously in Upper Silesia, Poland, the Donbass in the Ukraine, and the Ruhr Area of Germany from 6:00 p.m. to 2:00 a.m.

The ERIH has several problems:

- Funding: Like many cross European organizations, it is extremely short of money. While project funding can be obtained from the EU, the application process is lengthy and entails considerable work with high risks of failure. Membership fees bring in little money: few members can afford higher fees.
- Time: Working across Europe is expensive and time consuming. Current funding levels allow for only one member of staff.
- Lack of tourism knowledge and interest: Membership is dominated by heritage conservation interests, with very little knowledge of tourism. ERIH would like to change that, but has too few resources.
- The need to tackle key undiscussed problem areas: These include access to industrial heritage sites for those with disabilities; work on developing programmes for a range of school curricula, work to harmonize building and other regulations.

The European Textile Network

The European Textile Network was founded informally in Germany in 1989. Since 1993 it has been registered as a non-profit organization in Strasbourg. It emerged from a post 1960s growth in Artisan Textile production across Europe, a growing recognition of Europe as a textile culture region, and from the closure of many large scale production units. Initial funding came from the Council of Europe.

Members include textile artisans and artists, textile associations, museums and collections, designers, educators, schools, institutions and anyone interested in contemporary and heritage textiles. There are 400-450 members, from 40 European countries. Although "European", ETN also has members and partners worldwide, including Australia, Argentina, Canada and the USA. ETN makes special efforts to work with the "new" EU members. It publishes an extremely stylish and useful quarterly journal, "ETN Textile Forum", organises conferences and working groups - including one on Cultural Heritage and Museums. It aims to develop European co-operation, to strengthen regional identities and the idea of Europe· It is a lively organisation; its conferences buzz with animated discussions, and fascinating presentations.

Membership costs from €55 per year. The total turnover is €30,000 per year.

ETN ideas include:

- Textile linked industrial heritage is widespread across Europe. ETN wishes to conserve that heritage and see it used. Textilforum 3/94 sets out their main ideas.
- "In the interests of local producers, the preservation of the cultural textile heritage must urgently be updated", ... ETN proposes regional

textile visitor centres, courses, and summer academies. Textile museums and centres are often members of ETN.
- ETN has completed 2 European Textile Routes, working with ERIH. It is interested in working with farmers who produce fibres: there are potential links to rural tourism.

It follows, therefore, that ETN should have an interest in heritage tourism. Tourism skills could boost museum and centre visits. They could create local artisan producer trails to boost sales. There could be synergy between niche market tourism and niche market production. Yet ETN is not very interested in tourism. It does not see it as its business. This is in some ways understandable. But it exemplifies one of the reasons why some parts of the industrial and cultural heritage may be doomed. Given the likely lack of future public sector funding for textile cultural heritage, effective tourism links could be a valuable life line. Textile museums, centres and producers who understand the market and how to work with it could be the only survivors.

FEDECRAIL – the Federation of European Museum and Tourist Railways

The idea of a European federation of heritage railways emerged during celebrations for the 150 anniversary of Dutch Railways in 1989. FEDECRAIL was established in 1994 in Brussels, to monitor European legislation and seek amendments when they were likely to have an adverse impact on the industry and the Federation's members.

This has now evolved into 5 key aims and objectives to:
- Promote the rescue, restoration and operation of Europe's railway heritage.
- Represent its members' interests with international agencies, in particular the European Commission and European Parliament.
- Encourage the exchange of ideas across national and cultural boundaries and foster co-operation between museums and tourist railways involved in railway heritage.
- Provide advice and assistance for museums and tourist railways involved in railway heritage.
- Study and share solutions to problems in restoring and operating heritage railways.

Membership is open to all European national organisations whose members are engaged in the preservation and operation of historic railways. Individuals or non-European national organisations can also join the federation as 'Friends of FEDECRAIL', but have no voting rights.

Currently has 16 national umbrella organisations as full members and 33 'Friends', which encompass 27 European countries. FEDECRAIL represents 640 heritage railways and railway museums across Europe· The membership is predominantly from 'old' Europe; membership of the national organisations is generally higher in northern European and Scandinavian countries, probably reflecting the higher incidence of preserved industrial heritage in these countries.

Membership of most of the national member organisations has been stable over the last five years, with a small number seeing a modest increase.

Funding

The Federation is funded almost entirely from membership subscriptions which gives a turnover of only €25,000 per annum. The only other source of funding has been a small surplus generated by the annual conference and visit programme. The Federation council, managing committee and technical representatives are all un-paid posts and are drawn from the membership of the national associations. A full-time officer would be helpful in promoting the industry, but the majority of the individual railways and museums rely largely on volunteers, and feel unable to support such a position.

Funding from mainstream banks is problematic; there is partial support from the public sector. Other funding opportunities are also limited, although in the UK heritage railways have limited access to the Heritage Lottery Fund. Until recently it was possible to get grants from the European Regional Development Fund. The European Cultural Fund has to date tended to ignore heritage projects in favour of the performing arts.

Tourism

FEDECRAIL has no specific tourism policy but they are very aware of the importance of tourism to many of their members. They endeavour to raise awareness of the value that their member's railways bring to local economies.

A number of railways are open all the year round but none on a daily basis, with winter openings usually restricted to weekends and school holidays, reflecting the general peak/off-peak season for most of the tourism industry. There is considerable variation in the level of joint activity with tourism boards, in part reflecting the national structure of these organisations, but also the size and available resources of the national umbrella organisations.

FEDECRAIL and some of its members are very interested in pursuing skills development, but there are insufficient funds to develop a number of promising proposals.

Lobbying

Since 1994, FEDECRAIL has lobbied for changes to 15 directives, all successfully, ranging from additional safety measures to restrictions on specific working practices. The group hope for closer links with the European Parliament's Transport and Tourism committee in this area. Some national organisations are also actively engaged in promoting the industry at national level. A study has been commissioned in France to gain a better insight into the value of the industry to local and national economies.

External issues

Heritage railways face many of the same issues as businesses or enterprises in other sectors. However, it is the introduction of restrictions that impact adversely on traditional methods of operation and conservation in particular that is likely to impact on their industry. In general they accept most rules and regulations as these for the most part are accepted by most industries.

Member services

It publishes a quarterly bulletin and organises annual conferences for members, which discuss current issues facing the industry. Some of the national umbrella organisations also provide a small number of membership services, for example the Heritage Railway Association in the UK holds seminars twice a year to up-date members on safety regulations etc.

Future needs

- Research is needed to find how best to extend the season
- Economic impact studies should demonstrate the value to local economies
- Funding for a full-time officer
- Better funding opportunities, including for skills development

EuroGites: The European Federation of Rural Tourism

During the European Year of Tourism in 1990, rural and farm tourism national organizations including those from France, Germany, Belgium, Italy, Portugal, and Iceland met to discuss the creation of a European umbrella body. The proposed organization would be able to lobby at European level, provide a potential European wide marketing platform, and become a forum for discussion, best practice and new ideas. EuroGites was formally registered in 1991 in Strasbourg.

It is a non-profit organization, effectively owned and supported by its members, most of whom are also non-profits. Its prime supporter was Gites de France, then, as now, Europe's largest rural tourism organization, which provided office space and temporary staff. The EuroGites secretariat was based in Strasbourg, and its first President came from France. Following constitutional reorganization in 2002, the President is based in Spain.

EuroGites currently has 35 national members across 28 countries.

Continuity in work since 2002 has achieved:

- An English/French/German/Spanish language web site offering linked access to all its members' web sites, and a range of publications and news items. That web site has accumulated over 520,000 hits. It has a link to the web site of the European Travel Commission.

- Participation on behalf of its members in European level policy discussions, research projects, policy making forums, and formal advice structures to the Commission such as the Advisory Group on Rural Development or the TSG-Tourism Sustainability Group.
- Strong and proactive involvement in the preparation and implementation of the 21 actions of the European Tourism Policy – participating in several ad-hoc working groups and focus groups.
- Five major European conferences ("European Congress on Rural Tourism"), typically bringing 100+ international delegates and 200 local delegates together.
- A major Rural Tourism Quality Survey across a number of European countries in 2003-4 that resulted in the common European Assessment Criteria for Rural Tourism that were formally approved in 2005.
- These criteria and parameters were extended and updated in 2009-2010, in the context of a European-wide online quality assessment and training system for rural tourism70.
- The registration of its logo as a European Trademark.
- Four-monthly market and business survey about the evolution of rural tourism in Europe, in parallel with the UNWTO Tourism Barometer.
- Networking between professionals in the rural tourism field, and discussions about problem solving and innovation both through EuroGites meetings and directly between EuroGites members.
- Cooperation with other European transnational organisations, either as member or within specific projects.

Funding and Finance

EuroGites relies entirely on contributions - and sometimes support in kind - from its members. A basic annual fee of €400 is increased by additional payments of 40 Eurocents according each national body's member numbers, with total payments capped at €4,000. The total funds raised are just €19,000 per year. This minimal funding level allows very few new activities to be undertaken. EuroGites relies for its survival on the help and goodwill of its members and on the largely unpaid efforts of its General Secretary, Klaus Ehrlich. Project funding was practically impossible to achieve in the past due to the lack of specific EU opportunities for tourism.

Funding is limited because national members often wish to concentrate their expenditure on their domestic activities, and oppose any increase in money paid to EuroGites. The value of a presence and participation in EU structures is not understood, nor are the possibilities for new product ideas or markets.

EuroGites has not been able to source any money for research or the testing of innovative new products that could benefit European rural economies. Its members are all under financial pressures because much of their revenue comes from marketing - their marketing function is being increasingly lost to a range of online international booking agencies.

SOME KEY TOOLS FOR DEVELOPMENT

This section provides a critical outline review of a number of development tools used by both rural and industrial heritage tourism. An understanding of the role of development tools is essential if effective policies are to be devised for the development of these forms of special interest tourism. Particular attention is paid to Heritage Interpretation, however, because it is often misunderstood, badly used, but is essential in the experiential marketing context to both forms of tourism.

HERITAGE INTERPRETATION

Quality Heritage Interpretation is a key product development which could make a major improvement to the fortunes of both industrial heritage and rural tourism in Europe. Both rural and industrial heritage tourism sites and areas need an interpretation strategy and programme to explain, develop and make visitors enthralled by their unique selling point - their heritage. Interpretation is a concept which dates back to the 1950s. It was a concept developed with the US National Park Service by Freeman Tilden – the third edition of his classic text is still in print.

His key principles can be summarised as:

- Interpretation that does not relate what is being described to something within the personality or experience of the visitor will be sterile.
- Information is not interpretation. Interpretation is revelation based on information.
- Interpretation is an art – any art is to some degree teachable.
- The aim of Interpretation is not instruction but provocation.
- Interpretation addressed to children requires a separate programme.
- No device is as desirable as interpretation by direct contact with a person.

Since Freeman Tilden's days, the concept of interpretation has been widened. It is now used as a tourism management device to influence visitor behaviour. The positioning of visitor centres, which often contain interpretation materials, helps influence visitor flow patterns. The interpreter's message is recognised to be politically charged. And the interpretation system itself can become an attraction in its own right. Marketing can, and should, be linked to the interpretive system.

We also know much more about the many types of interpretation, about the use of themes and story lines, about linking to real life human stories, and to technicalities such as the 3 and 5 rule (not less than 3 pieces of information in any one story and not more than 5, – see Ham, 1992). All sorts of technology have been introduced, from interactive displays to QR codes and mobile phone apps. Well trained and even "old" humans are still remarkably good, however, and have lower capital costs. Both technology and humans need skilled management, support, training and updating.

There is a growing body of research available about how and why interpretation works, and how it can help build "place attachment" that can encourage repeat visits. It is becoming clear that Interpretation should link closely to the interests and values of the market as well as the site, should link to visitor experience planning and be the device to tackle cultural valorisation issues.

It should follow the sentiments expressed below:

- "The success of a tourism product depends on what the producers see as the needs of the consumer. However many tourist organizations are ignorant of the motivations of the people who purchase their products. First they design products, and then they try and find buyers, instead of designing their products to meet the needs of the market."

The dilemma is, however, how to retain the concept of authenticity through the above process. This is an on-going and fascinating dilemma in all partnerships between tourism development and cultural management.

Finally, it is important to note that no single enterprise in rural tourism can set up an effective heritage interpretation strategy for a wider area, or a destination. The subject needs research to learn more about the heritage, research to understand what the market wants, and co-ordination over a wide area to agree common themes and story lines, and to pay for the infrastructure necessary. Partnership is essential. Some larger industrial heritage sites can and do work independently, but usually partnerships can produce stronger products and brand images.

BRANDING

Branding is a feature of modern life. It helps consumers make decisions about which out of hundreds of products to choose. Brands are not just names, but quality marks, symbolising desired qualities and attributes. Many destinations have become brand names. Within rural tourism some brand names have appeared – usually geographical areas such as the English Lake District, the Irish Ring of Kerry, and the Salzkammergut in Austria. Austria's Farm Holidays – Urlaub am Bauernhof – group is now attaining brand status because of its close attention to quality and targeted marketing. Branding may have relevance to other rural areas and to Industrial Heritage Tourism and could be a valuable tool. But it is not an easy or quick fix for problems because it is not simply a name – it requires market knowledge, branding is closely linked to the self-image and identity of many customers. It must also align to the attainment of quality standards and quality delivery.

TRAILS

The Trail concept has become an increasingly popular one in the last twenty years. In many parts of the developed world, cycling and walking for pleasure have experienced growth. And the creation of trails, sometimes from disused or underused rights of way, sometimes from abandoned rail or canal routes, has become a passion for trails enthusiasts. In addition to non-motorised trails, there are some car based trails – the USA's scenic byways programme is the biggest example, using lightly trafficked rural roads to bring tourists to forgotten areas and communities.

The trail concept can be used primarily as a marketing device – the European Routes of Industrial Heritage network is of this type. There is also a broader version of the trail concept, the important activity corridor concept, bringing a broad corridor of activities together, sometimes with a spine route formed by a rail line, a road or cycle track. Activity corridors are increasingly linked to the slow travel concept.

The most successful trails can become cult destinations in themselves. Examples include the Danube cycle path, the C2C cycle route from west to east coasts in northern England, and the 780 km Caminio Frances walking/cycle trail to Santiago de Compostela in northern Spain. Many trails are not so successful: there is often little cross fertilisation between tourism and trails. Trails are often backed by non-profits and public sector agencies. Tourism is typically private sector. The former look to local users: the latter look to non-local users. And the trails which are developed are rarely conceived or designed and built with a market in mind. There is a natural synergy between trails and sustainable tourism, not least because most trails encourage slow travel by non-motorised means. But trails need professional and skilled management to maintain the infrastructure, to market the product and energise and co-ordinate the linear partnerships involved. Trails are easy to create but difficult to maintain.

The world leaders in trail development are the Rails to Trails Conservancy in the USA, founded in 1986 it is a well led and managed non-profit with over 150,000 members, working on over 32,000 kilometres of trails across the USA. Over the last 25 years they have evolved into a very professional group who, from beginnings in local and regional recreation, are slowly coming to terms with trail tourism. The Conservancy has a very wide range of publications, providing a factual and an inspirational base for many European trail makers.

Trails are not exactly the same concept as "routes" – see below. Trails are usually a rural tourism tool, but can be used in some cases for industrial heritage tourism purposes.

HERITAGE ROUTES AND HERITAGE REGIONS

The concept of heritage regions emerged in 1980s Canada, promoted by the Heritage Canada Foundation as a way of creating tourism and conservation groups across groups of usually scattered rural communities. They allow small communities to pool ideas, marketing and lobbying. In tourism they allow effective branding to take place, they create more viable destinations, and help promote a learning culture and innovation.

In Europe there has been an especially great interest in the concept of Heritage Routes, rather than regions. In part that interest comes from an extension of the Trails concept,, a concept inherited from religious pilgrimages, and one that takes the transport component of tourism activity and turns it into a product in itself. In part it is an attempt to link special interest sites in a meaningful way. And in part, in Europe, it is a political and educational statement, a way of getting neighbouring regions and countries to work together on a European level. European Transnational Routes were pioneered by the Council of Europe and are often funded and encouraged by the EU.

The expression of the Heritage Routes concept can be clearly seen in the routes developed by the European Routes of Industrial Heritage group. While this organization does much more than help develop routes, both transnational and regional, its title gives prominence to the routes concept in industrial heritage tourism. The big question that practitioners face, however, is: Do Heritage Routes work? Are the routes well used? Do they encourage tourism spend along the routes?

The Council of Europe has researched these issues in depth, publishing its 261 page provisional study "Impact of European Cultural Routes on SMEs' innovation and competitiveness" in 2010. The Cultural Routes programme of the Council of Europe was adopted in 1987. Since then 29 Routes covering 70 countries have been set up.

Eight points and quotations from that study are given below which point out very clearly the many problems with the concept, especially in relation to building tourist numbers and supporting enterprises and facilities:

- "The economic dimension of the Cultural Routes has never been one of their major aspects.... At the same time, tourism and sustainable development are clearly specified as part of the criteria for certification."
- "European networks make a vital contribution to transnational co-operation across diverse sectors of arts and heritage fields. A contemporary phenomenon, they represent a flexible and dynamic

way of working which brings together professionals across Europe who share common concerns."

- "Since there is no legal system to create a "European statute" for a non-governmental organisation and, therefore, most legal statutes have to be located in one European country, networks are already at a disadvantage when hoping to create an equitable transnational legal base for their work."
- "According to the analyses of the Cultural Routes conducted within the framework of this study, there are very few shared innovation projects across national borders. Cultural Routes have few regular shared events or activities that bind their work together and give shape and reason for the international network."
- "It is important to note that the Cultural Routes are not business organisations, which are usually considered as innovation hubs. The Cultural Routes are rather a means to preserve and showcase European cultural identities."
- "Our case study research found that even at local level, data specific to the activities of the Cultural Route were generally not being collected and thus there was little awareness of the value of the economic contribution being made to local economies, and in particular to SME growth and competitiveness... our survey also suggested that lack of resources, technical expertise and different approaches to data collection across the network was an issue."
- "Although the demand for Cultural Route tourism products is still very basic, the tourism offer along them is very diverse."
- "In summary, and according to this analysis, the following is a list of the most important issues concerning the Cultural Routes that need to be addressed:
  - There is low transnational connectivity of the Cultural Routes networks;
  - There is lack of co-ordination at European level in the developmental and promotional strategies of the Cultural Routes;
  - They have weak brand image and marketing strategies;
  - There is a low degree of quality and sustainable tourism standards development/ implementation;
  - There are very limited human and financial resources of the Routes;
  - There is a lack of expertise in the management of the networks;
  - There is poor exchange of good practices; and absence of network management and performance evaluation tools."

The Route/European Route concept, therefore, while a much used device, appears to have serious problems. This is hardly surprising. Most tourists seek a resort or a region that acts as a resort. There is little sign that this will change. A few routes do achieve cult status but they are very few. Is there an alternative?

The most likely alternative is the Heritage Region concept, pioneered in Canada, described earlier in this section, which creates a decentralised resort, builds local loyalty and involvement, is easily understood by visitors and has been copied on a micro scale at Blaenavon in Wales, and on a macro scale very successfully by Ruhr Tourismus in Germany. The Heritage Region is not a low-cost development; it requires skilled and long-term marketing and local partnership work. It does not automatically encourage European Networking. But it could do that, both by synergy marketing between related heritage regions, and by organised expertise exchanges.

VISITOR CENTRES

A concept created by the US National Parks Service 50 years ago, the visitor centre has been frequently used in Europe for both industrial heritage and rural tourism.

It can be, and should be, a multi-purpose development, informing visitors, channelling them into suitable routes, providing a tourism related retail outlet, offering local food, and centred on a wider region as well as a specific site. And if possible there should be provision for community use.

They are tangible, capital investments often attracting public sector funding, grants and support. They can contain administrative offices, keeping administrators aware of visitor needs and visitors aware of the activity of the administrators.

But Visitor Centres can have disadvantages. There is a danger that all sites feel that they must have a dedicated new centre: often the site or region could instead use local shops or cafes or bars as para-visitor centres. Visitor centres are expensive to build, and expensive to operate. They are frequently sited at inappropriate places (often due to pressures to use redundant buildings or cheap or publicly owned land).

They may be inflexibly designed, making multi-purpose use difficult. Many architects understand little about interpretation or visitor centres, leading to inappropriate designs. The visitor information is often poorly written, and expensive to update. The local community may be alienated by the capital costs and top down approach of the centre.

Current issues in visitor centre development include the need to link them to the concept of Heritage Regions, rather than as stand-alone entities; to involve local people as volunteers, and/or as franchisees of businesses within the centres, and the need to have "action exhibits", demonstrations, events, "living history", festivals etc. linked to the centres.

Visitor Centres are usually a rural tourism tool, but can also be in some circumstances a tool for industrial heritage tourism.

THE ROLE OF MUSEUMS

Museums were not "designed" to be part of a tourism industry, but they can transform their political and financial security if they can work with tourism. This is especially true in the current situation where public sector funding for museums is being cut back. The fundamental problem is that many museums function as repositories, led by trained curators, keeping objects safely for all time. Their role as interpreter and educator, as link between past and future, is still seen as secondary by some managers. Few curators have the necessary skills to engage in marketing or to work in partnership with tourism interests. But both sides of the potential equation would benefit from a re-assessment of their relationship and could take part in the development of heritage interpretation as a key tourism product. They may become related to the visitor centre concept, but great care must be taken not to lose their conservation and curatorial skills.

MANAGING SEASONAL TOURISM FLOWS

Traditionally, tourism in Europe was a very seasonal activity, peaking sharply between June and October. However, the seasonality problem has eased in recent years for many reasons, and is now much less problematic than in the past. This section explains how and discusses the management tools available to address seasonality.

Both industrial heritage and rural tourism have benefitted from the growing numbers of active older people, who are not tied to school holidays for their travels. Equally, many of the active old have sufficiently high incomes to take several holidays per year. And, for a variety of reasons, winter travel is no longer the feared experience that it once was – and has, for some, become fashionable.

On the supply side a range of management tools are available. Both forms of tourism have diversified and developed shoulder and low season activities to counteract seasonality problems. Beamish Industrial Museum and the work of Ruhr Tourismus are textbook examples of how to stage low season events and activities to spread tourism demand for industrial heritage. The rise of city tourism has also helped to ease the seasonality problem: much city tourism is now often at its height in the low season. Rural tourism has fewer ways out of wet/cold weather problems than the often indoor industrial heritage attractions, but has also found that the creation of events and new activities can be designed to reduce seasonality.

It has benefited enormously from better wet and cold weather clothing, with garments with breathable fabrics, effective insulation and quality design features: outdoor activity clothing has become a fashion item. The quest to keep fit by all season walking, cross country skiing and cycling has also helped; as has a range of new niche activities include ice climbing, orienteering and winter bird watching. Both forms of tourism are also beginning to employ seasonal price variation techniques, with low season offers. Beamish is a recent and successful user of variable pricing. In short, market knowledge, skilled marketing, product innovation and tourism management have, along with changing market requirements, reduced seasonality problems.

FESTIVALS

Festivals have become a common device in tourism and in the arts since the 1970s. They reflect an increasingly mobile and affluent population, who seek new and fashionable encounters with cultural experiences, and they also reflect an increasingly strong and effective series of marketing channels. They are used by both industrial heritage and rural tourism organisations to draw attention to their activities, to celebrate or launch new product areas, and, in many cases, to attract low and shoulder season audiences. They often use short term sponsorship as a funding source. They can be very successful indeed, but they can also be very demanding of supply side resources, and they can be temporary devices without long-term results. Capriella and Rotherham draw some interesting conclusions from Italy. They form part of a growing research and training discipline under the title of "events".

LOCAL DEVELOPMENT GROUPS

Local development groups are central to the work of much industrial heritage tourism and rural tourism. They form lobby groups, support groups, action groups and mechanisms to apply for and receive funding. They are normally voluntary but can employ paid staff especially on special project work. Understanding the psychology, motivations, strengths and weaknesses of groups is essential for their success, as is understanding that they are often short-term, which does not necessarily detract from their importance· The complications in creating and sustaining local groups are dealt with by Koutsouris based on Greek experience; despite the problems outlined, local groups can be very effective. The concept of local groups has been developed into the more formal and powerful paradigm of the LEADER group, and the Local Action Group: see 6.9 below.

LEADER

LEADER stands for 'Liaison Entre Actions de Développement de l'Économie Rurale', meaning 'Links between the rural economy and development actions'· Since 1991, the EU's Leader group concept and its associated Local Action Groups have become an important funding mechanism for rural development including rural tourism, and, in some cases, industrial heritage tourism in rural settings. Although now mainstreamed into national programmes, Leader Groups will continue until at least 2013, and longer in some areas. It is important to note their contribution here, and their hallmarks of the project method, grass-roots approach, innovation, integrated multi-sectoral actions, cooperation and partnership, area based approaches and cross-border networking. Leader groups have been very successful and while none have concentrated on tourism, they provide a proven management system for partnership operations within EU countries. Their power over the last 20 years has been such that much of the agri-tourism and rural tourism development in the EU has been related to rural development goals, rather than tourism goals.

ASSESSING THE PROBLEMS: INNOVATIVE SOLUTIONS

PROBLEMS AND POTENTIAL

This study has described two niche market tourism sectors and shown here them to be, in principle, well-tuned to fit the needs and aspirations of our modern and evolving society. They offer considerable benefits to local economies. Industrial Heritage Tourism is estimated to be worth well in excess of €9 billion annually; rural tourism is estimated to be worth at least €150 billion annually. Because of the widespread use of volunteers, it is difficult to assess the numbers of jobs provided by industrial heritage tourism; estimates show that rural tourism provides around 900,000 jobs. Both sectors provide many additional environmental and socio-cultural benefits for local society, plus wider benefits for society nationally, across Europe and, in some cases, worldwide.

Both have great potential for future growth. Europe has always been a leader, and the largest global provider, of rural tourism: it attracts professional study visits from other countries around the world. Europe is also very much the leader and largest provider of industrial heritage tourism in the world. It too is beginning to attract professional study visits from other continents. Section 6 has set out just some of a range of developmental tools that can be used, tested, evaluated and improved in both sectors. Rural tourism, in particular, is full of innovative ideas for development and marketing. It has a range of good practice examples. Industrial heritage tourism currently has fewer innovative ideas, but could adapt many of those that rural tourism has, and it too has a range of good practice examples.

Both tourism forms have strong potential to encourage low carbon recreation and tourism, and to make tourism more sustainable. Both can offer a useful contribution to EU policy to reduce the greenhouse gas emissions by 20 per cent by 2020.

Much more could be made of short-haul holidays, domestically and within Europe. There are numerous under-exploited markets domestically, including the increasingly active over 65s, and in the "traditional" export markets of North America, Australasia and Japan, and the new markets in Asia and the BRIC countries.

But within the above picture of success there are a complex series of pressing problems to be overcome before the potential described above can be developed and become sustainable. The background to the problems has been described in this study.

In brief:

- Both sectors are extremely fragmented, with few effective networking or partnership arrangements in place to gain economies in scale in market research and marketing, in training and in innovation. They both suffer from weak governance systems, with only a glimmer of hope coming from some protected area managements. Governance covers the issues of advice and assistance in many forms. National rural tourism organizations were once stronger and helped provide some advice and assistance, but, as this study has shown, many of those now have problems from online marketing competition and lack of both skills and financial resources. Pan European organizations in both sectors have very severe financial problems, and a growing lack of both resource and purpose.
- Both sectors have been shown to be somewhat unprofessional in their approach to tourism - and that has been shown to be especially true of industrial heritage tourism.
- Both face great competition from resurgent professionally managed resorts, from city tourism and from long-haul competition from low cost and exotic competition across the world.
- A series of hidden threats exist. In rural tourism many of the SMEs are owned by pioneers from the growth years of the 1980s and 90s who will shortly retire and leave their businesses. The nature of rural tourism often means that few SMEs sell their businesses on. In industrial heritage, many attractions face growing maintenance costs as their heritage ages beyond its life expectancy: the most successful part of industrial heritage, railway tourism, is especially at risk, because of its reliance on bridges, tunnels, earthworks and complex machinery. Good financial results are vital.
- Both sectors have been shown to be highly reliant on public sector support, rural tourism for its infrastructure and often for landscape protection, industrial heritage for direct ownership and support of the heritage itself. Public sector support seems likely to shrink, as rival demands in the health, educational and age related benefits sector grows.
- Both sectors need to respond to new technologies in marketing, heritage interpretation and business, but find those responses difficult.
- Research and development is not easily available to many small SMEs -yet is important for their future survival.

There is, however, great unused potential that could enable all the above problems to be overcome. Examples of very successful businesses and organizations have been illustrated in both sectors, examples which contrast sharply with the many less successful ones. There are many innovative ideas and techniques that have been discussed in this study could be used. There are innumerable academic researchers who could help educate and advise but are not organised or incentivised to do so. And en route to developing that potential there are many unsung benefits for the wider society - extending transferrable skills training for businesses, employees and volunteers, and helping keep people healthy by offering informal outdoor physical exercise through walking, climbing, cycling, etc.

This section of this study justifies intervention to solve the market failure issues that are likely to affect businesses, jobs, incomes, communities and investments made in infrastructure. Less directly, there would also be an important loss of heritage assets for future generations: tourism valorises heritage. And sectoral decline would make moves towards low carbon tourism more difficult.

Action at a European level is especially capable of finding solutions to these problems, because it can use best practice, researchers and practitioners across the EU to solve problems that would be too difficult to do nation by nation. The publication of the very comprehensive, practical and positive European Parliament Report *Europe, the world's No 1 tourist destination – a new political framework for tourism in Europe* in 2011 set the scene for a new era of change. The next section of this study outlines what could be done to fulfil the demands and suggestions of that for industrial heritage and rural tourism.

RECOMMENDATIONS

The recommendations aim to provide information to guide future investment policies in industrial heritage and rural tourism, develop means to guide and increase the competiveness of the SMEs involved, provide effective governance systems to help partnerships and networking and create ways to develop the social, economic and environmental performance of the sectors involved. In the past large sums of money were provided by the EU to assist capital projects linked to tourism.

The recommendations here concern much smaller sums to improve expertise, knowledge and operational change. It also suggests a range of delivery mechanisms to facilitate those changes. Those mechanisms should include at least two pan-European organizations as well as national organizations. The recommendations are modular and incremental. While ideally the virtual research and development centre should be developed first to service and evaluate the other six recommendations, each of the recommendations could be developed separately, and incrementally, as funds and time permitted.

A virtual research and development centre

The key recommendation is one developed from a point made in COM 352 final, and from point 20 in EU A7-0265/11, which called for a "Virtual Tourism Monitoring Centre". This foresees the creation of a virtual network to bring together research institutes and other key players to provide a research and advice base for all member states. While there might need to be only one network to serve both of the special interest areas under discussion, it would almost certainly be more useful if it was set up as two parts of one whole, because of the differences in product and style of industrial heritage tourism and rural tourism.

The proposal goes far beyond the dissemination of best practice. It seeks to create an organization to analyse and test performance and practice in detail, on the lines of the organisations that are used to test medical drug performance and value for money.

It also seeks to provide a mechanism to deliver research and advice and to incentivise its adoption. The network would provide a unique link between researchers, state and EU policy makers and practitioners, could work with the some of major pan-European organisations listed in Section 5.4, plus others if required, and provide an innovation and research hub for industrial heritage and rural tourism. Modelled on the several years of experience developed by ALTER-Net, it would operate virtually with only annual face to face meetings. It would be designed so that it could move towards economic self-sufficiency after a period of perhaps 5 years, again on the ALTER-Net model. It could also learn from the experiences of the long lived Commonwealth Government of Australia's Sustainable Tourism Cooperative Research Centre, which led the way in sustainable tourism research from 1997 until 2010, and is likely to be reincarnated shortly.

The ALTER-Net partnership was developed through a "Network of Excellence" as part of the European Commission's 6 Framework Programme. It undertakes long-term, European-scale, inter-disciplinary research on biodiversity, ecosystems and ecosystem services using its combined expertise in ecology, social sciences, economics, information management and knowledge transfer. Those areas of research, policy and practice application could be transferred to both rural and to industrial heritage tourism - researching effective governance models, creating programmes for market research that can be used by non-specialists, using Skype and webinars for consultations between group members, and bringing heritage interpretation to life in order to lengthen stay, spend and increase in-field enjoyment.

Four essential features should be included:

- Key research areas should be chosen by discussions between industry stakeholders, researchers and EU tourism experts. It is essential to include stakeholder input to avoid the problems that befell the

SPRITE project on supporting and promoting integrated tourism in Europe's lagging rural regions which appears to have been largely academic.

- The centre must research and test innovation delivery methods, including the use of selected national rural/agri tourism and industrial heritage tourism organizations.
- The centre should produce systems to help SMEs monitor their performance and visitor satisfaction.
- Incentives to take up Continuing Professional Development events, and to adopt innovation, should also be explored.

Eventual research areas could include:

- A detailed assessment of the state of the industrial heritage and rural tourism sectors.
- Carrying out basic market research – either by collating existing materials or collecting additional materials, or both.
- Field testing a range of questionnaire and analysis packages to allow sites, communities and regions to carry out quality surveys and produce results themselves.
- Detailed and critical evaluation of a range of marketing concepts for industrial heritage and rural tourism.
- An exploration and evaluation of a range of product development ideas and techniques, including for example visitor centres.
- Field testing of a range of market related heritage interpretation ideas and products.
- An exploration of the market for both types of tourism in the growing post 65 years of age market.
- An enquiry into the governance systems for both Industrial Heritage tourism and Rural Tourism on a national and regional basis seeking to provide best ways forward for regional governance and national governance. This is a necessity in its own right and in order to assess the problems currently faced by many, but not all, national associations.
- A critical evaluation of the concept of Heritage Regions against the concept of Heritage Routes.
- Work to assess in the industrial heritage sector how best skills training could be developed and if possible formalised. As the heritage railways group appear to be most advanced in this area, FEDECRAIL and its members may be a group to work with, perhaps working with the Council of Europe or others.
- A review of the definitions of industrial heritage tourism and rural tourism across European countries, initiatives to collect data on both subjects to common standards.

- Work to harmonise and simplify the legal requirements for small businesses in both enterprise areas.

Initial funding for the development of the proposal could come from Preparatory Actions, followed by an application to the successor to Framework Initiative 7, Horizon 2020.

A prototype Industrial Heritage Region project.

A second recommendation is to seek funding for the development of a prototype Industrial Heritage Region project, to use innovative governance, marketing, product development, interpretation and accommodation provision. The region could be chosen by competition - if possible - across Europe. Funding would be sought from the Structural Funds. This should be regarded as a demonstration project for good practice, with regular dissemination of issues encountered and successes as well as failures. Its assessment could be carried by the virtual centre.

A prototype Second Generation Rural Tourism region

The third recommendation is to seek funding, from the Rural Development section of the Agricultural Fund, for a prototype Second Generation Rural Tourism region, as a demonstration project using ideas related to those in 7.2.2 above. Its assessment could be carried by the virtual centre.

A demonstration project on Slow Tourism

The fourth recommendation is for a demonstration project on Slow Tourism to be a test bed for low carbon tourism techniques, regional development and behavioural change. While this is likely to be in a rural location, it should be remembered that there has been worldwide discussion of slow city tourism. Possible sites for a rural project include Austria – which has shown great interest in this type of development - Ireland, Portugal or Italy.

A Heritage Hardware Training programme

A number of industrial heritage organizations, in Austria, Belgium, the UK, Germany and the Netherlands, have discussed the concept of training young people - and others - in the repair and/or reproduction of heritage materials and hardware. That training would allow for example iron and wooden heritage items to serve museums, heritage architecture, and heritage equipment of all kinds to be conserved or replaced. A successful programme would require consultation and co-operation between heritage entities and educational organizations and qualification standards authorities. Mystic Seaport, USA, has a possible model in its maritime heritage training courses.

Tourism training is important but evidence given by national and pan European organizations indicate that it seems very difficult to establish a

"European normed" system. The recommendations given in this section could however, provide excellent training materials to be used across Europe in existing education and training institutions, and ALTER-Net has had success with skills building summer schools, especially in management and staff capacity building.

Innovative practice dissemination

A programme of dissemination of innovative practice – akin to a travelling exhibition with speakers – to tour EU members over a 5 year period to inspire change and development, to give added meaning to national and pan European bodies working in the industrial heritage and rural tourism. The programme would be backed by a web site offering research results and the developments in the demonstration projects.

Marketing for Asia and BRIC countries

The best of Europe's Industrial Heritage Tourism and Rural Tourism providers are of world class. While many of the recommendations in this section are concerned with raising the standards of those who are not quite the best, there is a case for also helping the best in class to develop new export markets. In part that would be a valuable Public Relations exercise for the EU and for the sectors concerned; in part it could be economically valuable.

A marketing initiative for Asia and BRIC countries could work with the European Travel Commission to explore the possibilities of selected components of industrial heritage and rural tourism being developed for these markets.

This could be done in conjunction with, for example, the growing industrial heritage interests in Japan, and with both the Korea and with the China Rural Tourism Associations. Such actions are foreshadowed in several places in the European Parliament Report *Europe, the world's No 1 tourist destination – a new political framework for tourism in Europe.* The experience of the New Zealand Tourist Board would be useful.

ISSUES AND COSTS

The main recommendation raises a number of important issues. One of them must be -would EuroGites and ERIH be involved with the research organization? The immediate answer is that they should be important advisers for the group, and they should receive funds to allow that advice to be given, but that they should not automatically be the managers or developers of that group.

A second question relates to decisions on the work programme and priorities of the group. Who should make the final decisions? That question is probably one best discussed with ALTER-Net and with a round table of key stakeholders under Preparatory Actions funding mentioned earlier. Sustainability indicators may also be a contested area, and it is felt that demonstration projects should include sustainability measures to test and demonstrate techniques rather than, at this stage, developing a contested European wide set of indicators.

Costs

What might be the costs of the above proposals? All recommendations are envisaged as relatively low cost and designed to be eventually self-supporting. Several of the recommendations could help regenerate pan-European development and support groups, and some national groups.

Each of the above proposals should cost less than €1 million per year, some much less than that sum*. Compared to the very large amounts spent on tourism related capital projects, that seems a low cost: ERDF funding alone related to tourism in the 2000-2006 programme amounted to €4.6 billion. Targeted and disseminated research to improve the economic, environmental, social and cultural returns from tourism or to improve its competitive position should repay its costs very quickly.

Bibliography

A Satish Babu: *Tourism Development in India : A Case Study*, APH Publication, Delhi, 2008.

Abha Lakshmi Singh and Shahab Fazal: *Rural Environmental Management*, B R Publication, Delhi, 2008.

Amit Gaur: *Adventure Tourism*, Sonali Publication, Delhi, 2011.

Anupama Srivastava and Keya Pandey: *Anthropology and Tourism*, Serials Publications, Delhi, 2012.

B S Badan and Harish Bhatt: *Adventure Tourism*, Commonwealth Publication, Delhi, 2007.

B S Badan and Harish Bhatt: *Travel Agencies and Tourism Development*, Commonwealth Publication, Delhi, 2007.

Banwari Lal Raheja: *Tourism Development Strategies*, Arise Publication Delhi, 2000.

Charlie Sampson: *Rural Tourism*, Discovery Publishing House, Delhi, 2011.

Devesh Nigam and Vinay Kumar Narula: *Rural Tourism : Emerging Issues and Challenges*, Shree Publication, Delhi, 2011.

Jack Randall: *Agriculture Tourism*, Discovery Publishing House, Delhi, 2011.

Jagmohan Negi and Gaurav Manoher: *Rural Tourism : Planning and Promotion*, Authorspress, Delhi, 2011.

Kailash Hariharan Iyer: *Tourism Development in India*, Vista International Publication, Delhi, 2006.

Lalita Sharma: *An Introduction to Ecotourism*, Centrum Press, Delhi, 2003.

Mahadev Kertwal: *Advertising in Leisure and Tourism*, Cyber Tech Publication, Delhi, 2012.

N. Jayapalan: *An Introduction to Tourism*, Atlantic Publication, Delhi, 2001.

O.P. Kandari and Ashish Chandra: *Tourism Development Principles and Practices*, Shree Publication, Delhi, 2004.

P. Siva Sankara Reddy: *Rural Tourism and Promotion of Handicrafts in India*, Kanishka Publication, Delhi, 2012.

Palash Handique, Hemanta Saikia and Ratul Kumar Lahon: *Tourism Development and Planning in India*, SSDN Publishers, Delhi, 2014.

Prateek A. Aggarwal: *Aspects of Crosscultural Interaction and Tourism*, Mohit Publication, Delhi, 2005.

R K Pruthi: *Rural Tourism : Challenges and Paradox*, Rajat Publication, Delhi, 2006.

Ramesh Raj Kunwar: *Anthropology of Tourism : A Case Study of Chitwan-Sauraha, Nepal*, Adroit Publication, Delhi, 2002.

Romila Chawla: *Agri-Tourism*, Sonali Publication, Delhi, 2006.

Rudra Prasad Upadhyay: *Readings in Rural Tourism*, Sunlight Publication, Delhi, 2008.

S Sutheeshna Babu; Sitikantha Mishra and Bivraj Bhusan Parida: *Tourism Development Revisited : Concepts, Issues and Paradigms*, Response Books, Delhi, 2008.

S.B. Verma, Shiw Kumar Jiloka and Potukuchi Thryambakam: *Rural Tourism and Tribal Development*, Deep and Deep Publication, Delhi, 2006.

Saurab Kumar Dixit: *Aspects of Tourism Development*, Mohit Publication, Delhi, 2005.

Sourabh Shrivastava and Santosh Shukla: *Urbanisation and Transformation of Rural Environment in Madhya Pradesh*, Readworthy, 2012.

Thomas Walsh: *Adventure Tourism*, Discovery Publishing House, Delhi, 2011.

V P Sati: *Tourism Development in India*, Pointer Publication, Delhi, 2001.

Yogesh Kumar Sharma: *Rural Tourism and Development*, Pointer Publication, Delhi, 2005.

Index

I

L

M

N

P

R

S

T

U

V

W

Z